China's New Engagement with Taliban and the Wakhan Corridor

China's New Engagement with Taliban and the Wakhan Corridor

Musa Khan Jalalzai

Vij Books India Pvt Ltd

New Delhi (India)

Published by

Vij Books India Pvt Ltd
(Publishers, Distributors & Importers)
2/19, Ansari Road
Delhi – 110 002
Phone: 91-11-43596460
Mobile: 98110 94883
e-mail: contact@vijpublishing.com
www.vijbooks.in

ISBN: 978-93-93499-71-4 (Hardback)
ISBN: 978-93-93499-72-1 (Paperback)
ISBN: 978-93-93499-73-8 (ebook)

Contents

Introduction

Pakistani Mullah Abdul Aziz of Lal Masjid in his recent interview with a local journalist (Quran orders to become terrorists: Maulana Abdul Aziz, SAMVADA-25 August 2021) communicated that the Holy Quran has ordained Muslims to become terrorists against enemies of Allah. His interview generated a new perception that now Pakistan wants to justify terrorism and jihad from the Holy Quran against non-Muslim states in Europe and Asia. His knowledge about the Holy Quran and Allah Almighty is shameful and deplorable but silence of all so called Muftis, religious scholars and political parties on his humiliation of the Holy Quran is underwhelming. In his Tweet, Vivek Sinha raised the question of Pakistani Mullahs silence on Maulana Abdul Aziz remarks: "Maulana Abdul Aziz of Pakistan's Lal Masjid says clearly that Quran orders Muslims to become Terrorists. Is this is not Pakistani state-sponsored terrorism? Moreover, Altaf Hussain in his Tweet also raised issue of Mullahs silence: "Qur'an ordains Muslims to become "terrorists", Decree by Lal Masjid cleric Maulana Abdul Aziz, Chief Administrator of Lal Masjid opposite "the ISI headquarter at Aabpara Islamabad. He generated controversies about Allah Almighty and the Holy Quran and clearly barricaded his stance on jihad against non-Muslim states. The Holy Quran never instructed or directed Muslims to become terrorists against the enemies of Allah Almighty. The Quran says: "When it is said to them: "Make no mischief on the earth," They say: "Why we only want to make peace. Of a surety, they are the ones who make mischief, but they realize (it) not". Al Baqara, 2:11).

Journalist Umar Farooq (*The Friday Times*, September, 21 2021) has noted his previous campaign that caused pain and distress: "Abdul Aziz's campaign against "immorality" was causing quite a stir in the city and created an impression of a crisis—which was serving the purpose of anyone who was bent on dislodging the politically and intellectually handicapped military ruler General Pervez Musharraf. There was a general consensus among political analysts in those days that the military top brass had decided to get rid of General Musharraf after he shot himself in the foot by colliding head-on with the judiciary and lawyers' community". On 19 September,

2021, a case was registered against Maulana Abdul Aziz in Islamabad for threatening policemen who came to remove Afghan Taliban's flags hoisted at Jamia Hafsa, a seminary run by the cleric's wife. Thus, Prime Minister Imran Khan's policy of appeasing radicals backfired while Lal Masjid Madrassa now openly inculcating young girls in the manner of beheading.

Expert and analyst, Mrityunjoy Kumar Jha in his analysis (India Narrative, 09-12-2021) noted the exponentially growing trends of suicide terrorism and beheading in Pakistan: "Pakistan's notorious Lal Masjid is back in the news again. In a viral video, the young girl students were shown how to behead a person who disrespects Prophet Mohammad (PBU). In the background, the slogan of hardliner radical Tehreek-i-Labbaik Pakistan (TLP), "Gustakh-e-Rasool ki ek hi sazaa, Sar tan se Juda, Sar tan se Juda" (Only one punishment for blasphemy against the prophet, separation of head from the body) was playing on the loudspeakers. It was the same slogan that supporters of TLP were chanting while they lynched and burnt the Sri Lankan factory manager Priyantha Kumara Diyawadana in Sialkot. Sharing the video clip, Pakistani journalist Gul Bukhari wrote on Twitter post, "Students of Red Mosque Islamabad practicing how to behead a person accused of blasphemy. Pakistan's "kamyab jawan" (successful youth) project is proceeding rather well," a reference to the Pakistani Prime Minister Imran Khan's project for youth of the country. "The Pakistan Taliban (TTP) will teach you all a lesson," he threatened them. The Islamic fundamentalist, Maulana Aziz had issued a "fatwa" that no one would attend the funerals of Pakistani soldiers and called for "agitations" against the government. As expected, Imran Khan had to surrender to him to keep the situation normal in the capital".

The concept of suicide attacks, or dying in order to kill in the name of religion become supreme ideal of Taliban and Pakistani madrassas. After the US invasion of Afghanistan, Taliban resorted to suicide terrorism to force the United States and its NATO allies to withdraw their forces from the country and restore Emirate Islami. Taliban and the IS-K became dominant forces in suicide terrorism to internationalize and justify it. Modern suicide terrorism emerged in Afghanistan after 9/11, but it was introduced in different shapes. Over the past two decades, the tactic of suicide terrorism in Afghanistan and Pakistan has been modified and justified by religious clerics. According to expert Assaf Moghadam (Suicide Terrorism, Occupation, and the Globalization of Martyrdom: A Critique of Dying to Win, published in 2006): "the growing interest in suicide terrorism in recent years has generated a steep rise in the number of books that address a topic that is inherently fascinating—a mode of operations that requires the death of its perpetrator to ensure its success".

Analyst and writer, Florian Weigand has noted (Afghanistan's Taliban: Legitimate Jihadists or Coercive Extremists?) that the Taliban wanted to introduce sharia and prohibit music and suppress women: "The Taliban are usually depicted as ideological fighters–religious extremists who want to introduce harsh rules in Afghanistan, including the prohibition of music and the suppression of women. Their mode of governance stands in stark contrast to Western ideals, with the fall of the Taliban government in 2001 being portrayed as a victory against terrorism and human rights abuses. However, the influence of the Taliban and other armed opposition groups is steadily growing again throughout Afghanistan. They describe themselves as 'jihadists' that fight against the government and its foreign supporters. According to a report for the United States (US) Congress, not even 60 percent of the country's districts were under Afghan government control or influence in 2017 (SIGAR 2017, 87). At the same time the US is welcoming direct peace talks with the Taliban (Tolo News, February 24, 2016). This development raises the question as to what the affected people – rather than the foreign interveners – think about the Taliban".

Experts and analysts, Ivan A. Safranchuk, and Vera M. Zhornist of MGIMO State University of International Relations, Moscow, Russia Institute for International Studies (The Taliban Enigma and the Polycentric World: The Benefits of Being Independent-Russia in Global Affairs, 0.31278/1810-6374-2021-19-3-10-24-Vol. 19, No.3, July – September 2021) in their research paper have noted symposium of jihadist internationalist in Afghanistan: "Jihadist internationalists represent a noticeable force in Afghanistan. They need the country as a basis for regional and global activities. They are in a state of constant struggle, which is tied to international ideologists and sponsors: in order to fight, they need encouragement from their ideologists and financial donations, and in order to receive them, they need to fight. Jihadists are inseparable from their external patrons, and the more they internationalize a local or regional conflict, in which they have intervened themselves or become drawn, the more successful they are. In this sense, jihadist internationalists are not independent despite all their desperation and eagerness to fight a bloody battle".

The Looting and ransacking of Afghanistan's natural resources by NATO and the United States, and their criminal militias suchlike the ISIS and Taliban terrorist groups, caused misunderstanding between the Afghans and International Coalition that they all were involved in looting of mineral resources of their country. The IS-K controlled parts of the country's rich mineral wealth, especially talc, chromite and marble. According to the Global Witness research report, several insurgents' groups, militias, Taliban and the ISIS were deeply involved in the plunder of these resources: "The Islamic State in Afghanistan (ISKP) controls major mining sites in eastern Afghanistan and has a strategic interest in the country's rich mineral resources, new Global Witness research shows–a powerful example of the wider threat posed by armed groups and corrupt actors in Afghan mining. The Islamic State in Afghanistan (ISKP) controls large talc, marble and chromite mines in the Islamic State stronghold of Achin district in the Nangarhar province of eastern Afghanistan–the same area where in April 2017 the US military dropped the 'Mother of All Bombs' against ISKP-held caves. Nangarhar was the deadliest Afghan province for US troops in 2017. An estimated 380,000 tons of talc was imported into the United States in 2017. On average around 35 percent of US imports are from Pakistan, according to the US Geological Survey. From our research we also estimated that around 80 percent of Pakistan's 2016 exports of talc actually originated in Afghanistan. Of those exports, 42 percent went to the US, and another 36 percent went to EU countries, especially the Netherlands and Italy".

The perception that Taliban are ideological fighter is totally wrong, the reason for that they are terrorists and act like terrorists, carrying out suicide attacks against civilians and destroying everything they don't like. They and the Pakistani ISI have committed war crimes, beheaded innocent Muslims, kidnapped women and children and used them for sexual exploitation. They are proxies of Pakistan's military establishment, barking for the American Army and ISI equally. They have established suicide brigades, and threatened Afghanistan's neighbours. The Taliban's relationship with al Qaeda and the IS-K further generated fear and consternation. As Afghanistan remained a top destination for foreign terrorist groups, Taliban entered into alliances with different groups. The fall of Afghanistan to the Taliban generated a new terror threat in South and Central Asia. The Taliban's close relationship with several Pakistani terror groups and its inability to govern the whole country may turn Afghanistan into a nest of terror militias. In Afghanistan, close cooperation between Daesh and some disgruntled Taliban groups added to the pain of the Taliban Government. The Khorasan terrorist group, which emerged with a strong military power in 2015, is in control of important districts in Jalalabad province. The group's military tactics include beheading, public prosecution, kidnapping, and torture, looting and raping, and also forcing families from their homes.

Due to the weakness of Taliban and local administration, the IS-K expanded its networks to all districts of Jalalabad. Some of the groups including Quetta Shura, Tora Bora Jihadi group, Gul Buddin Hekmatyar group, Salafi group, Fidayee Karwan, Sia Pushan groups (identified as black-clad and masked terrorists) were in clandestine collaboration with the Khorasan group, TTP, and Lashkar-e-Islam group. In Mohmand Agency, Jamaat Al Ahrar and TTP were operating in collaboration with ISKP. Afghanistan is still run by proxy militias of different internal and external stakeholders. In October 2015, Kunduz was destroyed by these militias which looted banks, markets and houses. After the Soviet invasion of Afghanistan, and emergence of Mujahedeen's militias in Pakistan and Iran, regional powers, US, NATO and the Arab world's military experts arrived in Pakistan to train, support, and arm every terrorist and extremist group to defeat the Soviet army in Afghanistan. All these private militias era is still dancing to different tangos in all provinces of Afghanistan. They receive financial support from different channels-challenging territorial authority of the national army of the country.

On 10 June 2022, Human Rights Watch reported Taliban's torture of civilians in Panjshir valley. "Since mid-May 2022, fighting has escalated in the province as National Resistance Front (NRF) forces have attacked Taliban units and checkpoints. The Taliban have responded by deploying to the province thousands of fighters, who have carried out search operations targeting communities. During search operations in other provinces, Taliban forces have committed summary executions and enforced disappearances of captured fighters and other detainees, which are war crimes. Taliban forces in Panjshir province have quickly resorted to beating civilians in their response to fighting against the opposition National Resistance Front," said Patricia Gossman, associate Asia director at Human Rights Watch. "The Taliban's longstanding failure to punish those responsible for serious abuses in their ranks puts more civilians at risk." Human Rights Watch noted. Afghanistan's ruling Taliban illegally detained and tortured residents in northern Panjshir province for their alleged links to armed opposition forces, Human Rights Watch reported.

"Taliban forces in Panjshir province have quickly resorted to beating civilians in their response to fighting against the opposition National Resistance Front," said Patricia Gossma, the associate Asia director at Human Rights Watch. "The Taliban's longstanding failure to punish those responsible for serious abuses in their ranks puts more civilians at risk," she added in the statement. However, Human Rights Watch on 07 July 2022, in its report noted: "Taliban security forces have summarily executed and forcibly disappeared alleged members and supporters of an Islamic State offshoot in eastern Afghanistan, Human Rights Watch said. Since the Taliban took power in August 2021, residents of Nangarhar and Kunar provinces east of Kabul have discovered the bodies of more than 100 men dumped in canals and other locations. Taliban forces have carried out abusive search operations, including night raids, against residents they accuse of sheltering or supporting members of the Islamic State of Khorasan Province (ISKP) armed group, the Afghan affiliate of the Islamic State (ISIS). During these raids, Taliban forces have beaten residents and have detained men they accuse of being ISKP members without legal process or revealing their whereabouts to their families. An unknown number have been summarily executed–shot, hanged, or beheaded–or forcibly disappeared. HRW noted.

The global human rights group has documented the alleged abuses in a report saying they were committed in eastern Nangarhar and Kunar provinces. "Since the Taliban took power in August 2021, residents of Nangarhar and Kunar … have discovered the bodies of more than 100 men dumped in canals and other locations [between August 2021 and April 2022]," the report said. The two provinces, which border Pakistan, are known for hosting active bases of the Islamic State of Khorasan Province (ISIS-K), the Afghan affiliate of Islamic State. Ayaz Gul reported. The possibility of sectarian violence will further disrupt the peace process as the Taliban targets everyone, every sect and every tribe. Expert and analyst, Ajmal Sohail (Afghanistan on the Verge of Religious Terrorism and Sectarian Warfare- July 22, 2022, documented Taliban atrocities against Salafies and other sects:

"In Afghanistan, the Taliban's position towards the Salafists has become punitive and ruthless once again. Albeit, followers of numerous religious Sects live in Afghanistan, such as Ismailia, Shia, Jafri, Ahle-Hadith/Wahhabis, and Sunni-Hanafi. The position of the Taliban militants concerning the Sunni-Hanafi religion is soft and the level of danger to its followers is very low and even zero, compared to followers of other religions. Nevertheless, there are three religious sects, whose followers are at utmost risk, and are under the greatest threat and danger. These three religious groups are particularly tarnished in Afghanistan, since they are assumed to be the elements of foreign intelligence organizations and are used for a common intelligence goal. The first category is the Shias, whose lives are currently under threat in the country, and there are always deadly attacks on their religious ceremonies. Even the Taliban militants intervene in their rites, while disrupting their religious rituals and beating them up. Meanwhile, attacks against the Shia religions by the Daesh group or using the name of this group have been intensified, while slaying them, are tactics of foreign intelligence, especially CIA. Steering an intelligence war tactics in the name of religion between Daesh/Salafi and Shia religions in Afghanistan, like Mosul and other parts of Iraq, which will in turn strain the relations between the new administration of the Taliban of Afghanistan and Iran, is part of the CIA's policy. Because it will force Iran to use the Fatimyun proxy group to defend the rights of the Shia religion's followers in Afghanistan. Thus, the practice of anti-Taliban armed forces and fronts against the Taliban to indirectly control the Taliban in Afghanistan is a special part of the US foreign policy. Nonetheless, if the US wants to directly control the Taliban, then they are supposed to intervene militarily, or apply tremendous external pressure on the Taliban, to get them to abide by the US policy.

Musa Khan Jalalzai

London

Chapter 1

Implications of the New Taliban Government for the Biden Administration

Richard J. Chasdi

Abstract

The August 2021 Taliban takeover of Kabul, and the prospect of Jihadi influxes from Afghanistan subject to Taliban government manipulation, elicits several international security challenges to the United States, and several international and domestic security challenges to several nation-states in close proximity to Afghanistan. Those countries include Tajikistan, Turkmenistan, Uzbekistan, Russia, Pakistan, India, China, and Iran. The threat from potential Jihadi influxes is examined, along with new opportunities for the Biden administration to improve relations with Iran's Ayatollah Khamene'i and President Raisi by means of what political scientists call "assurance games." It follows the use of an "assurance games" framework to help protect Iranian interests in Afghanistan such as the Hazaras for example, has the potential to influence the Joint Comprehensive Plan of Action (JCPOA) talks because issue areas in international politics are related. To further this goal, public U.S. administration support for the efforts by the Taliban government to protect Hazara communities in Afghanistan against ISIS-K terrorism is critical for a substantive re-engagement of American influence in Afghanistan. At the domestic politics level, this is also a prudent position for President Biden to take after his ill-conceived and costly withdrawal from Afghanistan

Keywords: Afghanistan Taliban India terrorism Biden

Introduction

In public discourse about the fall of Afghanistan, it is commonplace to note articles about the egregious human rights violations the Taliban commit, the plight of women and girls under the Taliban, and what the true face of the contemporary Taliban is all about. While all of those topics are critically important, there is precious little in the public domain devoted to even a broader analysis of some strategic threats for regional and international security elicited by the Taliban takeover of Afghanistan. This brief essay on Afghanistan after the fall of the Taliban seeks to fill that gap. The framework for discussion involves: potential Taliban manipulation of opium supplies to international markets; threat potential associated Jihadi extremist influxes to Tajikistan, Turkmenistan, and Uzbekistan; the potential security threat of such influxes to Russian republics in the Caucuses; security implications for India, Pakistan, and China; ties between internal security conditions in Afghanistan and Iran; implications for American security policy.

Overall, the danger the Taliban pose in Afghanistan has grown because the new government is in desperate need of domestic infrastructure and experienced administrators to run the country and police international borders. George suggests that whether or not such threats materialize depends on the capacity of the new Taliban government to access billions of dollars in frozen assets. Dixon states that overall Afghanistan Central Bank assets in U.S. financial institutions amount to approximately U.S. $7 billion, while another U.S. $460 million is held by the International Monetary Fund. For George, "many of the countries in control of that cash flow have said the group's actions regarding human rights, the rights of women and civil liberties will be key to their decision-making," in regards to Taliban access to those funds (Dixon, 2021; George, 2021). The underlying theme of this essay is that the Taliban government can manipulate Jihadi migration flows to countries in close proximity in pursuit of its national interests. One threat associated with potential Jihadi influxes across national borders involves increased opium production and trafficking. Taylor reports, "Afghanistan accounted for 85 percent of the opium produced worldwide last year, far outdoing rival producers such as Myanmar and Mexico …." (Taylor, 2021) If it is deemed to be in the national interest of Taliban leadership to increase drug flows because of revenue scarcities or other political dissatisfaction, terrorist migration and asset flows might include some mixture of assets linked to drug cultivation and distribution.

It seems reasonable that the degree of drug flow encountered would mirror the intensity of domestic problems in Afghanistan. To be more specific, that threat might reflect Taliban leadership perceptions about the likelihood and degree of future international money flows into Afghanistan from Asia and the West, from both state actors and non-state actor donors. If substantial economic problems for the new Afghan government materialize, drug production or distribution, as part of relocated terrorist assets, might work to produce new or enhanced middle-run economic and societal problems. Those problems could include worker absenteeism and crime, designed to augment traditional terrorism threats in some Central Asian states. The potential middle-run and long-haul effects this dimension of terrorist threat could elicit, contrasts sharply with the short-run effects that most single terrorist events and even nearly simultaneous multiple terrorist acts have, where political impacts tend to dissipate over time. Clearly, September 11, 2001 events constitute an exception where terrorist events in New York City, Washington, DC and Shanksville, Pennsylvania had middle-run and long-haul effects.

It follows the potential to flood drug markets with opium is a Taliban leverage point that could be used to access those international funds and otherwise fulfill Taliban government political demands and aspirations, and even sub-national interests linked to Taliban allied terrorist groups. It is important to note that some terrorist groups active in the region have had ties to the drug trade. For example, the Islamic Movement of Uzbekistan (IMU) was at some point involved in drug operations, even as its primary objective remained the replacement of Uzbekistan's secular government with an Islamic government. While the current chieftain of the Islamic Movement of Uzbekistan (IMU) remains unknown, the CIA reports the IMU was headed by Abdulaziz Yuldash until he was killed by the Afghan military in November 2020; it estimates the IMU has some 700 activists (Central Intelligence Agency, 2021c). *Appendix-T-Terrorism; terrorist group(s) – Islamic Movement of Uzbekistan (IMU)*; Saif, 2020)

The literature on drug cartel activity provides some additional insight into this threat dimension that emanates from Afghanistan. In Mexico for example, criminal enterprise drug distribution is enhanced by plazas or "corridors" that are geographical locales used for the safe passage of drugs en-route to American and other international markets. It follows terrorist groups might be compelled to pay rent to the Taliban for use of Afghanistan as a springboard for terrorism expansion in much the same way as drug lords who peddle drugs, "rent" drug corridors from other drug lords in Mexico to expand their presence in international drug markets. As previously noted, new enhanced Jihadi influxes are likely to reflect mixtures of

Taliban government national interest goals and the sub-national objectives of specific terrorist groups. Still, the prospect of traditional terrorism, not drug trafficking, is the most dire threat that Jihadi terrorist group influxes pose to the stability of nation-states in close proximity to Afghanistan. The local powers of the region, namely Uzbekistan, Turkmenistan, and Tajikistan are found to its north, in addition to two world powers – the Russian Federation, and China. The regional powers of Pakistan and India are found to the southeast of Afghanistan, while Iran is found to its west.

Tajikistan, Turkmenistan, Uzbekistan, and Russia

Tajikistan, Turkmenistan, and Uzbekistan are characterized by demographics where ethnic communities (i.e., nations) do not conform completely to nation-state borders. For example, in 2014, the CIA estimated some 84.3 percent of Tajikistan was composed of Tajiks, 13.8 percent of the population was Uzbek, while other ethnic groups comprised 2.0 percent of the total. In the case of Turkmenistan, the demographics breakdown was very similar in 2003, with Turkmens who comprised 85.0 percent of the population, followed by 5.0 percent who were Uzbek, 4.0 percent who were Russian, and other ethnic groups which comprised 6 percent of the total. In the case of Uzbekistan, a 2017 breakdown of ethnic minority groups was comparable. Uzbeks comprised 83.8 percent of the total, with Tajiks at 4.8 percent, Kazakhs at 2.5 percent, Russians at 2.3 percent, Karakalpak at 2.2 percent, Tatars at 1.5 percent, and other ethnic groups at 4.4 percent (Central Intelligence Agency, 2021f. *Explore All Countries – Tajikistan: Central Asia: ethnic groups, Central Intelligence Agency, 2021g. Explore All Countries – Turkmenistan: Central Asia: ethnic groups, Central Intelligence Agency, 2021h. Explore All Countries – Uzbekistan: Central Asia: ethnic groups*). Across these three countries, the rate of minority groups with potential for new or increased political mobilization due to internal or external agitation or both, was roughly comparable, taking into account the different years highlighted in CIA reports.

Those statistics also illustrate the incongruity found between state borders and ethnic population locales. Due to their demographics, those three countries resemble what Anderson in her work on the Middle East suggests are "society centered" countries, where "kinship groups – lineages and tribes" create loyalties that compete with loyalties to the state, thereby in effect working to detract from state power. For Anderson, such competing loyalties to the state, largely absent in the European historical experience of nation-state development, contributed to problems in the Middle East for the nation-state as a political and social construct to take hold and flourish

(Anderson, 1987; Hinnebusch, 2016). Even in Middle East countries with a history of centralized government and what Anderson calls "strong state apparatus" as found in states such as Iran, Turkey, and Tunisia, powerful ethnic and religious ties between groups traverse national borders to weaken the power of national and local governments (Anderson, 1987; Hinnebusch, 2016). One hallmark of supra-national ethnic or religious "kinship-lineage" ties in a particular region or across regions is their set of links to transnational movements such as Pan-Arabism and Pan-Islamism, and to transnational organizations, such as terrorist groups, that are non-state actors frequently emblematic of such political movements.

It is possible to extrapolate from Anderson's analysis on "kinship groups" to showcase how certain domestic terrorist groups in countries in Central Asia with ties to populations across state border could benefit from Jihadi influxes from Afghanistan. For example, according to the Emomali Rahmon government, the terrorist threat in Tajikistan emanates from Jammat Ansrullah, a domestic sourced terrorist group in Afghanistan established by Amridden Tabarov in 2010 and from "foreign based" terrorist groups that augment the terrorism threat such as the Islamic Movement of Uzbekistan (IMU) (Ahmadi, Yusufi, & Fazlidden, 2021; Lemon, 2014). As Afghanistan's population is some 27 percent Tajik, it is probably no exaggeration to say that Afghanistan could serve as a platform for increased "foreign based" Jihadi flows into Tajikistan as well (World Population Review, 2021).

Moreover, the structure and processes of terrorist groups can take advantage of "society centered" country dynamics in countries characterized by this poor fit between national borders and ethnic populations. Those processes include terrorist group permeability and the capacity of some terrorist groups to draw from multiple recruitment sources. The ability of terrorist groups to recruit from each other also seems to underscore Anderson's point about "society-centered" country effects and in this case, the potential for terrorist alliance shifts. For example, the Islamic State of Iraq and ash Sham Khorasan Province (ISIS-K) has recruited from the Islamic Movement of Uzbekistan (IMU), disaffected former Taliban activists, and from Tehrik-e-Taliban Pakistan (TTP) (Central Intelligence Agency, 2021d. *Appendix-T-Terrorism, terrorist group(s)–Islamic State of Iraq and ash-Sham-Khorasan Province (ISIS-K)*; Anderson, 1987). Furthermore, empirical patterns in the structural shifts of terrorist group alliances support this notion. For example, the Islamic Movement of Uzbekistan (IMU) is now closely affiliated with ISIS-K but it was once affiliated with the Taliban. In contrast, an IMU splinter group called the Islamic Jihad Union (IJU) has maintained close links to al-Qaeda and the Taliban, even against the backdrop of terrorist group permeability dynamics, where shifting terrorist loyalties, and in some cases multiple terrorist affiliations with terrorist groups, remain a hallmark of the terrorist group splintering process.

The Islamic Jihad Union (IJU) was headed by Najmidden Kamolitdinovich Jalalov until his death on September 14, 2009. As in the case of the Islamic Movement of Uzbekistan (IMU) described above, the current chieftain of the Islamic Jihad Union (IJU) remains unknown, but the CIA estimates the terrorist organization has some 100–200 activists (Central Intelligence Agency, 2021b. *Appendix-T-Terrorism, terrorist group(s) – Islamic Jihad Union (IJU)*; Gorman & Spiegel, 2009). It seems fair to say that condition of terrorist group permeability between many terrorist groups has the potential to help create opportunities for terrorist groups to expand and increase nation-state political instability. Terrorist splintering, itself a function of the interactive effects of personal rivalries, differences of opinion about a group's political direction, and government anti-terrorism policy, leads to the expansion of terrorist groups and can lead to changes in target selection, and intensity of terrorist assaults (Chasdi, 2002, 1999).

What is significant here is that terrorist group leaders with direct loyalties to the Taliban or al-Qaeda or both, or indirect loyalties through allied terrorist groups, could cause significant political instability in Tajikistan, Turkmenistan, or Uzbekistan, should terrorist group interests and Taliban government interests converge. In a similar vein, terrorist groups affiliated with ISIS-Khorasan or ISIS in the broader sense could also promote corresponding political instability in Uzbekistan, Turkmenistan, and Tajikistan, as well as in countries such as India, Pakistan, and Iran, all within the context of the fierce global struggle between ISIS and the Taliban. Turning to Russia, the prospect of Jihadi influxes from Afghanistan creates a set of especially dire challenges for the Russian Federation. President Putin has to contend with the likelihood that Jihadi influxes from Afghanistan will provide a springboard for new Jihadi migrations into the Russian republics of Chechnya, Dagestan, and Ingushetia, beyond the independent "near abroad" countries of Tajikistan, Turkmenistan, and Uzbekistan. Those Jihadi influxes could help bring Chechen and other wars of independence in Caucasus region countries closer to Moscow and other Russian cities.

India and Pakistan

With respect to India, a major strategic challenge to regional security is that Jihadis from Afghanistan could create what amounts to a corridor through Peshawar, bypassing Islamabad to make their way into Jammu and Kashmir. Jihad influxes would constitute what Jenkins calls a "force multiplier" to enhance India's "spiral of insecurity" vis a vis Pakistan. A substantial influx of Jihadis into Jammu and Kashmir would probably produce significant political destabilization, increasing the likelihood of yet another war – a fifth – between India and Pakistan. What is significant in this case are the powerful ties between terrorist groups with vested interests in Jammu and Kashmir and the set of permeable boundaries found presumably between at least some of those terrorist groups. That condition would work to amplify threat potential posed by Jihadi influxes into Jammu and Kashmir with the prospect that a new spate of terrorist assaults characterized by greater intensity, modified target preference or both, could become the emergent reality as a result of pooled resources.

For example, Harakat ul-Jihad-i-Islami (HUJI) advocates for full-blown Pakistani control over Jammu and Kashmir and has strong ties to al-Qaeda and to Pakistan. That is also the case for Harakat ul-Mujahidin (HUM), that itself is a Harakat ul-Jihad-i-Islami (HUJI) splinter group (Central Intelligence Agency, 2021a. *Appendix-T-Terrorism, terrorist group(s)– Harakat ul-Mujahidin (HUM)*). In addition, Lashkar-i-Jhangvi, Jaish-e-Mohammed (JeM) and Pakistan's Lashkar-e-Taiba organization all have solid links to al-Qaeda and now presumably to the Taliban government. Lashkar e-Taiba also has connections to al-Qaeda and strong ties to Pakistan's Inter-Service Intelligence (ISI) (Central Intelligence Agency, 2021e. *Appendix-T-Terrorism, terrorist group(s)–Lashkar-e-Taiba (LeT)*; (Fair, 2014; Pike, 2004; SATP, 2001). *Harakat-ul-Mujahideen (HuM): Assam))* Likewise, ISIS and terrorist groups aligned with it also have potential to send activists to Jammu Kashmir, perhaps to offset influxes of Jihadis with ties to the Taliban government and al-Qaeda.

Terrorist group penetrability is also critical to take into account to appraise existing connections between established terrorist groups in Pakistan. The reason why is because new Islamic extremist migration flows from Afghanistan in Jammu and Kashmir could also exploit opportunities to influence events back home in Afghanistan. For example, ISIS-K's parent organization, Tehrik-e-Taliban Pakistan (TTP) is characterized by activist support for both al-Qaeda and ISIS. While Tehrik-e-Taliban Pakistan (TTP) has proclaimed support for al-Qaeda in the past, the CIA reports some TTP activists have defected to ISIS-K.[1] Hence, it seems possible that certain TTP activists with allegiance to ISIS-K might collaborate with ISIS-K in Afghanistan in its efforts to commit terrorist attacks against the Shia Hazaras (Constable, 2021; Felbab-Brown, 2021).

This is still not a complete picture of the national security challenges that confront India's national government in Delhi. For Indian national security, the scope and depth of Jihadi influx threats moves well beyond Jammu and Kashmir. The reason why is the scope and numbers of Maoist organizations such as the Communist Party of India (CPI Maoist), and the very large number of national-irredentist terrorist groups found in India. Khemnar reports the South Asian Terror Portal (SATP) chronicled some 180 terrorist groups in India over the past few decades. Likewise, Sahni reports some 136 "militant groups" in Northeast India's sister state region, a part of India that borders several countries where Chinese influence is pronounced (Khemnar, 2018; Sahni, 2019).

Many of these Indian national-irredentist terrorist groups have adopted minority ethnic groups and promoted their interests, while simultaneously working to develop bases of constituent support and safe-havens. In many cases, those minority ethnic groups have experienced protracted conflict with India's national government in Delhi, and in some instances state government, over political and cultural issues associated with prolonged economic backwater conditions and systemic discrimination. That condition provides critical leverage for both Taliban leaders, who can influence migration flow directions, and equally important, to Chinese leaders who can support those Indian terrorist groups to promote Chinese national interests. Another dimension of the Jihadi influx problem into Pakistan is that Tehrik-e-Taliban Pakistan (TTP) could work directly to destabilize Pakistan's Imran Khan government if Tehrik-e-Taliban Pakistan leadership perceives, either rightly or wrongly, that Imran Khan's government has cooperated too closely with the Biden administration's "over-the-horizon" counterterrorism programs. For reasons detailed below, Pakistan will probably remain an important part of the counterterrorism puzzle that U.S. policymakers must confront for "over the horizon efforts" in Afghanistan, even though the exact role for Pakistan in U.S. counterterrorism plans remains ill-defined.

The reason why Pakistan remains in the alliance picture is the Biden administration has some leverage over Prime Minister Imran Khan due to the large numbers of refugees expected to materialize on Pakistan's western border at the Durand Line. Pakistani leaders know there is real potential to mask terrorist group and asset movement across the border as terrorists intermingle with legitimate refugees who seek a safe haven from the Taliban. Even if terrorist group crossings into vulnerable areas under the cover of legitimate refugee flows is minimal, the overall pressure refugee influxes create for government abilities to maintain order and provide social services is enormous. Those government capacities, already strained in western Pakistan, would probably increase violence potential and for some desperate refugees, the process of radicalization. All of the foregoing provides incentives for Pakistani leadership to reach out to international organizations that Washington heavily influences, and to the Biden administration directly for help. Having said that U.S. foreign policymakers are on the horns of a dilemma with Kabul's fall to the Taliban. While it is critical for U.S. policymakers to craft a new range of security arrangements with India, it is equally important to balance security planning with India with clear policy objectives and recommendations about what to request from Pakistani leaders to buttress security at the Durand Line. Plainly, subsequent talks with Pakistani leaders will amount to intensive bargaining over concessions; that will probably involve a set of lowered expectations on both sides because of the strained relationship between American and Pakistani leaders since 2001, made more pronounced with the volcanic shock waves produced when Osama Bin Laden was found in Abbottabad (Wagner, 2007).

China

The potential Jihadi influx from Afghanistan also increases the nation-state security dilemma and corresponding "spiral of insecurity" between India and China, a spiral that is already extremely high because of recent border skirmishes in the Himalayas. As previously mentioned, President Xi Jinping might obtain active or tacit Taliban support for Chinese assistance provided to Indian Maoist or nationalist-irredentist terrorist groups in conflict with India's national government. The links between geography and geopolitical interests are stark in this case. The reason why is because of the geographical proximity of several countries to India that are heavily influenced by Chinese national interests. Thus, the Chinese are in a position to exert influence on terrorist groups fighting against India's national government. Those countries include Nepal, Bhutan, Bangladesh, and Myanmar, and some of those countries have been used in the past as a conduit to extend Chinese aid to terrorist groups (*Meghalaya Times* (India), 2013. Trader escapes unhurt in militant firing; Gohain, 2007)

In the broader sense, analysts point out that with the fall of Kabul, Chinese and Afghan national interests dovetail well, in no small part because each set of national interests is framed within the context of authoritarian political systems. In the short-run, President Xi Jinping is compelled to work with the Taliban because the Taliban have an ace up their sleeve – the Chinese fear an Afghan Jihadi group corridor of their own, flooded with Islamic extremists working their way into Xinjiang province to support and train Uighur activists. Leaving aside such negative inducements and the leverage they produce, the Chinese and Afghans have a range of economic interests that converge in the middle-run and long-haul intervals, in no small part because the Chinese want additional territories to expand their Belt and Road Initiative. In turn, the Taliban want Chinese investment monies that could be accessible, perhaps through the Asia Infrastructure Investment Bank (AIIB). As previously mentioned, Taliban leaders need experienced bureaucrats to run the country. Thus, for both sides, some fundamental political goals in each country's national interest agenda seem achievable. From the standpoint of Chinese and Russian leaders, the political shockwaves of the Taliban government borrowing from AIIB rather than the World Bank or the International Monetary Fund (IMF) would be considerable because it might jump start even closer AIIB involvement with countries with egregiously poor human rights records that are in basic need of financial assistance. Indeed, that pattern of AIIB borrowing might affect international economic assistance sources for decades to come.

Iran

The Iranian dimension of the Taliban's victory in Afghanistan also needs to be taken into account by U.S. security planners. Velda Felbab-Brown provides a solid account of Iranian Fatemiyoun military outfits in Afghanistan, geared toward the protection of Iranian interests in Afghanistan. The author notes Iranian leaders have an underlying national interest in efforts to protect Afghanistan's Shia Hazara communities from ISIS-Khorasan (ISIS-K) terrorist assaults, attacks designed to exacerbate Sunni-Shia tensions in Afghanistan and ultimately, to disrupt and undercut Taliban political control (Felbab-Brown, 2021). Velda Felbab-Brown also reports that should ISIS-Khorasan (ISIS-K) intensify terrorist assaults against Afghanistan's Hazaras, or should ISIS-K terrorist attacks happen closer to the Iranian-Afghan border, those Fatemiyoun outfits might be mobilized by Iranian President Ebrahim Raisi (Felbab-Brown, 2021). Against the backdrop of Iranian-Pakistani-Chinese relations, it is also important to note that an effective and sustained Iranian campaign against

17

ISIS-K could also stimulate TTP actions in Pakistan against the Imran Khan government to try to reduce or alter the range of Iranian military responses in Afghanistan against TTP's own splinter group, ISIS-K.

In addition to the challenge of protecting Iranian interests, the Taliban takeover of Kabul also provides opportunities for President Ebrahim Raisi and the Biden administration to take advantage of converging national interests. What is tantalizing is that with such cooperation, there is the prospect of positive effects across interconnected foreign policy issue areas. For example, should conflict involving the Hazaras in Afghanistan develop further, or that likelihood is appraised as high by U.S. policymakers, opportunities for cooperation with the Raisi government might materialize. In other words, a lurking conflict between Iranian Fatemiyoun outfits and the ISIS-K in Afghanistan might provide an opportunity for what Lawson might call American-Iranian "assurance games" (Lawson, 2018).

For Lawson, who draws on the work of L.L. Martin, "assurance games" involve "informal cooperation" between adversaries over specific issues fraught with threat potential. It follows such "assurance games" might include U.S. confidence building measures (CBM's) offered to Iranian leaders to support those Iranian military outfits in their struggle against ISIS-K (Lawson, 2018). Simultaneously, the value-added component of such CBM's would be to demonstrate American willingness to support Taliban government national interests, thereby in effect setting the stage for future American -Taliban political interactions. What is significant is the time-honored notion that issue areas in international politics are related. Therefore, it seems possible that the continuously evolving security condition in Afghanistan could be used to leverage Iranian concessions about a new iteration of the now moribund Joint Comprehensive Plan of Action (i.e., JCPOA 2.0).

United States policy response

All of the foregoing underscores the imperative for good U.S. intelligence compilation. It is probably fair to say that effective and sustained "on-the-ground" intelligence compilation is perhaps best accessed through Pakistan because intelligence operatives can cross the Durand Line and blend in well with local populations due to those operatives having Pashtun or Tajik culture and languages in common. Having said that there are problems to tackle. First, within the context of strains and tensions between the United States and Pakistan, there is no indication, at least for the time being, that Pakistani leaders would agree to close collaboration, including the use of

Pakistani bases for U.S. "over-the-horizon" counterterrorism operations. Second, U.S. policymakers must confront the realities of Pakistan's time-honoured alliance with China. Those close political ties to China suggest that Pakistani leaders might respond to significant Jihadi influx problems into Jammu and Kashmir and into parts of uncontested India in ways that are less than satisfactory from American and Indian security perspectives.

Another challenge for U.S. foreign policymakers revolves around Chinese and Russian cooperation. The political elite in China and Russia are likely to coordinate foreign policy inclusive of economic assistance to the Taliban to the detriment of American interests because it is that fundamental commitment to the Taliban that will keep the U.S. on the political fringes of involvement in Afghanistan for years to come. This puts President Joseph R. Biden in a weakened position where he will have to provide some incentives for the Russians to blunt the effects of such triangulation, perhaps with concessions. That might involve concessions about Russian natural gas energy distribution to Western Europe or Ukraine, greater recognition of Russian "near-abroad" interests, or greater concessions to Russian leaders in parts of the Middle East such as Sudan, where Russian national interests are pronounced (Washington Post, 2021. Disputed Nord Stream pipeline completed; Al-Jazeera, 2021. Military chief says Sudan reviewing naval base deal with Russia). Still, Putin might agree to work with the Biden administration in addition to the governments of Tajikistan and Turkmenistan to supply more seamless protection against Jihadi migration threats into the Caucasus, depending on the potential scope of the problem. The political vulnerabilities of Tajikistan, Turkmenistan, and Uzbekistan to Jihadi migration might actually provide a series of POE's (points of entry) for American-based intelligence assets into Afghanistan from Tajikistan or Turkmenistan or both, that would also benefit Russian security. However, that type of security cooperation seems unlikely to develop fully because both Chinese and Russian national interest in providing assistance to the Taliban dovetail so well.

Final reflections

What seems especially important at this juncture is not so much whether President Biden was right or wrong to leave Afghanistan in the way he did, but whether or not Biden senior administration officials are taking into account the subtleties and nuances of these interrelated foreign policy issue areas where connections create threat amplification effects throughout the region between sub-national actors. In addition, connections between state actors such as Afghanistan, Russia, China, India, Pakistan, and Iran, and various non-state actors must be taken into account with emphasis on policy work to identify anticipated and unanticipated effects that stem from those that complex set of direct and indirect connections between stakeholders.

For Biden, statements to convey to the American public that those complex and connected issues are under review should not be a difficult task because President Biden does not have to offer anything more to the public at this time than acknowledgment of those complexities and assurances that his administration is focused on them. Such acknowledgment would be good political capital for President Biden, to offset an ill-conceived and costly withdrawal from Afghanistan. It would also pave the way for implementation of new "over-the-horizon" counter-terrorism programs, and multilateral efforts to confront problems in the region that include terrorist threat potential, and other related challenges that Afghanistan's new Taliban government could bring to Washington's doorstep.

No potential conflict of interest was reported by the author(s). **Richard J. Chasdi**, *Ph.D. is a Professorial Lecturer in the Department of Political Science at The George Washington University. He is a Senior Fellow at the Global Peace Institute, London, U.K. and also an Adjunct Senior Fellow at the International Centre for Political Violence and Terrorism Research (ICPVTR) at the S. Rajaratnam School of International Studies (RSIS) at Nanyang Technological University, Singapore. Prior to that Dr. Chasdi was a Professor of Management at Walsh College in Troy, Michigan. He received his B.A. in Politics from Brandeis University in 1981, his M.A. in Political Science from Boston College in 1985, and his Ph.D. in Political Science from Purdue University in 1995. He has published four books on terrorism and counterterrorism, and several book chapters and refereed academic articles. Chasdi's first book, Serenade of Suffering: A Portrait of Middle East Terrorism, 1968-1993 (Lexington Books, 1999) received Choice magazine's "Outstanding Academic Title" in the field of international relations in 2000. Dr. Chasdi serves on the editorial board of Armed Forces & Society, on the editorial board of Perspectives on Terrorism: A Journal of the Terrorism Research Initiative, and serves as an Advisory Council member to the Digital Marketing Certificate Program at the School of Business, The George Washington University. In 2017, Chasdi was a Fulbright Specialist at RSIS at Nanyang Technological University, working as a Visiting Fellow at the International Centre for Political Violence and Terrorism Research (ICPVTR). He has served as a news consultant for National Public Radio (NPR), Al-Jazeera, Al-Sharq TV, China Global Television (CGTN), and Radio Sputnik. The International Journal of Intelligence, Security, and Public Affairs Volume 23, 2021 - Issue 3. The International Journal of Intelligence, Security, and Public Affairs (formerly known as Inteligencia y Seguridad: Revista de Análisis y Prospectiva), founded in 2006, began as the first*

Spanish scientific journal dedicated to the study of intelligence. It has since then joined Taylor & Francis' robust stable of intelligence journals and began publishing exclusively in English in 2016. The journal is characterized by a clear international vocation and perspective. It aims to disseminate original academic and professional articles on matters related to intelligence applied to security, defense, business and the financial-economic environment. Taylor & Francis make every effort to ensure the accuracy of all the information (the "Content") contained in our publications. However, Taylor & Francis, our agents (including the editor, any member of the editorial team or editorial board, and any guest editors), and our licensors, make no representations or warranties whatsoever as to the accuracy, completeness, or suitability for any purpose of the Content. Any opinions and views expressed in this publication are the opinions and views of the authors, and are not the views of or endorsed by Taylor & Francis. The accuracy of the Content should not be relied upon and should be independently verified with primary sources of information. Taylor & Francis shall not be liable for any losses, actions, claims, proceedings, demands, costs, expenses, damages, and other liabilities whatsoever or howsoever caused arising directly or indirectly in connection with, in relation to, or arising out of the use of the Content. Implications of the New Taliban Government for the Biden Administration. Richard J. Chasdi. Pages 425-438 | Published online: 22 Dec 2021. The journal's main goal is to investigate and study intelligence for decision making in a broad sense. It is a meeting point for professionals and academics where they tackle rigorously a wide range of subjects in this field, including issues related to the practice of intelligence in democratic societies. To cite this article: Richard J. Chasdi (2021) Implications of the New Taliban Government for the Biden Administration, The International Journal of Intelligence, Security, and Public Affairs, 23:3, 425-438, DOI: 10.1080/23800992.2021.2011071 To link to this article: https://doi. org/10.1080/23800992.2021.2011071 © 2021 The Author(s). Published with license by Taylor & Francis Group, LLC. CONTACT Richard J. Chasdi rchasdi@aol.com Department of Political Science, George Washington University, Monroe Hall Ste 440, 2115 G Street NW Washington, DC 20052 THE INTERNATIONAL JOURNAL OF INTELLIGENCE, SECURITY, AND PUBLIC AFFAIRS 2021, VOL. 23, NO. 3, 425–438 https://doi.org/10.1080/23800992.2021.2011071 © 2021 The Author(s). Published with license by Taylor & Francis Group, LLC. This is an Open Access article distributed under the terms of the Creative Commons Attribution-NonCommercial-NoDerivatives License (http://creativecommons.org/licenses/by-nc-nd/4.0/), which permits non-commercial re-use, distribution, and reproduction in any medium, provided the original work is properly cited, and is not altered, transformed, or built upon in any way

Chapter 2

China's Engagement with Taliban after American Withdrawal: Implications for Pakistan

Jalal ud Din Kakar and Asad ur Rehman

Abstract

The United States' sudden withdrawal from Afghanistan created a huge power vacuum in the region and induced serious repercussions for all regional states. China is especially facing a new situation in its backyard that has the potential to disrupt its Belt and Road Initiative. Afghanistan's location makes it an important place connecting eastern and western parts of BRI. This study by delving into primary and secondary sources concurs that China is thinking about a serious engagement with the new regime in Afghanistan. Using the analytic engagement and conceptual framework of geo-economics it brings out the potential avenues of cooperation between both countries and what it means for Pakistan. From the Chinese perspective this paper informs about Chinese intentions to engage with the Taliban regime in economic and security related spheres. It aims to understand the potential avenues of cooperation that exist between both countries, of which one has no international recognition. Lastly, the paper also included discussion on China-Taliban's engagement and its implication for Pakistan and argues that Pakistan's national security is heavily dependent on both China and Afghanistan.

Keywords: China, Taliban, Afghanistan, United States of America, Geo-economics, Pakistan

Introduction

At the global scale, it seems, both the U.S. and China are competing for domination over the world. The situation is forcing both countries to make alliances to achieve their national goals and protect their national goals in the macro-region of the Global Indian Ocean (Hass R. , 2021). The US's interests in Afghanistan were predicated upon a strict national security paradigm legitimized by normative ideas underpinning liberal political order spearheaded by the United State since the end of the 2nd world war. Notable objective of this intervention was to bring political stability, end protracted civil war and destroy the safe havens of groups working against American interests. However, the sudden American withdrawal from Afghanistan is creating a domestic power vacuum and anxieties for the region. Both factors offered opportunity and space for diplomatic manoeuvring to China (Hass, 2021). It is now seriously considering investing in its economic ties with Afghanistan to achieve the same ends, its own national security. It is argued that a stable Afghanistan is more crucial for its newly envisioned long-term objective to make China the largest economy of the world (Glazbrook, 2021).

China has its eagerness in a similar case shown in Iran and agreed to invest $400 billion in the Persian Gulf State, over the period of 25 years (Fassihi & Myers, 2021). In fact, In Pakistan, under the vision of the flagship Silk Road Project, China had already invested more than $73 billion in 'China's Pakistan Economic Corridor' (Hillman & Sacks, 2021). Not only this investment will be saved and get more premium if Afghanistan will also join the BRI (Belt and Road Initiative). The unique and attractive geo-graphical location of Afghanistan has created interest in China. On the other hand, The United States and its NATO (North Atlantic Treaty Organization) presence in the backyard of China, has created a a 'security dilemma' for her. China sees the U.S and its military presence in its backyard is a direct threat to China's national security. The most pertinent objective of China in Afghanistan is to secure its long-term interest in the region and beyond through peaceful means. Thus, China wants the United States execution from the region, and only when the withdrawal is responsible and not left a chaotic and uncertain prevailing situation in the region. (Sun, 2020). Similarly, there are legitimate concerns in China and Pakistan fearing that some semblance of stability will not get restored in Afghanistan. It will not only aggravate the stability inside Pakistan but also put Chinese's investment in the region at stake and future geo-economic plans of integrating the regional economies of Asia. After the blitz-like Taliban takeover of Kabul, the United States' two-decade long efforts ended in a withdrawal and a new strategy of engagement with twin countries of Pakistan and Afghanistan or (Af-Pak). Amidst this sudden chaotic withdrawal and to total annihilation of Ashraf Ghani led Afghan regime all eyes remained focus on Taliban and United States.

There is a little or no discussion on Chinese intentions, options, and opportunities to fill in the gap left behind by American withdrawal. This is what provided inspiration to us to try to understand the existing Sino-Taliban/Afghan relations and how American withdrawal can affect it (Kaur, 2021). Afghanistan is a landlocked country, yet it did not remain aloof from the rest of the world since the time of Alexander. However, with the arrival of the modern era the country had turned into a classic case of a prisoner of geography (it describes the impact geography can have on international affairs) There is a plurality of narratives that define and describe the position of the country in regional and global history. To celebrate the resilience and steadfastness of the people of Afghanistan against the foreign invasions it has been eulogized 'graveyard of empires.' From the times of Kipling to Khaled Hosseini the literature world sees it as a land of brute force where jaggedness and wilderness are not features of physical geography but also of its people (Benjamin, 2020). In fact, its history reflects that many great powers have miserably failed to conquer it or keep a direct control on it. It is as correct for contemporary powers as it was true for the likes of Alexander and Genghis Khan, (Benjamin, 2020).

However, this narrative oversimplifies or misses some nuanced details of the affairs between empires and the nature of their engagement with the Afghan country. Especially with the rising British influence and sovereignty in 19th century the region served as a 'buffer zone' between Great Britain and the then Soviet Union. And in the process lost its unique position of political eminence, it enjoyed until the 18th century, and turned into a weak state dependent on its neighbours for even sorting out domestic challenges. Starting from the British shadow of 'shared sovereignty' has not left Afghanistan. Later on, the Soviet Union, US, Pakistan and Iran pulled over their weight onto the domestic politics and even state-formation inside Afghanistan (Laskin, 2021). The United States' hurried withdrawal is not first of its nature and it could be compared with the USSR military drawdown from Afghanistan in 1988. The ill-planned military withdrawal had created a political vacuum in the country with dire consequences for the region is swamped by bogey of cross-border (inter-region) terrorism and strong presences of sectarianism and political stability caused by an 'ungovernable' Afghanistan. The manner in which the United State of America had set its 'feet of clay' (in the words of Trotsky) and later the way it has changed (or changed) its nature of engagement with the Af-Pak region is yet a satisfactory answer. (Kissinger, 2021).

The United State of America and Taliban has no one-dimensional history of engagement nor a stable ideological or transactional relationship. Relations between the United State of America and the Afghan Taliban have not been good in the past. The United State of America provided logistical, financial, and moral support to the Mujahidin, smiling and shaking hands with President Reagan at White House. Then it kept in direct relationship with Taliban mediated by Pakistan to achieve certain guarantees for protecting the economic interest of its oil Companies (Rashid, 2010). The nature of engagement and a closer look on its evolutionary trajectory could help situating the current withdrawal in a relatively longer period of engagement between the two countries adhering to two strictly opposing ideological worldviews. In February of 1989, the USSR (The Union of Soviet Socialist Republic) pulled out from Afghanistan handling over power to Dr. Najeeb Ullah. He tried his best to end the internecine conflict between the warring factions of Afghan tribal elites. He tried to use the power of the state to bring some social modernization to reduce the burden of conservative value-system that was inflaming the conflict. However, despite the disintegration of the USSR and relatively more liberal credentials of Dr Najeeb (Dutta, 2021).

The United States continued supplying weapons to the Mujahidin. This civil war continues and in 1992, Taliban won the civil war in Afghanistan. In 1996, the Taliban established Islamic Emirate of Afghanistan. They emerged as a major political force in Afghanistan. Their victory influenced the domestic and regional politics in multiple manners. For example, the enforcement of religiosity through state, imaginary of Khilafat and implementation of Sharia (in practice code of Pashtun wali) have transnational and continental consequences i.e., the event of 9/11. Especially religion becoming the key ideational force lying down conditions for any political arena. Predominantly Sunni, the interpretation of religion, politics, and sociality. They were offering was not acceptable to the minority Shiite sect, who was also ethnically different from the Pashtun dominated Taliban movement. The authorities and rowdy culture of rural Pashtun pushed the Taliban to inscribe the same code of ethics and system of values to a diverse pool of sects, tribes, and ethnicities. It ended up creating moral to political chaos and consolidation of authoritarian

25

impulses into the Emirate-e-Afghanistan (Maizland, 2021). The United State during the whole period was merely a spectator and tried to keep its hand away from making a direct military, diplomatic, or any other kind of intervention. In the due period the Islamic outlook of Taliban regime, its porous control on territory and population and the purposive use of symbol of PanIslamism led to the consolidation of forces and organizations that were latter designated as terrorist by the home security department of the US (Emily, 2021).

In reaction to the event of 9/11. On Oct 7, 2001, American forces joined by NATO allies (North Atlantic Treaty Organization) entered Afghanistan with a pretext to overthrow the Islamic Emirate of Afghanistan which was sheltering wanted terrorist of Al-Qaeda (It is a multinationals militant Islamic group composed of Salafist Jihadists). This new engagement of US with Afghanistan was coded as "Global War on Terrorism" with purpose of bringing "enduring freedom" to extirpate the menace of terrorism from its root. The proclaimed objective of this militaristic intervention was to hunt down the Osama Bin Ladin and to penalize Taliban for giving safe sanctuaries to the Al-Qaeda top notch in leaders in Afghanistan. However, despite continuous pressure and the threat of invasion, the Taliban were not persuaded to breakage their linkage with Al-Qaeda. The Taliban unwillingness to return Bin Ladin forced the United Sates to dismantle the Taliban regime (Zucchino, 2021). The United State of America's interests and nature of its indirect, mediated and latter direct militaristic engagement with Afghanistan were always predicated upon the strict national security concerns. However, for drawing in the legitimacy for its action it also used Normative-Liberal discourse of Human Rights violation and women freedom to justify its action. However, this veneer was simply lifted. In 2021 by, President Joe Biden by counting that, "United State of America led NATO force cannot fight a war that the people of Afghan and its military are not willing to fight for themselves. The US has spent our trillions of dollars and well trained and equipped the Afghan army of some 3 million large force."(House, The White, 2021). Similarly, after the blitz like swift takeover of Afghanistan on 15 Aug 2021, the United States' two decade long protracted direct engagement were ended in an agreed yet ill-planned withdrawal. Once, the Afghan Taliban was back in action and the Afghan army had shown no spine to stand before a rowing band of the Taliban troops. It received to a humiliating defeat at the hands of Taliban and all the vestiges, institutional as well as ideological, smoked into air with a swish of the hands. All the investment which was done by the United State of America on Afghan army, was fruitless (Acemoglu, 2021). An authoritarian scholar in the field, Dr. Shoaib Pervaiz, explained this setback in following terms, "This is very big loss for the United State of America itself, it has invested over $3 trillion in Afghanistan to stop them (Taliban) from taking over. So that project is completely in disarray. Similarly, the win heart and mind strategy of General Petraeus, former Director of Central Intelligence Agency and the next General who took over the command of American forces. It is in shamble because that strategy has really failed." In fact, the Afghan Taliban made a strong come back to the helm of power in Afghanistan after the two decades of long war consist of pitched battles of mind, nerves and strategy. After the total annihilation of Ashraf Ghani led government all eyes of the international community are fixed on the Afghan Taliban.

While on the ground the situation for this Taliban regime is facing now one of the worst political, economic, climate, and humanitarian crisis. The Afghan economy is in shamble, and even no money is available in public exchequer to pay salaries of public servants. Taliban lacked in the organizational capacity to manage these monumental challenges in the after math of US withdrawal (Nagesh , 2020). Given the nature of inconsistent nature of US-Taliban relations. China's role attains much significance not only for Afghanistan but also China. China is an emerging economic power of Asia trying to protect this success into ideological and political domains. China is seriously considering the region and revitalizing its old silk road through the One Belt and One Road Initiatives. Therefore, stable Afghanistan is very important to ensure its futuristic ambitious of building a chain centric hegemonic model of pragmatic political economy without any agenda for imparting a social change in Afghanistan. However, there is not clarity of both ambitions and conduct and that is question that inquiry would like to probe.

Geo-Economic Perspective

Geo-economics lay down the emphasis on promotion of trade and economic cooperation among the states to bring them closer to achieve the national interests. While according to classical geo-politics the national interest and power can be gained and maintained through the physical control of territories. Therefore, the concept of geo-economic is antithesis to the classical geo-political theory as both approaches follow different mechanism to achieve the same goals (Bura, 2012). According to Mikael Wigell, geo-economics is an approach which can be attributed to the both an analytical approach and a foreign policy strategy. Geo-economics put emphasis on economic cooperation to gain and maximize power, and this concept is a new tool for the scholars to analyze the international relations. In geo-economics one could analyze how economic tools are employed by the states to achieve a specific strategic objective in a particular geographical area as the state using economic means to meet foreign policy goals. And this study heavily borrows on the work of Mikael Wigell (Wigell, 2018).

Conceptual Framework

Afghanistan boasts of a unique geographical location as it connects central Asia, South Asia, and the Middle East. Its unique geography creates geo-strategic and geo-political interests for China. Owing to the unique topography of Afghanistan, which mainly consists of mountains, terrains and valleys, China or any other powerful state cannot achieve geo-strategic interests through classical approach, which believes in the use of military power and occupation to achieve goals. Therefore, China has wielded a geo-economics approach to procure its geo-strategic and geo-political goals. There are a myriad of geo-strategic and economic interests that China wants to acquire in Afghanistan to enhance its power. Firstly, China wants to jettison the security risks that are posed to China due to instability in Afghanistan. China shares a border with Afghanistan and the latter has been the hub of terrorists since a long time. Those terrorists in Afghanistan poses a serious threat to the sovereignty of China, and China has the aspiration to get rid of these terrorists. Therefore, the Chinese leadership wants economic cooperation with Afghanistan so that a robust government of Afghanistan cooperates with her to achieve her security interest in Afghanistan. Secondly, China launched BRI in order to increase its influence in the region. China is an emerging global power on the map of the world, and the world has recently witnessed the bitter animosity between the USA and China. The USA evacuated Afghanistan last year which provided relief to China. China cannot afford to have any other global power sitting next to its door which could prove a hurdle in the way of its national interests. Due to this reason China envisages a stable and robust Afghan government so that there would be no room for any foreign power to invade Afghanistan.

Thirdly, China aspires to have an influence in the Middle East, and she has made a huge investment in Iran. Iran is a geo-strategic partner of China; however, both partners have no ground connection. Afghanistan provides a road connection between China and Iran. China has a special interest in the Middle East; therefore, she wants economic cooperation with Afghanistan. Thus, China wants a prosperous Afghanistan so that it can help China to exert her influence in the Middle East. Fourthly, the instability in Afghanistan poses a serious threat to China's BRI (Belt and Road initiative) project and especially to the CPEC project, the flagship project under the umbrella of BRI. China wants to extirpate all security risks associated with its developmental projects. Therefore, China is investing in Afghanistan so that a stable Afghanistan helps China to achieve her economic and strategic goals in the region. China wants to achieve the above --mentioned objectives through geo-economics tools. China wants economic cooperation with Afghanistan to procure its interests by creating a stable and prosper government in Afghanistan that serves her interests. To begin with Afghanistan's unveiled underground natural resources. China has offered economic and technical assistance to Afghanistan to parlay the underground resources to cash. It will prosper the Afghan government which will ultimately serve the interest of China. Similarly, China wants infrastructural development in Afghanistan which will result in connectivity of the region. China wants to invest in infrastructural development in Afghanistan as it will help China to achieve geo-strategic and geo-political objectives in the region. Moreover, the road connectivity with Iran will help China to exert its influence in the region. Similarly, China wants to dole out economic assistance to Afghanistan so that a powerful Afghan government crush the terrorists who pose threat to the economic interests of China. To cut the story short, China has employed geo-economics theory in Afghanistan to safeguard its geo-political and geo-strategic interests.

Potential Avenues of Cooperation

After the US evacuation, Afghanistan is inundated with a plethora of problems; but, worn-torn Afghanistan also offers numerous opportunities for the neighbouring countries, especially for China. The nascent Taliban led government is desperately looking for friends in the international political arena who could help them to rehabilitate their country, and it is appropriate time for the regional players to extend their hands towards Afghan people before they get exploited by terrorists or extra-regional players for personal gains. To this end, China, an emerging global and regional power, has struck the right path by starting diplomatic ties with the Taliban regime, the current rulers of Afghanistan. The current Chinese approach towards Taliban is antithesis to its 1990s approach when they shunned diplomatic ties or relations with the Taliban regime. China has altogether changed her approach towards the Taliban regime owing to securing its geo-strategic and geo-economic interests which are contingent upon peace and stability in Afghanistan. There are certain areas of mutual cooperation and benefits for the both countries, China and Afghanistan.

Political and Economic Alignment Both Chinese and Taliban leadership believe that the United States is responsible for the current chaotic situation in Afghanistan. The leaders of both countries aspire for a peaceful and stable Afghanistan. Moreover, the Taliban leadership is resolute that they will not interfere in the affairs of other states and also not allow any terrorist to use their land against any other country. When the Chinese spokesperson Yi met the current acting deputy Prime Minister, Abdul Ghani Baradar, promised that "The Afghan Taliban is committed to refrain from activities that directly or indirectly destabilize another country. And the Taliban would honor its commitment to an open and inclusive Islamic government." And the Chinese leadership has also ensured that they will not interfere in the domestic affairs of Afghanistan. Non-interference is the potential avenues of co-operation between China and Afghanistan. Mr. Wang Yi, China foreign ministry spokesperson stated that "China has never interfered in the internal affairs of Afghanistan " (MFAPRC, 2021). Historically, it is also an established fact that China has never interfered in the internal matters of other states. Similarly, the Taliban leadership and their people are tired of prolonged war, and they do not want to indulge themselves in any proxy war. One of the religious scholars from Afghanistan explained to me, China wants one thing from the Afghan people: that they must not interfere in the domestic affairs of the other countries and we will do the same. In reality this is the objective of Islamic Emirate of Afghanistan.

The formation of an Inclusive government is also the potential avenues of Cooperation between China and the Islamic Emirate of Afghanistan. China also asked the Taliban leadership to make an inclusive government so that Afghanistan should not fell prey to the civil war. The Taliban leadership also assured the international community that they will form an inclusive government (MFAPRC, 2021). The unique geographical location of Afghanistan has created special interest for China in Afghanistan. The Chinese leadership envisions the idea of connecting the region. Afghanistan is the gateway to central Asia from south Asia, and it connects Central Asia with the Middle East. Security analyst in the field, Retired Lieutenant General Javid, stated, "Though, China's financial engagement has been less in the past. However, now according to the president Xi Jinping vision i.e., under the One Belt and One Road Initiative, cross border economic activities will provide greater opportunity for China to remain in the region and to promote interest of the China". China has envisaged a plan to connect the world through roads, railway networks and sea, and to this end, she began BRI (Belt and Road initiative) a few years back in 2013. This project of China is highly laudable as it will overcome the trade barriers and will bring prosperity in the world; however, there are certain hurdles in the way of BRI completion. China has poured billions of dollars in the BRI project, and she cannot afford to risk her investment. One of the largest threats posed to the BRI project is regional instability.

Afghanistan has remained the ground for terrorist outfits and in the current decade several new terrorist organizations are rearing their heads in Afghanistan like ISIS, IS Khurasan etc. These terrorist organizations pose serious threat to the BRI. But also create an opportunity for China and Afghanistan to work together to uproot these terrorist organizations which pose serious threat to the BRI project. Current Afghan regime is also willing to cooperate with China in this regard as this project will help Afghanistan to build new infrastructure and stable its economy. The official spokesperson of the Islamic Emirate, Zabiullah Mujahid also welcomed the BRI in these words. "China is our main partner and represents a fundamental and astonishing opportunity for us because it is ready to invest and rebuild our country" (RFERL, 2021). The Foreign Minister of the People's Republic of China, Wang Yi said "The BRI (Belt and Road Initiative), warmly welcomed and actively participated by Afghanistan, has brought benefits to both Afghanistan and China and the region beyond" (Embassay C.-A. , 202O).

Moreover, Afghanistan is also enriched with untapped natural resources and rare earth minerals like copper, chromite etc. Unfortunately, Afghanistan does not have financial resources and modern machinery to extract underground minerals. And, it creates another opportunity for both the countries to work mutually. Afghan leadership is looking for China's assistance to parlay its underground resources into cash. However, China has little investment in the 'Anyak Copper Mine' and 'Amu Daraya Basin Oil' projects, the religious scholar from Afghanistan, explained to me, "the Anyak copper mine, has been slowdown for many years due to U.S. presence in Afghanistan; however, we will expedite it now". The cooperation between China and Afghan leadership will robust the Afghan economy. An official spokesperson of Islamic Emirate of Afghanistan, Zabiullah Mujahid, stated "Afghanistan has rich copper mines and untapped natural resources, which, thanks to the Chinese, will be modernized. Finally, China represents our ticket to the market around the world." The Taliban

31

leadership wants to cooperate with China so that it can heal the wounds of its people, which are inflicted by two-decade protracted war, by making them financially stable. Similarly, China also wants to help its neighbor as the prosperity in its neighbor servers her interest.

Additionally, Afghanistan produces surplus fruits especially dry fruits which is one of her major exports. On the other hand, China has highest population in the world, and to fulfill the food needs she imports food items from other countries. Thus, it creates another opportunity for the both countries to work together. The Taliban leadership is looking towards China as the largest export market, and it will also help China to overcome food shortages problem. One of clergies of Afghanistan Shura (consultation committee of Islamic Emirate of Afghanistan) has expressed his thoughts during interview with me as, "Afghanistan is also an agrarian country and a great number of our people are linked with the occupation of agriculture. We produce surplus fruit especially dry fruit but we have no market to export our goods." Moreover, China can also help Afghanistan to improve the quality and production of agricultural items by sharing new and sophisticated technology as she already employed in her country. In a nut shell both countries have multiple avenues of economic cooperation. If both countries cash these opportunities, this region will become prosper in letter and spirit.

Strategic Calculus of Security

China is located in the far northeast of Afghanistan. China is an emerging global economic power while Afghanistan is at war since the last four decades. Afghanistan remained a hub of terrorist outfits for many years. China views instability in Afghanistan a threat to its geo-strategic interests in the region. The Taliban leadership, who mainly represents Pashtun community, has not yet included Tajik and Uzbek in their interim government. There is a fear that if Taliban leadership does not incorporate Tajik and Uzbek communities in the government, they might join ETIM East Turkistan Islamic Movement. It is also said that the ETIM has tentacles in China; however, it is mainly based in Badakhshan, Afghanistan. ETIM is a separatist and terrorist organization which poses a serious threat to the sovereignty of China and this organization is also against the Taliban regime. The threats posed by ETIM creates another potential avenue of cooperation. To this means, presence of any security threats may pose a strategic threat to the long term strategic and economic interests of China and Afghanistan. Therefore, they are ready to address the issue of security threat in in order to safeguard its long-term interests in the region

(Amy, 2021). Additionally, China and Iran, which is located in the west of Afghanistan, have recently signed a 25-year comprehensive strategic agreement on 27 March 2021. This agreement will provide a relief to the torpid Iran's economy which is in doldrums owing to the US sanctions. This deal will weak the US hegemony in the region and it will also help China to exert its influence in the Middle East. Both geostrategic partners, Iran and China, do not have any land boundary with each other. Afghanistan provides a land connection between China and Iran; therefore, it creates another opportunity for the Afghan and Chinese leaders to work together. Retired Lieutenant General Javid state that, "Afghanistan boasts of a mountain's terrain and fertile valleys.

Each valley is separated by mountains and rivers and have its own different culture and norms. There is no land connection between these valleys as there is no infrastructural development. These mountains make it difficult for any foreign power to conquer the whole Afghanistan". This mountains terrain does not only provide natural defense against foreign invaders but also hinder national cohesion. Historically, it is an established fact that no local ruler of Afghanistan has ruled all over Afghanistan due to diverse ethnicities living in their valleys, which are separated from each other by mountains. The Taliban leadership is also cognizant of this fact that infrastructural development is imperative for national cohesion. It creates another potential avenue of cooperation between China and Afghanistan. The roads and infrastructure development under the Belt and Road Initiative will provide national cohesion in Afghanistan, and it would also make it easy for China to access its geostrategic partner, Iran, through road link.

China-Taliban Relations

Implications for Pakistan Afghanistan has remained the hub of great game and proxies since the last four decades. Pakistan has claimed on multiple occasions in the past that Afghanistan provides the safe heaven to those who want to destabilize Pakistan. Pakistan has also tried convincing the USA during the latter's presence in Afghanistan that Afghan land is used by its adversaries. However, the USA always rebuffed this claim advertently or inadvertently. After the takeover of Kabul by Taliban. This fact was endorsed by Senator Dr Jahanzeb Jamal Dini affiliated with Baluchistan National party (Mengal), stated, "It seems the situation has been turned in favor of Pakistan as the Taliban leadership has assured the international community that they would not allow its soil to be used for terrorist activities against any other country". Therefore, Pakistan has also welcomed the growing ties between China and Afghan leadership. The cooperation between Afghanistan and China will ultimately help Pakistan as Pakistan enjoys cordial relations with China. Moreover, the growing cooperation between the China and Afghanistan will eliminate the security risk to the CPEC. The growing ties between the Taliban and Chinese leadership are endorsed by the Pakistani political elite because China and Pakistan have mutual geo-strategic and geo-economic goals.

Additionally, the peace in Afghanistan will provide a chance for regional cooperation, regional connectivity and regional prosperity. Afghanistan is located at the heart of Asia. It connects central Asia, South Asia and Middle East with each other. It is the crossroad to many countries. This truth was properly reflected by Dr Shoaib, an independent scholar in the field, stated, "Peaceful Afghanistan will guarantee the completion of China's dream of connecting the whole region. The regional connectivity will open the doors for regional cooperation and trade, if China involves itself in Afghanistan, China gives a lot of economic opportunities to the regional connectivity". The continent of Asia has the largest population which makes it the largest trade market of the world and a house of the biggest manpower. Therefore, the trade and cooperation in the region can potentially make it the 21st century an Asian century. However, peace, prosperity, connectivity and cooperation of the region depends upon the stability in Afghanistan. Therefore, Pakistan welcomes the Chinese special interest in Afghanistan. China is also cognizant of the fact that peace and prosperity of the region is linked with peaceful Afghanistan. Moreover, due to high demand of electricity and energy, Pakistan has made deals with central Asian states to import energy. The CASA-1000 (Central Asia- South Asia power project) is an under construction project that will allow for the export of surplus electricity from Tajikistan and Uzbekistan to Pakistan through Afghanistan.

Similarly, the TAPI (Turkmenistan-Afghanistan-Pakistan-India) pipeline will allow Pakistan and Afghanistan to import gas from central Asian states to meet their energy demands. One of the greatest threats posed to the completion of this project is the security risk in Afghanistan. An independent expert in the field, Dr Waqar, stated, "The Taliban comeback will prove beneficial for both sides. It will bring both sides closer and well helping to bridge the gulf and enhancing trust between the two countries". There is also a positive sign for the completion of these projects as the Afghan leadership has assured all the stakeholders of this project that they will provide security to these projects. The completion of these projects will help Pakistan and Afghanistan to meet their energy demands which will ultimately robust their economies. It is an established fact that trade between two countries helps to resolve other conflicts as well and economic dependency on each other will enhance cooperation between the states. On the Eastern border Pakistan has a bitter rivalry with India due to border disputes especially in Kashmir. Pakistan also blames India for proxy war in Afghanistan to destabilize CPEC through proxies in Afghanistan. An independent scholar in the field, Dr Shoaib, stated, "Pakistan and China cannot do tangible progress without Afghan help. If Afghanistan is in shamble. Pakistan will be in shamble. If Pakistan go astray the whole China-Pakistan Economic Corridor and Belt and Road initiative will be out of window."

It creates another area of strategic cooperation where the Taliban leadership and China can work together to extirpate India's presence in Afghanistan in order to secure their geo-strategic and geo-economic interests. The Afghan leadership has reiterated it multiple times that they would uproot the proxies from Afghanistan altogether so it will help Pakistan in eradicating any security to destabilize CPEC. Pakistan is located to the south and East of Afghanistan, and both countries are separated by Durand line, the border between Pakistan and Afghanistan was drawn during British rule over India in 1893, however the tribes near the border on each side have same ancestral roots and also have identical ethnicity. The state of Pakistan and Afghanistan has a long border dispute over border demarcation. It creates an opportunity for China to play the role of mediator between Pakistan and Afghanistan. Therefore, an authoritative expert in the field, Dr Waqar, stated, "China has always sided with Pakistan in many of its dealings, so Pakistan and China will solve a realistic and substantial plan to solve the problems, which will ultimately serve its geo-economic and geo-strategic interests." Pakistan is a geo-strategic and geo-economic partner of China. The CPEC (China Pakistan Economic Corridor) project is the flagship project of China's OBOR (one belt one road initiative), and it provides access to China to the Arabian Sea.

On the other hand, if Taliban leadership fail to form an inclusive government, it will have severe implications for Pakistan and the region. There is a fear that if Taliban do not form an inclusive government, there are chances of breakout of a civil war that will harshly impact the whole region. Firstly, there will be the mass exodus of refugees from Afghanistan to Pakistan. Pakistan's economic conditions do not allow it to host immigrants. In case of civil war, the emigrants will add burden to the already struggling economy of Pakistan and concomitant problems will make the state vulnerable. Another independent expert in the field, Shakeel Ramay, stated, "Pakistan cannot afford uncertainty in Afghanistan. As Anarchy and civil war in Afghanistan will result in mass departure from Afghanistan to Pakistan, Afghanistan will again become the center of proxies and terrorism. It poses a serious threat to the national security of Pakistan." Pakistan has already sacrificed a lot during war on terror in terms of financial and human losses. Thirdly, the smuggling of narcotics and weapons to Pakistan will engender more issues and further aggravate the problems for Pakistan. Pakistan is already trying to come out of the predicaments that are caused due to instability in Pakistan. The Pakistani leadership knows peace in Pakistan is directly linked with the peace in Afghanistan.

Conclusion

The sudden U.S. withdrawal from Afghanistan has created a vacuum in the region. This time, China has become quite assertive in the region, the new scenario in the region will be completely different from the earlier one, and China will bridge this gape through massive economic development. China is increasing its economic rapprochement and ties with Afghanistan aimed at to bring the region into BRI and counter American threat in the region. However, Pakistan's security being dependent on the stability of Afghanistan has a massive concern over the instability. If Afghanistan remains unstable for long, Pakistan and China will also not be exempted from the consequences. Thus, if Afghanistan and China continue to work on its landmark project, the Belt and Road Initiative (BRI), Pakistan would be benefited to further its increase economic ties with Afghanistan. It will be beneficial for both Pakistan and Afghanistan.

China's Engagement with Taliban after American Withdrawal: Implications for Pakistan. Jalal Ud Din Kakar M.Phil. International Relation, University of Management and Technology Lahore Asad ur Rehman Assistant Professor, Department of Political Science, and IR, University of Management and Technology Lahore asadrehman@umt.edu.pk. Pakistan Journal of Social Research ISSN 2710-3129 (P) 2710-3137 (O) Vol. 4, No. 2, April-June 2022, pp. 526-536. www.pjsr.com. pk. Pakistan Journal of Social Research (PJSR) [2710-3129 Print; 2710-3137 Online] HEC Recognized Y Category Journal which is run by a registered society "Health Education Research Foundation" and provides a platform to the academicians, researchers, policy makers, practitioners, professionals, and research students for a comprehensive analysis, innovation, transformation, and rigorous debate in the form of high quality empirically and theoretically sound research articles, case studies, review based papers, and book reviews.PJSR encourages the young researchers, scholars and students to get published their scholarly work for the better policy recommendations in resolving the social issues across the world. PJSR welcomes the contributions from the scholars from all regions of the world while focusing any of the domain of social sciences and allied disciplines. Scope and Mission. Pakistan Journal of Social Research (PJSR) is an academic, peer reviewed and referenced journal that functions as a platform for Social Scientists to showcase their original research. Published quarterly, the journal covers a wide variety of topics from all fields of Social Sciences including Economics, International Relations, Political Science, Sociology, Anthropology, History, Law, Gender Studies, Defense Studies, Archaeology, Psychology and Business Studies. The focus of the journal is to publish scholarly and cutting-edge research articles with an emphasis on the issues of developing countries. PJSR is open to different methods of scientific inquiry and welcomes qualitative, quantitative, as well as mix method research. The journal publishes genuine theoretical and analytical research in all fields of Social Sciences. Open Access Policy. The PJSR is an open access journal which means that all content is freely available without charge to the user or his/her institution. Users are allowed to read, download, copy, distribute, print, search, or link to the full texts of the articles, or use them for any other lawful purpose, without asking prior permission from the publisher or the author. This is in accordance with the BOAI definition of open access. Aims and Objectives. To publish and acknowledge original contribution in various fields of Social Sciences. To ensure wider dissemination of latest developments in Social Sciences particularly with reference to Pakistan and South Asia. To promote interdisciplinary research within various fields of Social Sciences. Contact Us. All correspondence shall be addressed to the Chief Editor, Dr. Sarfraz Khan Assistant Professor, Department of Sociology, Quaid-i-Azam University, 45320 Islamabad Pakistan (email: sarfraz@qau.edu.pk) or at the office address of the journal, The Chief Editor, Pakistan Journal of Social Research, Office No. 2, HE-12/F, I&T Center, G6/1-4, 44000 Islamabad Pakistan (email: editor@pjsr.com.pk). http://creativecommons.org/licenses/by-nc/4.0/

Chapter 3

China's New Engagement with Afghanistan after the Withdrawal

Feng Zhang

Abstract

China's historical relationship with Afghanistan is marked by three periods: estrangement during the Cold War (1955–1990), rising concern with Uighur terrorism emanating from Afghanistan (1991–2000), and evolving activism in Afghan affairs following the US invasion (2001–2020). Since the withdrawal of US forces in Afghanistan in August 2021, Beijing has formed a new, five-pronged engagement policy toward Afghanistan: pragmatically and cautiously accepting the Taliban's dominance in Afghan affairs, preventing the re-emergence of Afghanistan as a safe haven for terrorists, facilitating an inclusive politics in the country, demonstrating a greater degree of humanitarian concern, and shaming the US and the West for forfeiting their responsibility. Shaping this new policy are four factors that have affected and will continue to affect Chinese policy in the future: security and stability in Xinjiang and China's western border region, Afghanistan's place in China's overarching international strategy, great power politics involving the United States, and the economic value of Afghanistan.

Keywords: China's policy toward Afghanistan; China Afghanistan relations; terrorism; Uighur; Sino-American relations

Introduction

The ignominious departure of the United States from Afghanistan in August 2021 after a 20-year intervention left China as the biggest regional country capable of playing critical role in future Afghan affairs dominated by a resurgent Taliban. What is China's policy toward Afghanistan after the US withdrawal? To what extent will it seek to exercise its influence? I argue that China has formed a new, five-pronged engagement policy toward Afghanistan: (i) pragmatically and cautiously accepting the Taliban's dominance in Afghan affairs; (ii) preventing the re-emergence of Afghanistan as a safe haven for terrorists; (iii) facilitating an inclusive politics in the country; (iv) demonstrating a greater degree of humanitarian concern; and (v) shaming the US and the West for forfeiting their responsibility. However, although China's policy has certainly become more active and constructive, it is still hemmed in by major constraints, not least its misgivings about the Taliban and its growing rivalry with the United States. I begin by sketching the historical background to Sino-Afghan relations, distinguishing three phases of this relationship from the founding of the People's Republic of China in 1949 to the US withdrawal in 2021: (i) estrangement during the Cold War (1955–1990); (ii) rising concern with Uighur terrorism emanating from Afghanistan (1991–2000); and (iii) evolving activism in Afghan affairs following the US invasion (2001–2020). I then examine four factors that have affected and will continue to affect Chinese policy toward Afghanistan: (i) security and stability in the northwestern province of Xinjiang and China's western border region; (ii) Afghanistan's place in China's overarching international strategy; (iii) great power politics involving the United States; and (iv) the economic value of Afghanistan.

These factors determine the continuities and changes of Chinese policy after the US pullout. Afghanistan is likely to receive more attention from policymakers as a result of the priority of neighbourhood diplomacy in China's overall foreign policy. But the precise degree of its rising importance will be determined by policymakers' perceptions of China's interests and its vulnerabilities in the country. Among its interests, security and stability in Xinjiang and along the wider western border region will continue to dominate economic considerations. Among its vulnerabilities, the most salient are the nature and competence of the Taliban regime and the strategic posture of the United States. China is acutely aware of the limits of external intervention in influencing the Taliban, so its future contribution to Afghan reconstruction, while it will undoubtedly grow, is going to be limited by such realism. China is critical of the US strategy of quitting Afghanistan so as to concentrate on competing with it in the Indo-Pacific, with China seething at both the mess that Washington has left in Afghanistan and its recalibration of strategic offensive against it. The surging rivalry between the two countries is preventing them from meaningfully cooperating over Afghanistan, despite the fact that cooperation is obviously needed and would, if successful, help to ease their rivalry.

The Historical Background

Afghanistan established a formal diplomatic relationship with the People's Republic of China in January 1955, becoming one of the first few countries to recognize the new Communist-led government in Beijing. The relationship became more distant from the late 1970s to the end of the 1980s, as Afghanistan fell under the Soviet sphere of influence and as China broke away from its alliance with the Soviet Union after the 1960s. During the 1980s, Afghanistan became a battleground, with China collaborating closely with the United States in a common effort to thwart the Soviet invasion of the country, and with additional help from Pakistan it provided Soviet-style arms to Afghan insurgents. The Sino-Afghan relationship during the Cold War thus was dominated by great power rivalry[1]. This became less so after the Cold War, although, as we shall see, great power rivalry—now played between China and the United States—has reemerged as a severe constraint on Chinese policy.

The evolution of the Sino-Afghan relationship in the post–Cold War period can be divided into three phases. In the first phase, from 1991 to 2001, Afghanistan did not play an intrinsic part in Chinese foreign policy making. At this time, Beijing's interest in Afghanistan was in terms of protecting Xinjiang against terrorist threats and developing relations with the post-Soviet Central Asian republics. Uighur terrorism acquired policy salience for the first time in April 1990, when a group of Uighur men conducted an armed uprising against Chinese police and security forces in the township of Baren with the aim of establishing an "East Turkestan Republic[2]". Meanwhile, Afghanistan was mired in a civil war between the regime of President Najibullah and various mujahideen units, forcing China to withdraw its embassy staff in 1993. In 1996, the Taliban took control of the country, but China refused to establish diplomatic ties with the new regime. The triumph of this fundamentalist Islamic movement greatly heightened Chinese anxiety, because it had no scruples about providing a safe haven for a variety of radical Islamists. These included not only the Islamic Movement of Uzbekistan that launched attacks mainly into Central Asian states, but also the Uighur-centered East Turkestan Islamic Movement (ETIM) that demanded independence for Xinjiang.

Consequently, China took bilateral and multilateral measures. Bilaterally, it sought to deal directly with the Taliban through the intermediary of its long-time ally, Pakistan. Multilaterally, it found common cause with Russia and the Central Asian states to create a new regional security institution—the Shanghai Five—which was established in 1996 with Russia, Kazakhstan, Kyrgyzstan, and Tajikistan. It expanded, becoming the Shanghai Cooperation Organization in 2001, with Uzbekistan as an additional member.

The second phase of China's post–Cold War policy toward Afghanistan lasted from 2001, when the United States invaded Afghanistan in the aftermath of the 9/11 terrorist attacks, to 2021, when, after a 20-year misadventure, Washington decided to entirely withdraw its troops from the country. For the first 10 years of this period, China adopted a largely reactive attitude toward the US intervention, offering limited engagement with the new US-backed Afghan government and rejecting any direct security involvement in the country. After the Obama administration made clear its intention to withdraw US and NATO forces from Afghanistan, however, China was forced to come to grips with the consequences of a post–US controlled Afghanistan.

So, after 2012, Beijing ramped up its diplomatic, security, and economic engagement with Kabul. It secured an observer status for Afghanistan in the Shanghai Cooperation Organization and upgraded the bilateral partnership to a strategic and cooperative partnership in June 2012. In September 2012, Zhou Yongkang, a member of the Standing Committee of the Politburo responsible for internal security, visited Kabul, an unmistakable sign that Beijing was seeking greater security and counterterrorism cooperation with the Afghan government to insulate Xinjiang after the US withdrawal[2].

China greatly intensified its bilateral and multilateral diplomatic activities after 2014 when the United States withdrew the bulk of its combat troops. The year 2014 is seen by many observers as a crucial year in China's policy evolution[3,4]. In that year alone, two senior security officials—Minister of Public Security and State Councilor Guo Shengkun and the People's Liberation Army (PLA) Deputy Chief of Staff Qi Jianguo—visited Kabul, while Afghanistan's newly elected President Ghani visited China. Soon, security and intelligence cooperation between China and Afghanistan took concrete—and in some cases, publicly acknowledged—forms. China sent its People's Armed Police troops to join their Afghan counterparts in patrolling the northeastern Afghan province of Badakhshan and offered to support a mountain brigade for the Afghan National Security Forces, while

Kabul handed over Uighur detainees in an effort to persuade China to use its influence with Pakistan to help start negotiations with the Taliban. On the multilateral front, three trilateral mechanisms took shape during this period: China–Afghanistan–Pakistan, China–Russia–Pakistan, and China–Russia–India dialogues. In October 2014, China hosted the fourth ministerial conference of the Istanbul Process (also known as the Heart of Asia) on Afghanistan, attended by 46 countries and international organizations, with the United States participating as a "supporting nation"[5]. Finally, and notably, China joined the Quadrilateral Coordination Group with Afghanistan, Pakistan, and the United States in January 2016.

Factors and Calculations

Before examining China's policy changes after the August 2021 US withdrawal, it is useful to consider the main factors affecting Chinese policy toward Afghanistan. Three factors deserve particular attention: security and stability in Xinjiang and China's western frontier region; Afghanistan's place in China's overarching international strategy; and great power politics involving the United States. The first two factors have remained more or less constant through 2021, so they impart a degree of continuity to Chinese policy. The third factor, however, has undergone major changes and is mainly responsible for new shifts in Chinese policy. The economic value of Afghanistan, especially with regard to its natural resources, may be considered a fourth factor. But it is much less important than the first three factors and is far from a main driver of Chinese policy.

Terrorism

The first and most important factor is Chinese concern with security. China is focused, above all, on the threat Uighur terrorism and separatism poses to the internal security and stability of Xinjiang province and the Chinese interior, as well as broader concerns with border security in the vast western frontier region. Xinjiang is China's biggest province by area, constituting one-sixth of the country's landmass, and borders Pakistan, Afghanistan, and the Central Asian republics of Tajikistan, Kazakhstan, and Kyrgyzstan. Any one of these countries could become a breeding ground for Uighur terrorism. Afghanistan has emerged as a particular menace because, as noted earlier, the Taliban regime has previously accommodated Uighur terrorists, including the ETIM, and allowed them to join Al-Qaeda affiliated terrorist camps. Chinese authorities estimate that hundreds of Uighur militants underwent training in Afghanistan when the Taliban controlled the country from 1996 to 2001[6].

They were mostly forced out after the US invasion and fled to Pakistan. After their safe havens were squeezed by the Pakistani army, they returned to Afghanistan and maintained a crucial presence in the north of the country, including the Wakhan corridor, where the ETIM chief was believed to be operating. This was one of the main reasons for Chinese interest in patrolling Badakhshan and in supporting the aforementioned building of a mountain brigade for Afghan security forces. In the 2010s, Chinese authorities reported a number of Uighur terrorist attacks not only in Xinjiang but also in China's interior regions, including a suicide attack at Tiananmen Square in October 2013 and a mass attack at the Kunming Train Station in March 2014. Between 2010 and 2014, terrorist attacks either in Xinjiang or linked regions (such as the Kunming attack) claimed the lives of 468 people and injured 548. China fears the potential of Uighur terrorism and separatism to fan out from Afghanistan and Pakistan to Central Asia and the wider Middle East region, destabilizing its western frontier. The emergence of the Islamic State (ISIS) as a major regional force in 2014 deepened these anxieties, as the movement declared its aspiration to extend its self-declared Caliphate into Xinjiang, and with some Afghans associated with the Taliban calling for establishing an ISI style regime in Afghanistan[6].

In February 2018, ISIS issued a direct threat against China, releasing a video in which Uighurs vowed to return home to carry out attacks[7]. The joining of forces between Uighur terrorists in Afghanistan and other terrorist groups in Afghanistan, Pakistan, and Central Asian countries would constitute a security nightmare to Beijing. Terrorism and instability in Afghanistan affect not only China itself but also the Central Asian frontier regions, whose states together share 2,300 kilometers of borders with Afghanistan and 3,300 kilometres of borders with China. The terrorist and extremist threats confronting Central Asia are both internal to regional countries, such as the Islamic Movement of Uzbekistan, and external, of which Afghanistan constitutes the greatest menace. If the Central Asian states are infiltrated by terrorists from Afghanistan, the threat may spill over from their long and porous borders into Xinjiang.

Unlike the Wakhan Corridor separating China from Afghanistan, which is difficult to traverse due to its harsh climate and formidable topography, China's borders with Central Asian states cannot be closed. Beijing has thus pushed the agenda of countering the so-called "three evil forces" of separatism, terrorism, and religious extremism with Central Asian states, and with notable success. Pakistan is a thorn in the side of China's fight against Uighur terrorism. A close ally of China's since both countries' founding in the late 1940s, Pakistan is notorious for providing a safe haven for Islamic extremists, including the Taliban and Uighur militants. In recent years, China has also fallen victim to attacks against its personnel and infrastructure by Pakistani extremists in Balochistan, where the China-Pakistan Economic Corridor (CPEC)—a flagship project of the massive Belt and Road Initiative (BRI)—is being developed. Beijing has tried to pressure Islamabad to repel Uighur militants based in the Federally Administered Tribal Areas of Pakistan adjoining Afghanistan and to safeguard the security of Chinese projects inside the country. However, the repeated terrorist attacks in Balochistan and the resurgence of the Afghan Taliban have reduced Beijing's confidence in Pakistan's ability to do so.

Grand Strategy

The second factor affecting China's policy toward Afghanistan is the country's place in China's overarching international strategy. Before President Xi Jinping assumed office in late 2012, Afghanistan was barely relevant to Chinese grand strategic thinking. As noted above, it only mattered when it impinged on China's security, as when it was invaded by the Soviet Union in the 1980s and when it accepted Uighur militants in the late 1990s, but hardly more. Since 2013 however, two new developments have elevated Afghanistan's importance in Chinese policy, although still only to a limited degree. The first, as the Chinese scholar Zhao Huasheng notes, is the rising prominence of neighborhood or periphery diplomacy (zhoubian waijiao) in Chinese foreign policy[5]. In October 2013, China held its first-ever conference on diplomacy toward countries on its periphery. President Xi emphasized the need to strive for achievement in neighbourhood diplomacy so as to ensure a favourable regional environment for China's development. Attended by representatives from the party, local and central government, the military, state-owned enterprises, and the diplomatic corps, this conference was a milestone in raising the profile of neighbourhood diplomacy in modern Chinese foreign policy.

The distinguished Chinese scholar Yan Xuetong argues that it indicated a strategic shift in Chinese foreign policy from "keeping a low profile" to "striving for achievement." In his view, it put an end to the debate about whether Xi was following the approach of Deng Xiaoping, the mastermind behind China's reform-era foreign policy, in keeping a low profile and ushered in a new era of a more activist regional strategy[8]. The second development is the much-vaunted BRI, a globe-spanning connectivity program advanced by President Xi in September–October 2013, exactly at the same time as the new neighborhood diplomacy was announced. The Belt part of the BRI seeks to connect the whole Eurasian continent from East Asia to Western Europe, while the Road attempts to link the Western Pacific, the South China Sea, and the Indian Ocean. By one account, the BRI network encompasses 4.4 billion people (63 percent of the world's population), 64 countries, and a combined economic output of 21 trillion dollars (29 percent of global GDP), requiring a gigantic investment of 20 trillion dollars in its first 10 years.[9] It is China's global economic strategy and is frequently asserted by observers as President Xi's grand strategy[10, 11].

Of these two developments, neighbourhood diplomacy affects China's policy toward Afghanistan more than the BRI does. Once the leadership has determined that foreign policy must be more proactive on the regional front, the diplomatic establishment must find ways to implement this new directive. Such an imperative must have been filtered through the policy process to bear on Afghanistan, although, of course, the specific manifestations of a more activist Afghanistan policy are determined by practical conditions. With respect to the BRI, however, the significance of Afghanistan is open to doubt. Some observers think that Afghanistan could be a central hub for the Belt linking Central Asia with South Asia, at least as it appears on the map. In 2016, officials from Afghanistan, China, and Pakistan mooted the possibility of extending the China-Pakistan Economic Corridor to Afghanistan.[12]

As China seeks to integrate Xinjiang and utilize its geopolitical position to overcome Uighur separatism and terrorism while facilitating a China-centric Eurasian geoeconomic system, Afghanistan ought to receive greater attention from Chinese strategists [2]. Even if this is true, Afghanistan can by no means attain centrality to the BRI in Central and South Asia simply by virtue of its geography[13]. In fact, Afghanistan is bypassed by two corridors of the BRI to its south and north, respectively: the China-Pakistan Economic Corridor and the China-Central Asia-West Asia economic corridor, which runs through the five Central Asian republics as well as Iran and Turkey. In other words, Afghanistan is dispensable in the whole scheme. A prominent Chinese analyst asserts that when it comes to economic significance Afghanistan is of no account to the BRI[14]. Those who tout the geopolitical value of Afghanistan and advocate the building of a strategic corridor linking China with Iran through Afghanistan overlook the massive costs and risks of doing so[15]. In terms of both geopolitics and security, Beijing considers Afghanistan largely in a negative rather than

45

positive light: it is a problem to be managed and contained rather than an asset to be leveraged and exploited.

The Great Game

The third factor affecting Chinese calculations toward Afghanistan is great power politics in Central and South Asia and, since 2001, Sino-American relations in particular. China's perceptions of the role of the United States and NATO in Afghanistan have undergone several interesting shifts. For roughly 10 years after the US invasion in 2001, Beijing was predictably apprehensive of US motives, in keeping with its general suspicion of a US intention to constrain or even contain China's rise. Hardliners in China's strategic community, especially the PLA and security agencies, were apt to see the US military presence in Afghanistan as a threat to China's national security and an instrument of America's encirclement strategy toward China. Partly as a result of such thinking, Beijing ignored US requests for cooperation, such as entreaties to assist Washington in developing alternatives to the increasingly fragile supply routes via Pakistan for the delivery of materiel to US and NATO forces. As Washington decided to withdraw its forces, however, Beijing began to see the US presence in a more favourable light. It was no longer averse to the idea that the US presence might, after all, be in China's interests because it allowed China to free-ride on Western stabilization efforts.

So Chinese officials started expressing concern that the United States should not leave too hastily[16]. Its anxieties about US encirclement were superseded by fears that Afghanistan might once again become a safe haven for Uighur militants and so destabilize China's western frontier. Underlying these changing perceptions is a conflicted mindset that simultaneously views the US containment of the Taliban as a positive outcome for Xinjiang's security and the strategic and military presence of the United States in Afghanistan as a geopolitical threat to China's national interest. As Andrew Small observes, China "wanted neither a Western victory that might entrench a US military presence in its backyard, nor a Taliban victory that would pose risks to Xinjiang and the wider region[17]." Consequently, between 2001 and 2014, it provided only tokenistic financial and political contributions to Afghanistan, aimed as much to avoid alienating anyone as to help rebuild the country. Such a conflicted mindset can only be resolved by a much greater willingness to intervene in Afghan affairs and to take matters into its own hands, or by the unfolding of one of the two dreaded outcomes— a US victory or a Taliban victory. As it turned out, it is the latter that Beijing now has to confront after the events of August 2021.

Economies

Before moving on to the new Taliban challenge, it is important to clarify the significance of economic considerations in China's policy toward Afghanistan. It is well-known that Afghanistan is richly endowed with a range of valuable natural resources including oil, natural gas, iron ore, gold, copper, cobalt, lithium, and other raw materials worth nearly $1 trillion[18]. It is natural to think that if China could import these resources through the BRI, it will be able to diversify its imports away from more distant, volatile, or unfriendly countries. Trade with Afghanistan will also promote the economic growth of China's western provinces as well as the neighboring countries of Pakistan and the Central Asian republics. These considerations of Afghanistan's economic value must be weighed against the costs and risks of doing business with and in Afghanistan.

The $20 billion Afghan economy runs largely on opium production and narcotics trafficking, as well as international aid. Sino-Afghan trade is negligible in the context of China's trade with its neighbours, amounting only to a meagre $550 million in 2020[19]. Afghanistan lacks the political stability, domestic security, and decent economic system necessary to create an adequate environment for Chinese investment. Its seemingly never-ending wars and civil conflicts, corruption, and decrepit infrastructure, as well as other problems, cannot but deter large-scale Chinese investments. It is instructive that China's two biggest investments in the country so far— the Metallurgical Corporation of China's $3 billion investment in the Aynak copper field and the China National Petroleum Corporation's investment in the Amu Darya oil project—have stalled, barely effectively running, let alone turning a profit. The Aynak copper field is located in Logar, one of Afghanistan's most violent provinces, and is now widely seen as a failed investment. Lessons of this kind have taught Chinese companies to be as risk averse as their Western counterparts.

A New Engagement Policy

The four factors examined above will enable us to develop a good explanation for the continuities and changes of China's policy after the US withdrawal from Afghanistan in August 2021. This policy may be described as China's new engagement with an Afghanistan that is once again governed by the Taliban. It consists of five main elements: (i) pragmatically and cautiously accepting the Taliban's dominance in Afghan affairs; (ii) preventing the reemergence of Afghanistan as a safe haven for terrorists; (iii) facilitating an inclusive politics in the country; (iv) demonstrating a greater degree of humanitarian concern; and (v) shaming the US and the West for forfeiting their responsibility. The first four elements contain clear continuities from past policies, but all of them have been advanced with a greater degree of urgency. Shaming the United States was meant in part to vindicate China's longstanding criticism of interventionist US foreign policy, but also to prod Washington to bear responsibility for Afghan reconstruction after the withdrawal.

Although China did not establish official relations with the first Taliban government of 1996– 2001, it established contact with the regime in the late 1990s and has maintained channels of communication ever since. A Chinese ambassador to Pakistan even met with the Taliban's leader, Mullah Muhammad Omar, in November 2000 17. Unlike the United States and some other Western countries, China has long taken the view that the Taliban are and will remain a core political actor in Afghanistan, and it has tried to avoid antagonizing it by refusing to side openly with US and NATO positions. Although the Taliban's rapid seizure of power in August 2021 surprised China as much as it did the United States, Beijing had not doubted its ability to secure a prominent role in Afghan affairs. On 28 July, before the Taliban took control of Kabul, State Councillor and Foreign Minister Wang Yi received a high-level delegation headed by Mullah Abdul Ghani Baradar, the deputy leader of the Taliban. Wang described the Taliban as "a pivotal military and political force in Afghanistan," thus offering, for the first time in public, China's acceptance of it as a legitimate and dominant player in Afghan affairs.[20]

Conditionality

Such acceptance, however, is made on pragmatic grounds and seems to be conditioned on the expectation of the Taliban's willingness and ability to combat terrorism and forge a viable political settlement, the second and third elements of China's new engagement policy. After all, the Taliban is an Islamic fundamentalist movement with no intrinsic respect for the secular notions of sovereignty and territorial integrity associated with modern statehood. Beijing's caution is manifest in the fact that, at this writing in February 2022, it has withheld official recognition of the new Taliban government. As no other country around the world has done so, China is obviously in no hurry. But recognition may have also been held up as leverage against the Taliban over issues of major concern, especially counter-terrorism and political stability. China's concern with Uighur terrorists and separatists operating from their bases in Afghanistan was heightened by the US withdrawal. In all of their public pronouncements about Afghanistan in 2021, Chinese officials never failed to point out the Taliban's responsibility to cast aside the ETIM and other forms of terrorism on Afghan soil. In the 28 July meeting with Mullah Baradar mentioned earlier, Wang Yi managed to elicit a pledge that Afghan territory will not be used by any forces to harm China.

In late October, meeting with Baradar again in Doha, Wang stated in unmistakable terms that China wanted the Taliban to completely sever ties with the ETIM; in response, Baradar repeated the promise of never allowing any forces to use Afghan territory to do things that will harm China.[21] Chinese officials are likely to take such promises with a pinch of salt, because they have been given several times before. Beijing knows precisely what the Taliban's track record on this actually amounts to— limiting ETIM activities somewhat but still providing them with a protected environment—and now it wants more. Therefore, in addition to directly pressuring the Taliban, China has made a renewed appeal to regional multilateralism, particularly the Shanghai Cooperation Organization and various coordination mechanisms with neighbouring countries, including Pakistan, Russia, Iran, and the Central Asian republics. In late October, Wang Yi declared that these countries need to form an "anti-terrorism united front.[22]" It is not clear to what extent China would enlist the United States in this endeavor, but any assistance Washington could render in counter-terrorism would be welcomed by Beijing, whatever their differences in other areas.

Facilitators

Chinese efforts to facilitate an inclusive political process in Afghanistan began long before the final US withdrawal. Before the Taliban's triumph, however, it was framed as "reconciliation" between the Taliban and the US-backed regime in Kabul. In 2010, Beijing stated for the first time that the Afghanistan reconciliation process needs to be "Afghan-led and Afghan-owned." In 2014, it began to bring the warring parties together for talks, with the hope of achieving inclusive political reconciliation, enhancing counter-terrorism capability, and maintaining communication and coordination with the United States. It was not, however, truly able to take on a mediation role, owing to a lack of in-depth knowledge about the actors and issues involved. Since August 2021, China has continued to espouse the "Afghan-led and Afghan-owned" principle, except now that the Taliban's dominant position is accepted as a fait accompli.[23] Accordingly, Beijing no longer sees its role as a quasi-mediator but rather as a facilitator who will help orient and urge the Taliban to take political reconstruction seriously.

Chinese officials emphasize in particular the need for the Taliban to create a broad and inclusive political framework, to adopt moderate domestic and foreign policies, to disown and combat terrorists, and to develop friendly relationship with neighboring countries.[24] These messages are clearly geared toward protecting China's security interests in Xinjiang and the wider western border region, as elaborated earlier. China's discourse also exhibits interesting continuities and changes. The continuities reflect longstanding foreign policy principles as applied to Afghanistan. These include respect for the sovereignty, independence, and territorial integrity of Afghanistan; support for the Afghan people's choice for their development path; and non-interference in Afghanistan's internal affairs. Starting in mid-2021, however, Beijing began to promise that it has no geopolitical designs on Afghanistan and that it will seek neither "private gains" nor a sphere of influence in the country. This was clearly meant to preempt a possible outside suspicion that China would fill the strategic vacuum left by the US withdrawal.

Aid and Assistance

The fourth element of China's new engagement policy is greater humanitarianism, and this too flows naturally from earlier policies. China has provided Afghanistan with material aid and other kinds of humanitarian assistance since 2002, as well as waiving all of the country's earlier debts. Initially modest, China's financial contribution dramatically increased after 2014, with the total amount between 2014 and 2017, valued at $326.7 million, exceeding the total of that given between 2001 and 2013. In addition, China supported the building of hospitals, schools, and other high-profile reconstruction projects, as well as providing educational scholarships and training the country's officials in diverse areas. China's post-2021 humanitarian approach is notable for its wider range of concerns. In early September 2021, Beijing announced that it was giving emergency aid of goods worth more than $31 million, as well as donating 3 million doses of COVID-19 vaccines, with more to come as required. By contrast, Western countries were struggling to find ways to channel funds in ways that would circumvent the Taliban, even though the total volume of Western aid still dwarfed that of China's. Chinese aid threw a shameful spotlight on the Biden administration's February 2022 decision to use half of Afghanistan's foreign reserves ($3.5 billion) frozen in US banks to compensate American victims of the 9/11 attacks.[25] China has not limited its aid to material goods. It has begun to emphasize the rights of women, children, and minority groups inside Afghanistan as well as the proper handling of refugees.[26] These belong properly to the realm of human rights, an area in which China has been repeatedly criticized by the West.

The United States

The final, inescapable aspect of China's new policy concerns the United States. As we have seen, between 2001 and 2020 China's attitude toward the US role in Afghanistan reflected two distinct kinds of worry—an initial worry about an entrenchment of the US presence that would "encircle" China and a later worry about a premature or disorderly US withdrawal that would threaten China's security by allowing terrorists to regroup. As the latter worry became real in August 2021, China's perception of the United States turned into a mix of scorn and indignation. The scorn was manifest in its censure and mockery of the chaotic US withdrawal. In June 2021, when the Biden administration was planning the withdrawal, Wang Yi expressed hope that it be carried out in a responsible and orderly manner to prevent the worsening of Afghanistan's security situation and a relapse into terrorism.[27]

In early July, he blamed the United States for causing problems in Afghanistan and pressed it to ensure a stable transition of Afghan affairs. Washington, he averred, should not allow its withdrawal to breed chaos and conflict.[28] In early September, as the debacle of the US pullout shocked the world, Wang pinned Washington down for its "inescapable responsibility for the peaceful reconstruction of Afghanistan," all the while admonishing it not to create new problems for the country or to cause new instabilities that would harm the interests of Afghanistan's neighbouring countries.[29] China's rebuke carried a clear double message—a triumphant pummelling of the failure of the US policy of armed intervention and nation building as well as a forceful exhortation for Washington to fulfil its post-withdrawal obligations to Afghanistan. The latter may be seen as a variant of the Chinese belief held after 2014 that some US presence in Afghanistan in fact serves China's interests. More important, China's position revealed a strong sense of indignation about the United States that went far beyond the mere fact that Washington had left a total mess in Afghanistan for China and other regional countries to clean up. There was also fury that the Biden administration justified its Afghanistan exit on anti-China grounds, a fury that would severely constrain its activism toward Afghanistan and limit its cooperation with the United States over Afghanistan.

On 4 September, in a telephone call with the Iranian foreign minister, Wang Yi noted the US assertion that the purpose of its withdrawal from

Afghanistan was to better concentrate on the challenges from China and Russia. Not only was this an attempt to find an excuse for its failure in Afghanistan, Wang protested, but it once again exposed the nature of US power politics around the world. If the United States did not learn lessons from Afghanistan and completely change its foreign policy approaches, it was bound to suffer even greater defeats in the future. "Great defeats" was no doubt intended as a warning against the US strategy of competition toward China that was spearheaded by the Trump administration and has been adopted in large measure by the Biden administration.[30, 31] Two schools of thought have emerged regarding Washington's position on Afghanistan in the context of its relations with China. One school holds that the fiasco of the US withdrawal demonstrated once more—after the Iraq War, the global financial crisis, and a string of other policy failures over the past 20 years—the decline of US power and competence.

According to this thinking, a strategic opportunity has opened up in Afghanistan, and China should fill the vacuum with alacrity. In particular, China needs to scale up the BRI by using Afghanistan to link up Central and South Asia, so as to achieve a better balance in the western and eastern elements of the strategy.[32] The second, opposing school of thought is nowhere near as sanguine. Instead, it presents a foreboding analysis that posits an insidious anti-China US agenda. This view holds that the US withdrawal from Afghanistan was a deliberate step in Washington's overall grand strategic shift from focusing on the Middle East to targeting China in the Indo-Pacific region. What is especially insidious in the US move is that by leaving Afghanistan, Washington was intentionally creating a gap to entice China to move in and devote more resources to its western borderlands. In effect, Washington was setting up a strategic trap by which to lure and ensnare China in the west so as to subvert its strategy on the eastern maritime front.[33]

Thus, the Biden administration was believed to be trying to lull China into a false cooperation with it over Afghanistan by talking up China's responsibility for Afghan transition. The obvious conclusion of this analysis is that China should not take the US bait. Rather than falling into the US trap and foolishly shifting its strategic resources to the west, China should instead compete even harder with the United States in the east. In all likelihood, the second view had the upper hand in 2021 and may well continue to dominate policy debates in the near future. There was no evidence of China actively taking up the US place in Afghanistan in the second half of 2021. It is true that Chinese officials mentioned the prospect of greater economic relations, including assisting Afghanistan to participate in the BRI [22]. But despite this rhetoric, there were no specifics about how that might be done, and all the questions about extending the BRI to Afghanistan raised in the previous section remain outstanding.

China has certainly become more active and constructive in Afghan affairs since the US pullout. Bilaterally, it has renewed a cautious engagement with the Taliban; multilaterally, it has taken a leading role in regional multilateralism to facilitate Afghan reconstruction, including building new coordination mechanisms, such as the Foreign Ministers' Meeting of the Neighboring Countries of Afghanistan. But its activism still has major limits. Apart from its misgivings about the Taliban and Afghanistan's notoriety—proved once again by the failure of US intervention— as the "graveyard of empires," rivalry with the United States is the most important external source of these limits. Beijing's traditional vigilance toward the United States, now heightened under the new condition of strategic competition between the two countries, constrains the degree to which it can cooperate with Washington over Afghanistan. In the 2010s, China cooperated with the United States over capacity-building programs in Afghanistan, including police training and demining.[34]

Into the 2020s, Beijing certainly will not reject communication with Washington or rebuff US counter-terrorism efforts, but any great degree of joint intervention in internal Afghan affairs, especially of the armed kind, will be out of the question. In the 1980s, when the two countries collaborated closely on military and intelligence matters over Afghanistan, they successfully thwarted the Soviet invasion. Now, if they could inaugurate a new round of cooperation, they may well pull off Afghan reconstruction. Alas, such is their surging enmity that this is all but impossible.[35]

Conclusion

In terms of the future role Afghanistan is likely to play in Chinese foreign policy, its importance is likely to rise further, owing to the priority that neighbourhood diplomacy has been receiving from decision makers since 2013. But the precise degree of its rising importance will be determined by policymakers' perceptions of China's interests and vulnerabilities in Afghanistan. As we have seen, China's predominant interest in Afghanistan is ensuring its own security and stability—above all in the restive Xinjiang province but also in its vast western border region abutting Central and South Asia. Combatting Uighur and other associated forms of terrorism, separatism, and extremism must and likely will remain a central goal of its

Afghanistan policy. The severity of these threats and the effectiveness of the Taliban regime in controlling them will, to a large degree, determine the tempo and substance of Chinese policy. In contrast, despite the popular hype, China's economic interest is far less prominent and certainly not one that will plunge it into the war-torn country. At any rate, China's assessment of the economic value of Afghanistan is intimately bound up with the internal stability and security of the country, and it will commence large-scale investment, BRI-related or otherwise, only after Afghanistan has achieved more or less the same degree of tranquillity as in Pakistan or the Central Asian republics. China's security interests in Afghanistan generally call for a more activist approach toward the country, but perceived vulnerabilities are likely to constrain such activism. Two dominant vulnerabilities are the nature and competence of the Taliban regime and the strategic posture of the United States. China's pragmatism toward the Taliban, as we have seen, is mingled with great caution and conditioned by the future direction of the Taliban's internal and external policies. Above all, China wants a moderate Taliban government that will maintain domestic stability and will forge friendly relations with neighbouring countries.

But it is acutely aware of the limits of external intervention in influencing the Taliban. Herein lies a great difference between its approach to Afghan reconstruction and that of the United States. The forceful, root-and-branch US approach of armed intervention, democracy promotion, and nation building is anathema to China. China will be compelled to be more active and constructive in Afghan affairs as its interests dictate, but it will never opt for interventionism of the US kind. We are likely to see greater Chinese contribution to the reconstruction of Afghanistan, but only as much as Beijing feels comfortable with. China has always worried about the US presence in Afghanistan. In early years following the US invasion, it feared that Washington's dominance of Afghanistan might help it to complete its strategic encirclement of China in the west; later, it fretted that a premature US pullout might give terrorists a new lease on life. The vulnerability it felt after the US withdrawal in 2021 is that Washington is scheming to adjust its strategic focus and to compete with China in the Indo-Pacific by leaving a mess in Afghanistan for China to clean up—and perhaps also by creating a vacuum to entice and suck in China's strategic resources. The tragedy of Afghanistan is that it has been racked by continuous wars and conflicts for the past forty years, whose prospects of peace and prosperity are often at the mercy of the great powers. The tragedy of Sino-American relations with respect to Afghanistan is that their new rivalry is preventing them from launching meaningful cooperation over a country where cooperation is obviously needed and which, if successful, would help to ease their rivalry.

To cite article: Zhang F. China's New Engagement with Afghanistan after the Withdrawal. LSE Public Policy Review. 2022; 2(3): 10, pp. 1–13. DOI: https:// doi. org/10.31389/lseppr.52Acknowledgement: I wish to thank Andrew Small for his incisive comments and suggestions, Zhu Yongbiao for his observations about China-Afghanistan relations, and Xing Jiaying for her research assistance. The author has no competing interests to declare. Author Feng Zhang is Professor of International Relations and Executive Dean of the Institute of Public Policy at the South China University of Technology in Guangzhou. He is the author of Chinese Hegemony: Grand Strategy and International Institutions in East Asian History (Stanford, 2015) and, with Richard Ned Lebow, of Taming Sino-American Rivalry (Oxford, 2020) and Justice and International Order: East and West (Oxford, 2022). Feng Zhang orcid.org/0000-0002-6758-4333 Institute of Public Policy, South China University of Technology, CN. Focus and Scope: CORRESPONDING AUTHOR: Feng Zhang Institute of Public Policy, South China University of Technology, CN zhangfeng@ ipp.org.cn GUEST EDITOR: Michael Cox Emeritus Professor of International Relations and Founding Director of LSE IDEAS, UK m.e.cox@lse.ac.uk. LSE Public Policy Review is an open-access, peer-reviewed journal which is published quarterly and draws principally (but not exclusively) on authors from across the LSE's 19 departments. Issues are thematic and concentrate on a key topic at the heart of current debates in public policy. Public policy challenges bring to the fore cross-cutting questions which require a global perspective and a focus on their interconnectedness. Articles in each issue take different disciplinary perspectives, encouraging interdisciplinary collaboration and analysis at the forefront of current thinking. As a result, each issue presents a comprehensive approach to the specific theme and an analysis that is academically rigorous but also readily accessible to all readers. All issues are initially proposed as public symposia, with symposia leaders outlining the main themes, suggested papers and authors. The LSEPPR Commissioning Editors regularly review a range of proposals for future issues, and decide amongst them based on the relevance of the topic, the fit of the proposed approach with the aims and scope of the journal and the level of scholarship of the proposed contributions. Given the thematic nature of the LSE Public Policy Review's issues, we cannot accept open submission of individual manuscripts. **Types of outputs accepted.** The LSEPPR publishes original research papers, conceptual articles, review papers written for a general readership, in non-technical language aimed at a wide audience including government, business and policy-makers, as well as academics and students. LSEPPR seeks to actively contribute to the study and development of public and social policy, public administration and public management. Publication Frequency. The journal publishes four issues quarterly online throughout the year. 'Guest' issues are welcomed and will be published as part of the normal schedule. Open Access Policy: This journal provides immediate open access to its content on the principle

Chapter 4

Writing War, and the Politics of Poetic Conversation

James Caron and Salman Khan

Abstract

This article's premise is that war is ontological devastation, which opens up questions as to how to write about it. The paper contends that even critiques of war, whether critical-geopolitical analyses of global structures or ethnographies of the everyday, center war in ways that underscore erasures of non-war life, and therefore risk participating in that same ontological devastation. Engagement with extra-academic conversational worlds, both their social lives and their intellectual ones, is ethically necessary in writing war. To that end, this article examines poetic production from one front in the US-led "Global War on Terror": Swat Valley, Pakistan. Poets in Swat have produced an analysis of war as ontological devastation, but also protest their reduction, in the minds of others and themselves, to the violence-stricken present. This intervention is not an intellectual critique alone. Focusing on a new genre of "resistance" poetry, this article shows how poets resist war by maintaining worlds partly beyond it. In this, the critical content and the social lives of poetry are inseparable.

Keywords: Violence counterinsurgency poetry politics of knowledge war on terror

Introduction

From 2007 to 2009, the upland region of Swat, in what was then the Northwest Frontier Province (NWFP) of Pakistan, experienced widespread insurgency, then Taliban rule. As the paramount branch of Pakistan's fissiparous Taliban movements, the Swat Taliban's leadership negotiated a power-sharing deal with the Pakistan government in 2009. Then very soon, as this deal broke down, everyday Taliban repression was compounded by devastating Pakistan Army operations and state violence. Two and a half million people were displaced; countless lives destroyed.[1]

Initially, we identified two vantage points in literature on the US-led global War on Terror: top-down and the everyday. Northwest Pakistan has been ruled as a frontier by multiple securitized states, and academic knowledge of it has often reflected these states' self-universalizing vantage points – a more general result of academic disciplines that emerged in institutional fields tied to imperial states.[2] As Magnus Marsden and Ben Hopkins illustrate in their introduction to the edited volume Beyond Swat (2013), conflict on the frontier has frequently been seen as the normal state of an aberrant region: much literature has assumed that a default condition of civility is disrupted by the pathological character of an area that is seen by others mostly in terms of its status as a frontier problem. This critique resonates with recent work in interdisciplinary studies of war. Tarak Barkawi notes the Eurocentrism involved in the main categories that scholars in his field, war studies, have used to think about war, including the idea that war and peace are binaries and the idea that the basic unit in war is the nation-state. Instead, Barkawi sees war as a contingent manifestation of an underlying long-term dynamic, the violence of international hierarchies. He suggests replacing the "war/peace" binary with a "battle/repression" model "in which the use of force is an integral, not extraordinary, dimension of politics" in a world textured by empire.[3] Complementing the material side of this, Tarak Barkawi and Shane Brighton note how war, in this more expansive sense of the use of force as politics, produces its own ontology that expands throughout societies – producing "relations between war, knowledge, and power" throughout society that they call "War/Truth," in institutions and in knowledge formations alike.[4] Global violence creates the reality in which it operates.

From a bottom-up direction, some scholars in fields such as anthropology, critical geopolitics, and development have decentered accounts of the agency of states and systems, and turned toward the "implements" of violence and the "discursive-material practices" of actors distributed throughout society.[5] Feminist and subaltern scholars have emphasized affect, embodied knowledge, and inter-relational positions rather than individuated ones. Such work, centered on the everyday, considers geopolitical violence but highlights subaltern representations of it that researchers hope can inform metropolitan theory.[6] In her work situated in Anbar Province, Iraq, Kali Rubaii draws on everyday interlocutors' responses to changes in the material environment. In a warscape built by counterinsurgency, even less-than-lethal violent material change destabilizes meaning via affect, making preexisting modes of life unthinkable and unlivable. Viewing counterinsurgency from the position of the population targeted for intervention, Rubaii's Anbari farmer interlocutors cannot differentiate between a positive-constructive and subtractive-destructive face to it: For them, counterterrorism is a modus operandi that affects whole populations in the same way torture strategies may affect an individual, by distorting their world until they cannot make meaning out of anything.[7]

Both these lines of inquiry shape our own thinking in writing about the War on Terror and our intervention is additive, not polemic. Our point is that we largely have found either holistic reckoning with structures of global violence as seen by critical theorists, or carefully drawn textural views of everyday knowledge as seen by participant ethnographers. Both perspectives pay attention to long-term histories and to how war creates metaphysical reality itself, on multiple scales. Ethnographies of war also describe ways that everyday life resists this, building temporary new subaltern realities in the interstices. Furthermore, ethnographic work also generally incorporates top-down views. But what has been missing is the middle.

As we read poetry and talked to poets and others from Swat, we noticed that poetry took place in social spaces that were not top-down, nor interstitial, nor exactly subaltern. Indeed, the poetic critiques we discuss here are not dominant in Pakistan or on its frontier, but they could be called mainstream in Pashto. Larger than the everyday, poetic conversation about war in Swat and the frontier highlights society-wide connections from before and outside the 2009 war. The War on Terror has not been a rupture; it is a neoliberal-era evolution of existing colonial and Mughal state-frontier processes, and poems in Pashto (not only from Swat) written since the recent Swat conflict locate this moment within just such longer histories of repression. But Swat's contemporary poetic communities seek to exceed even this long-term war. Their poems at once describe, and exist as a product of, long-term social conversations that have resisted War/Truth all along by exceeding it in space, in remembered pasts, and in aspirations for a future informed by these worlds rather than by War/Truth.

War, we argue, is ontological destruction in service of large-scale civilizational projects: the breaking of existing local patterns of meaning to create a blank slate on which to write a new future. Ceding the frame excessively to war destruction, whether focusing on its long-term global structures or on everyday responses in the ethnographic present, reinforces the centrality of War/Truth at a time when there exist long-standing local intellectual-cultural-social formations that consciously position themselves beyond it. This opens up a moral question: might not a general transdisciplinary tendency toward either top-down or everyday views contribute, even in a small way, to that very same erasing effect of war by centering it, even in critique?

In contrast, centering middle ground critical-poetic conversations in society presents insurgency, military, neoliberal geopolitics, and even the War/Truth of counterterrorism as characters, but does not allow them to colonize the story, displacing local society as protagonist or erasing the large-scale, non-war worlds it painstakingly builds. In this article, we show that local theories of war parallel much of the above insights about ontological destruction, but also that this critique is inseparable from actively maintaining the life of a cultural formation in a militarized frontier society. Poetic critique and poetry's social organization are two parts of the same thing. We show this through a study of poems, poets, and their networks in Swat from 2005 to the present, particularly exploring the rise of a new genre of muzāḥimatī ("resistance") literature.[8] This genre is inseparable from the violent present, but nonetheless is animated by, and reanimates, older conventions and life from outside War/Truth. We spoke to men and women from across greater Swat's oral-written literary formation,[9] including academics, cultural organizers, journalists, musicians, publishers, bookstore owners, and poets from all class backgrounds. We asked about changes in performed and written poetic styles, audiences, and wartime life.[10] Our Pashto and our experience with poets, performers, publishers, audiences, and texts in what we here call the "literary formation,"[11] the fact that we had read, watched, or listened to (as relevant) these poets' available work beforehand, and (in Salman's case) a life in the community all helped our conversations start from shared assumptions and vocabularies.[12]

In what follows, we draw on conversations, excerpts from printed works, and descriptions of live poetry exchanges (mushā'ire) to build a four-way analysis of this conflict supplied by our interlocutors: linkages between material violence, affect, poetic language, and social fields. We argue that meaning-making in poetry is inextricable from rapid destruction on several fronts. The salient selfhood of Swat and the frontier has been displaced by a War on Terror-era othering that has rendered Pashtuns' self-representation newly difficult in Pakistan. More than that, though, voicelessness has been fostered by violent interventions in the material-sensory environment, which create ambiguity, displacement, and powerlessness. This violence has been physical but, as we show, Swati poets see in it a strategic destruction of meaning, destabilizing people's affective-emotional-cognitive worlds, and making any reality apart from the Pakistan Army's hegemony, or Taliban counter hegemony, hard to imagine. Swati poetry reflects upon such material/epistemic colonization as a matter of course. Like other regional trends, this literature draws a view of conflict centered on "visceral lessons of [ongoing] colonialism in the habits of mind and emotive reflexes of the postcolonial subject."[13] We underscore that this is about more than representation. This poetry describes violence, but also pushes back to create new meaning amidst violence – new senses of how things, emotions, and concepts in the world fit together. If a loss of meaning is an active strategy of war, as our poets theorize, then the very act of speaking poetry in publics – the act of collective meaning-making – pushes back against this.

These conversations take place among actual people in a concrete society, not in an abstract conceptual world alone. We must attend to their sociological life to draw out poetry's full resistivity. Literary exchange in Swat, in hybrid oral and written spaces, builds publics that cross class, gender, and other divides. Across varied sectors of society, poetic-emotional investment in worlds beyond war generate feelings aimed at realizing not just conceptual critiques, but also feelings of solidarity, responsibility, and social service, as well as anti-hierarchy and skepticism toward power. This all has played out in the social action of networks built upon this ethos. In the second half of our essay, we examine how poetic networks have built institutions, brought together wider interests in them, and invigorated non-literary social-service organizations with such sentiments, too. This has remained so, even as anti-war poetry started getting bound up in neoliberal peacebuilding and counterinsurgency. As we demonstrate, poetic networks have engaged national and global development institutions tied to such programs but have resisted co-optation even when using peacebuilding initiatives to expand. This is another way that poetry creates alternate worlds.

Part I: Poetic visions of devastation

In this section, we present poetry that explores how material violence of war is inseparable for residents in war zones from a destruction of reality. Poets problematize this destruction and, in so doing, fight against it by unmasking it, thus reducing some of its impact, and by preserving landscapes of images from outside war, even amidst the devastation. What follows is kaleidoscopic more than linear, but two trends recur throughout: poets point to ontological devastation, and they seek to preserve life-potential and to create meaning larger than War/Truth.

Amjad Shahzad: Displacement as cultural loss

Beginning in 2002, in the wake of George W. Bush's proclamation that in the War on Terror, all members of the world community were either "with us or with the terrorists,"[14] Pakistan's military chose the former path. President/General Musharraf outlined a policy officially called "Enlightened Moderation," with US encouragement. Enlightened Moderation combined economic and cultural liberalism with politically-neutral Islam, and aimed to subjectify Pakistanis as rational, moderate, and individual citizen-subjects.[15] The government extended unprecedented freedoms to civil society activists and formerly-repressed provincial parties, so long as they avoided questioning the military's political-economic supremacy, or the increasingly violent war in Pakistan's northwestern borderlands. At the same time, anecdotally in both authors' everyday conversations from 2005 onward, was a widespread feeling in the region that the state also actively promoted conservative Islamic groups in those borderlands. The sense was that the state did so to foster zero-sum competition between Pashtun nationalist tendencies and pan-Islamic (potentially pro-center) sentiment, and to manage conservative elements in the province. Finally, the existence of the figure of "extremist" or "terrorist" as internal enemy helped in conjuring an image of the military as "enlightened" for both domestic and international consumption.

From a Pashtun nationalist view, both the central authoritarian state and pan-Islamists were hegemony-seeking imports to the region which conspired to devastate local histories. These themes appear especially strongly in the following poem written by Amjad Shahzad in 2012:

> Our houses, hujras, mosques burned; our libraries were ruined
>
> When war was announced from Lahore's minarets
>
> The clang of Khushhal's sword has left Pashtun ears
>
> Amidst Jalandhari's songs, they forgot those lessons of honor.
>
> How many bodies will I weep for; or martyrs will I count?
>
> O you who care about the nation, O leaders safeguarding our heads?

This will require resolve, a reckoning must come

We'll draw a line in the sand, and say this categorically

I won't carry the corpses of a failed state on my shoulders

I won't offer any more martyrs to that green flag

Whether Boots or Turbans, let all hear my words

I'll neither fear nor flee these honorless armies

There's no other solution; the one path is liberty

We must walk the path of unity, but always for liberty[16]

Amjad composed this poem after Bashir Bilour – a Member of Parliament for the Pashtun-nationalist, secularist, and center-left Awami National Party (ANP) – was assassinated by a suicide bomber in Peshawar, the capital of the former NWFP, of which Swat is part. Amjad read this poem at Bilour's wake.

A musician and poet, Amjad is among the region's most prominent entrepreneurs of arts education. He runs school-based programs for youth, and trains adult musicians and poets. Like many poets who choose Pashto as their medium, Amjad appreciates many ANP positions even if he is not a party member: Pashtun identity, anti-authoritarianism, executive and legislative decentralization, secularism, and liberal democracy. These concepts inform his poem's agonized defiance, as Amjad uses "boots" and "turbans" as metonyms for forces warring in Swat. In describing the announcement of war as coming from "Lahore's minarets," both militarized state power and militarized religious reform become alien impositions from Pakistan's metropole, and intimately connect parts of one phenomenon: destruction of local history and society. Amjad also calls attention to the physical landscape and how it is connected to intangibles, such as how the destruction of libraries destroys local self-knowledge. Destroying mosques and hujras (sitting rooms that function as public discussion forums in Pashtun society) breaks public space where local collective conversation thrives. On the Pashtun frontier, increasingly defined as a warscape, the military's message is material destruction and erasure of existing modes of speech. The only speech available, says Amjad, is refusal.

Refusal alone, though, only cedes ground to War/Truth. Hence the specific form of this protest. Amjad invokes Hafeez Jalandhari, the Urdu-language poet of Pakistan's national anthem, often accused of sycophancy toward

Pakistan's 1960s military ruler Ayub Khan. Amjad juxtaposes Jalandhari with Khushhal Khan, the seventeenth-century Pashtun polymath whose poetic condemnations of Mughal Emperor Aurangzeb are remembered as vividly as his anti-Mughal armed skirmishes, but whose Pashto-specific forms of knowledge are also a touchstone for Pashtun historians at odds with Pakistan's official state narrative. Amjad therefore highlights destruction of the past and its forms of life, but in doing so, recalls that same past in both intangible (poetic) and tangible (hujra) modes, resurrecting them in the collective imagination.

Didar Tahir: Displacement, and structures of devastation

Poets with less involvement in elite circles voice some of these same concerns, though their systemic perspectives are less embedded in the formal political field. Rather, they often focus on structures that enable ontological devastation and on that devastation itself. Didar Tahir is a retired schoolteacher from Batkhela, a medium-sized market town. He participates in local literary circles organized around informal meetups. Unlike Amjad, Tahir's concern is not ethnonationalism, though Tahir expresses just as much a feeling of responsibility to Pashtun society in conversation. Rather, this poem, from his 2010 collection, is about empire:

> This era has no Nimruds, this era has no Pharaohs
>
> This era has no Hishams, this era has no Hamans
>
> No Alexander and no Darius, no Yazid and no Shimar
>
> In this era there's no Bakhtzaman, no murderous Hulegu Khan
>
> Still, red fires burn everywhere, burning red coals rain down
>
> Oppression, violence, tumult, rivers of red blood flow in every direction
>
> These subcontractors of peace are snakes hiding in our sleeves
>
> These doctors, saying they'll cure any patient Are traders in heads
>
> War-chief and manager, both at once: That's the sort who rules this world[17]

Drawing a lineage of autocrats from antiquity to the Mongols, Tahir breaks off; in the modern world violence abounds, but one cannot pinpoint individual folk-demons. Instead, one must look at systems. As Tahir explained to us in interview, "contractors of peace" refers to the US, and its pressure on Pakistan's military-state.[18] The commonplace Pashto epithet da dunyā ṭekedār ("the world's subcontractor") avers that the US government, directly or outsourced, arrogates to itself a role of peacebuilding on behalf of peoples worldwide, but enforces solutions that actually fuel violence. Neoliberal structures reproduce fractally, as Faisal Devji argued in a 2009 article for The Guardian:

The Army ... is a corporation that owns vast tracts of land, industries, and commercial enterprises, of which the military forms only a part ... For their part, the Pakistani Taliban and other militant groups no longer speak the language of Islamic revolution or an Islamic state ... Instead they behave like private companies or NGOs, claiming to provide good governance or ethical lifestyles in areas that have been taken over from the state and transformed into militant versions of the model communities and special economic zones that also proliferate ... [19]

Having attended to structure, Tahir flips the view in his book's next poem toward local affective change:

> Our rose-garden has become a Land of Thorns, our date orchard's become a desert
>
> Our peace, our abode of tranquility has gone, like Iraq and Afghanistan
>
> The Jamiʿa Ḥafṣa school became a killing ground; our Red Mosque, a graveyard
>
> Every primary school of ours, Damadola; every city, Waziristan
>
> Everywhere, bombs, cannon, and rifles; every public square, gunpowder-stan
>
> If the rifle is our Raja, our country's become Rajastan
>
> We're all each other's enemies; our village lanes and homes are now Rebel-stan
>
> Where do we go; where do we hide? Even our duvet's now a Deathistan
>
> Our Swat, more beautiful than Paradise's garden: became a graveyard for flowers
>
> What name should I coin for it, Tahir? This whole land is a Land of Death-Throes[20]

While the War on Terror had long affected the Pashtun borderlands, the Army's July 2007 siege of the Red Mosque in the national capital, Islamabad, marked the point when Pakistan's national media first paid attention to the human pain in that War on Terror.[21] Tahir moves from his own space to the global War on Terror, down to the national-scale Red Mosque, then back to a local, intimate geography of traumas, as outsourced state violence in a neoliberal era sparks local violence. Finally, he mentions Swat. In the hundreds of poems we have read and listened to, this is one of a very few that specifically names events and localities. This is part of his point. He describes the destruction of place and a rendering of home as alien and painful. But at the same time, he preserves a prior Swat by mentioning its name, against all the new identities this dystopian war-scape has taken on.

Neelum Arzu and the breakdown of meaning in a war-scape

Neelum Arzu's poems are yet more self-reflective in exploring society-wide change on the level of cognition and emotion. They focus on subjectification and affect, linking physical violence to psycho-cognitive trauma. In an interview, Arzu linked this to her perspective as a young woman who observes strict physical gender segregation (parda), but one whose family is supportive of her intellectual life and her career as a womens' college chemistry lecturer.[22] For her, the constrained immediacy of parda, juxtaposed against her interactions (via her profession) with life outside, is what leads her to link everyday violence to larger patterns. In the following poem, Arzu describes war violence as an abusive marriage, to draw out multifarious connections between both. She contrasts the confused "blackness" of violence with the "red" of her interiority. The cosmetic beauty-mark, a common romantic symbol in Pashto literature, is replaced with blood:

> I reside in your love's blackness; that's why I beauty-mark myself with red

> I reside in darkness's oppression; that's why I beauty-mark myself with red...

> In pitch-blackness, black surroundings, what value can a black beauty-spot have?

> I reside in my suffering's heat; that's why I beauty-mark myself with red...

> This separation from sensation is a white burial shroud of hopes

I reside in a living grave; that's why I beauty-mark myself with red

This art, with its lacerated tongue, gives voice to Arzu's desire

I reside in lamentation's fire; that's why I beauty-mark myself with red[23]

Arzu explained to us that the darkness of war, a deprivation of any meaningful sense in the world, parallels the restricted experience that many women must adapt to around the age of 15, and linked this restriction to limits on how far women can imagine the world. Drawing her connections out, both military and Taliban violence (like the violence of some families) rendered existing chains of meaning in the world unavailable. Even more, Arzu describes a loss not only of meaning but of any recognizable feeling. Attention given to a population by a military organization, for instance, may be care of a sort, and Pakistan's military made these connections itself: one of its 2010 anti-Taliban campaigns was titled Operation Khwax ba de Sham ("You will come to love me"). Of course this is care in a violent, dominating, unrecognizable form. In a transformed reality, responses to care from before (a marriage, a war) no longer fit with what one feels. All is dark obscurity. Emotions no longer make sense. Bodily-affective symbols like the blood scar, replacing a traditional tattooed beauty-spot, are the last echoes of a past so horrifically transformed as to be inaccessible.

Take a moment before moving on to the following poem. In this one, Arzu looks outward, linking emotional devastation to the conflict's legacy of fracturing society – exacerbating and giving new significance to disparities of class, region, gender, and political access. This is again so destructive that it results in the loss of capacity to find any connection, or even meaning, in an alien new world:

If the world smiles, let it; there's no ban on that

As for me, I cry; I have no home or burial shroud

I see the gold threads across your velvet finery

My clothes are patched; there's no embroidery on my hem

In this thief's beard I see not one hay straw, but a bundle

But unfortunately, there's no effect in saying so

O my land, what flowers would your flamed earth sprout?

There's not one piece of your body without gunpowder on it

These ones in white clothes go about performing uprightness like falcons

While there's not one wispy thread of nobility on their bodies

My spirit's left my soul; I just drag my wounded heart around

Smiles confront me everywhere; that's why I have no home

Arzu, I'll keep the bird of poetic-images[24] locked up at home

For now, let's not write songs; there's no garden here.[25]

In conversation with us, Arzu carefully bracketed this poem as general commentary. Still, it conjures specific images, especially of rank-and-file Taliban. Consisting of local youths disaffected during the pre-war era, "Falcon Forces" began as insurgent cells during initial Taliban mobilizations in 2007.[26] When Taliban rule in the region began in 2009, these groups were deployed as morality squads, and their authority to search homes served as pretext for plunder of all sorts – displacing feelings of domestic security, robbing houses of any sense of home. Arzu also said she composed this poem when refugee displacements were highest. The fusion of these two displacements is startling: the predatory gaze of militant youth blend into mainstream Pakistan's distant empty smiles toward refugees. Together, they hollow out the pre-existing selfhood of the population, and recast Swatis – even to themselves – as powerless, even faceless.

In her poem, Arzu tells us that life has become so hostile to previous senses of reality that imagination itself is precluded, as Swatis' individual and collective prior experiences are no longer relevant. The "bird of poetic-images"–creative thinking-feeling – flees from body to soul to thought, and ultimately is locked up, isolated. The place for this bird is a conventionalized Indo-Persian landscape of sublime garden imagery, one that emerged in the poetic conversations of an older world that had the capacity to generate continuous new thoughts about the world through reflections on these images. Both that image-world and its companion social world are now gone.

How is poetic thinking resistance?

Though she is particularly incisive in drawing links between violence, affect, cognition, and destruction of reality itself, Arzu was far from the only one making these points. The following excerpts are from an interview with an influential non-poet figure in the literary formation:[27]

[Poets] vocalize the war's emotional impact on Swati society and Pashtuns generally. They express disgust, distrust, helplessness, exploitation, anger. These feelings come from practical life, our surroundings.

For instance, during the curfews, the army occupied numerous schools to use as bases, and utterly destroyed them and their libraries. One felt the army was maybe the bigger enemy of knowledge [than the Taliban]. Or, one morning, I saw a Frontier Corps soldier's head hanging from an electric pole and his body on the ground below. The Taliban pinned a message on, threatening violence if he was removed before eleven am. And army personnel carriers surrounded this, guarding, waiting for eleven am! Whose side was who on? Sights generated visceral terror, long-lasting trauma, and distrust in the army's motives. This is how the Taliban spread their message in the public mind. Not words; images. But leaving the body there exhibits to the world how deadly the conflict is and justifies the army's actions too. Both sides wanted the media to see. Both used ambiguous material things like this against us, too.

An army officer claimed it was impossible to close the Taliban's FM radio station [which they used for broadcasting decrees and demands, as well as individualized threats against enemies]. So, they lacked the technology to jam low-frequency radio, when any technician in Swat could do it? This is how our whole environment was anxiety, trauma, distrust, alienation. Apart from what the radio said, it was just there, invading daily life, and the army left it on. Things like this got people suspecting that the army and Taliban were on one page, united in conspiracy against the local people.

There would be gunfire and shelling all night, and come morning, it was innocent people who were dead, not Taliban like we expected. As bodies piled up, we felt exploited, and more and more uncertain as to what was what. You have strategic objectives, but you could inform people beforehand. Why sacrifice ordinary people to keep everyone in the dark?[28] This insight, that material violence communicates its own non-meaning and erases other meaning, is striking in the way that it mirrors Rubaii's vision of war as described in the introduction. Earlier ecologies of signification and feeling were rendered unfamiliar by violent new surroundings, fostering feelings of anxious confusion – of being in the dark – that this interviewee relates. And this interviewee also concretizes the idea that the violent fog of confusion can be deliberate. This mirrors work on military intervention elsewhere in Pakistan.[29] It is a way to paralyze resistance and it aims to create a situation in which the military or Taliban's preferred futures are the only ones, if any, that are imaginable.[30]

Much poetry written since 2007 has been preoccupied with heavily concrete images, reflecting a proliferation in material life of violent objects like corpses, boots, gunpowder, rifles, bullets, bombs, fire, thorns, and chains. Poets use these images to build a dystopic, superficially senseless image-landscape. This is often juxtaposed against a pre-war Indo-Persian image-landscape of gardens, birds, and trees, at a time when meanings were stable, the same landscape that Arzu invokes as absent. In interviews, poet after poet claimed that their new poetic symbol-set, and the emergent muzāḥimat genre it defines, was necessitated by the wholesale society-wide transformations in emotion that have resulted from traumatic changes in material-social relationships during war. All noted destruction of previous life-worlds, and of the ability to even create meaning in this new one. Arzu, again, sums up this loss in the following poem:

> What a lovely time it was; poets used to write songs
>
> There was none of this stench; thoughts would write the morning breeze
>
> Today, my faculty of image-creation is sacrificed on the pyres all around[31]
>
> Pens are no help in writing when every hand is trembling... [32]

But Arzu's pen and hand are writing these couplets. And even if they are doing something new, it is not entirely new. Indo-Persianate ghazals, the most widespread and prestigious genre in contemporary Pashto literature, rely on concrete figures relating to and constituting each other in a landscape, stereotypically a garden of birds, flowers, trees, and the morning breeze. As poets over centuries created new permutations of how these figures' interrelationships play out, chains of meaning emerged as culturally embedded ways of understanding how the world works.[33] In contemporary poetry, this millennium-old garden-scape often appears only to be destroyed and replaced by an apocalypse. But this new external landscape is in turn subjected to the same conventionalized rules of poetic meaning-making applied to the garden, even as the birds and trees are replaced by new violent objects. In so doing, poets make sense of life. Even meaninglessness itself is encapsulated as a poetic object that can be grasped and politically analyzed: defusing that particular war weapon by positioning the poetic vantage point, in its capacity to make meaning, beyond and above the destruction. Finally, in mentioning a garden lost, do not Tahir and Arzu remind their audiences and themselves of this? Even as it turns into a supplement to a violent new normal, keeping the garden alive in memory allows one to hold on to extra-war patterns of conversation, collective feeling, and metaphysical reality. All this provides ground to stand on, amidst the destruction.

Part II: Poetry's social lives: how affects and institutions together resist war/truth

All this is not only a phenomenon in the imaginal world. The preservation of an imaginal garden-scape and an active, conscious resignification of the exterior world are organic to a corresponding rise in social-activist sentiment. Interviewee after interviewee narrated desires to "be useful," and to "do something." Hence the label muzāḥimat for this genre: "resistance," derived from the affect-heavy word zaḥmat, "exertion; effort." The interview that we excerpted above began with a question about the ways in which the conflict had affected poetic culture, and this was the interviewee's response:

The conflict generated a power to act. It generated a new genre of resistance (muzāḥimatī) poetry against war, terrorism, and the ongoing countrywide treatment of Pashtuns, and this replaced the earlier romantic trend as predominant in Swati poetry. The organization of region-wide aman mushā'ire [peace-themed poetry slams] and the proliferation of poets' associations are features of Swat's landscape, post-conflict. Such mushā'ire are not restricted to a particular school of thought, and people from all walks of life participate. In these mushā'ire, poets vocalize the war's emotional impact on Swati society and Pashtuns generally. They express feelings like hatred, distrust, helplessness, exploitation, and anger. These feelings come from practical life, they come from our physical surroundings.[34]

As poets processed their feelings from the material world, reflected on them, and worked them into new meanings, they recognized they were building tools that could help others examine their own new experience to interrogate this physical dystopia's deeper structures, and to realize alternatives. But poetry does not exist independently of its networks, and we cannot build an account on transparent readings of poetry separate from their socio-political lives. Poets do not restrict themselves so, as the above quote illustrates. Pashto poetry emerges within geopolitical interplays of affect, discourse, and institutions, and in so doing aims to reshape them. Anti-war poetry can go in many directions. Individual poetic exploration of war might emphasize subjectivity and trauma at the expense of attention to structures that generate violence. Of course, this contention is difficult to sustain in the cases of Arzu, Tahir, and Amjad, but it is the case with a

71

range of other works we heard, particularly at poetic-musical performances. In these cases, we identified some cooption of anti-war poetry to larger projects, particularly army-led efforts at liberal peacebuilding, in league with transnational organizations. Nonetheless, this was not the case with much muzāḥimatī poetry, even that which could be seen as apolitical. Its social context prevented such a reading.

From local activism to liberal peacebuilding

Interviewees described how the war initially dispersed poets and curfews dampened vibrant literary associations. Much as Zarin Anzor described Pashto literary circles amidst the earlier Afghan-Soviet war, these organizations devolved into a plethora of small, informal circles, each developing idiosyncratic conversations and symbolic vocabularies.[35] But this also led to re-combinations. For instance, Akbar Siyal usually gathered a circle of around two dozen poets from greater Swat at his Islamabad residence. In his poetry Siyal tends to emphasize individualized lyrics re-inflected with the trauma and confusion other poets note, but he also devotes attention to longer trends engulfing the entire borderland region. As early as 2000, Siyal (among a few others) popularized poetic attention to the Afghan war's fallout, with his collection Pa Jang de Or Olagī ("Let War Itself be Burned") In his 2009 collection, Zamūṅg pa Kilī kxe Fasād ma Joṛawa ("Don't Spread Discord in our Village") he interrogates both trauma and historical structural violence while lamenting the atomization of alternative visions. This formerly individual set of preoccupations was adopted more broadly as the muzāḥimat genre rose.

Poetic cross-fertilization amidst the new Swat crisis linked multiple Pashtun space-times together. Phrased in Indo-Persianate ghazal registers, many poets articulated pre-war worlds, as noted above (as well as what Taimoor Shahid calls "precapitalist" ones).[36] Though he was based outside Swat, Siyal's circle had cross-cutting links with a range of others located there. Poets from one circle attended others' events, in social practices that also built on precapitalist processes. Amjad, for instance, said he attended many mushā'ire not for professional reasons, but to fulfill what he called adabī gham-xādī, a literary version of the webs of solidarity and reciprocity forged in social networks as people from different families, villages, and even regions physically attend to each other in moments of sorrow and celebration.[37] Others said that amidst the army curfews, these networks fulfilled a basic need for sociability itself. Literary exchange was at once a social-bonding activity and a way to talk about pain. As the War on Terror progressed, even informal poetic networks did not go unnoticed.

Additionally, some networks were already more institutionalized than others, and state actors and international donors sought to co-opt these into liberal peacebuilding initiatives.

By 2010, the Pakistan Army had dismantled the Taliban in Swat. The situation remained tense, but still, attempts at revitalizing Pashtun arts and culture in non-political "cultural heritage" modes, were afoot. The center-left, secularist ANP had won the 2008 provincial election, replacing an Islamist party coalition. Pashto heritage enthusiasts in the UK diaspora, including a Conservative Party MP, raised funds for an event that persuaded the new provincial government to reopen Nishtar Hall – Peshawar's largest performing arts venue – after it had been closed for eight years by the previous government for "promoting vulgarity." This inaugural event intersected with a two-year project called "Protection, Preservation and Revival of Local Culture, Arts and Heritage" that an ANP-linked body, the Baacha Khan Trust Educational Foundation, had created with funding from the Norwegian Embassy. This encompassed visual and performing arts, poetry, handicrafts, and village festivals. Part of the remit was to create vibrant, non-political public connectivities on the frontier to help fill a vacuum of sociability that was presumed to have enabled the rise of militancy.[38] This too, aimed at social re-engineering of an assumed empty space, a liberal form of War/Truth.

Networks of Swat-based activists like Usman Ulasyar and Amjad Shahzad had been holding similar events privately, despite Taliban reprisals. Unlike some others, Ulasyar and Amjad's networks had even mobilized resources to train musicians and poets. Around the time the Nishtar Hall inauguration was being planned, Ulasyar and others planned a major public event in Swat, but the army vetoed this just before it happened, ostensibly for security reasons (more likely, our interviewees suspected, in fear that some performers might speak subversively). So, their event was moved to Peshawar under provincial civilian-government sponsorship and combined with province-wide performers with Norwegian funding. This thus subsumed the Swati networks' event into the globalized Nishtar Hall inauguration project. Broadcast province-wide on FM radio, the combined event was reframed by the emcees both as a non-political celebration of Pashtun culture and a special tribute to Swat and its trauma. All this indexes how Swat-based networks' power-to-act[39] began adapting to various external forces, and then began exerting productive new liberal hegemony over mass cultural production in the Pashto-sphere.

Liberal peacebuilding: institutions

Underneath layers of this depoliticized celebration of Pashtun culture, involvement by muzāḥimatī (resistance) poets and singers from Swat gave this Nishtar Hall event undercurrents of protest. Nonetheless, the mostly depoliticized nature of this event emerged from a new cultivation of Pakistani civil society under President/General Musharraf. Thousands of local organizations formed, nationwide.[40] Some campaigned on specific political issues that fit with moderation generally. Others provided goods, services, and technical solutions to social problems, outside the domain of politics or the state. While this upswelling of NGO activity occurred mainly in the urban centers of Punjab and Karachi, it also encouraged and, through institutional links, fostered the emergence of a strategic action field[41] in the NWFP, including Swat, with funding from newly available national and international sources. The Nishtar Hall event, and Ulasyar's and Amjad's careers, came to be tied to this field, even if not fully determined by it.

In our interviews, Ulasyar emerged as a paramount cultural-heritage entrepreneur of Swat. In 1989, he and his college classmates established the Swat Art and Culture Association for the "intellectual and artistic development of poet, writer, and musician friends," holding mushā'ire that attracted some of Swat's most prominent poets.[42] Activities were financed by members, but as they graduated and moved on, Ulasyar formalized the organization. Renamed the Suvastu Art and Culture Association, he registered it under the Societies Act, branched out, and made links through the 1990s and 2000s with other civil society activists. Particularly important has been Khpal Kor Foundation (KKF), an orphanage, educational, and social welfare group on whose board Ulasyar serves. KKF in turn partnered with UNICEF and the AkzoNobel Foundation[43] to build institutional capacity. Ulasyar organized several Suvastu mushā'ire in KKF's hall during the 1990s and 2000s. These attracted sizeable audiences of intellectuals as well as influential people from business and social development sectors.

In 2010, under the umbrella of an international project,[44] Suvastu was commissioned to work with poets and writers while Amjad Shahzad was brought on to work with musicians who performed poetry and folklore. Amjad and his family had already established a small organization, Da Hunar Kor, which held local 'aman (peace) mushā'ire' – poetic-musical gatherings specifically designed to frame the ongoing situation. This was part of a larger trend of similar activities organized by local associations. When the project took off, Amjad's small organization gained a much larger institutional capacity that could encompass the entire frontier. In an interview he recalled:

We set the project's direction. We thought to activate all the poets of all the tribal regions: Mohmand, Waziristan, Bajaur, etc. We acquired a list of poets, and registered literary associations with the project. We gave them representation, and funds for conducting activities. We also centrally organized two or three events in Peshawar every month – mushāʿire, music – and invited poets from all over. We wanted people from different districts to develop interactions with each other. In those events, we selected poems suitable for musical performance [and matched them to singers]. We wanted to give a chance to established musicians who'd fallen from visibility [in such difficult times]. We facilitated them financially and recorded that poetry, from the monthly events, in their voices. Second, we tried to give opportunities to new singers. For that, we conducted auditions in each district.[45]

Eventually, they produced 90 recordings which were broadcast province-wide on commercial FM radio, the widest possible venue at the time. External patronage meant that most of these recordings were politically safe and emphasized beauty, entertainment, and the return of "springtime" to the "garden" of Swat. This in turn influenced public poetry more broadly. The majority of these songs lamented war generally without much analysis, simply asking listeners as individuals not to choose violence while remaining mute about the structures generating it. This liberal way of speaking also heavily textured aman melas (peace celebrations), including ones organized at camps to mark the return of refugees. Both state and global institutions attempted to assimilate local critiques, and both the United Nations Development Program (UNDP) and the Provincial Relief, Rehabilitation, and Settlement Authority (PaRRSA) sponsored high-profile events of this sort, often with Army support, over the next years.

Liberal peacebuilding: hearts and minds

The depoliticization of even sharply political poets' activities cannot be explained by sponsors' influence and expectations alone. Nor can this be explained by government demands or repression, though these played roles. Instead, one must relate this to the way that even critical actors in the literary ecosystem negotiate a warscape in which "hearts and minds" are a primary arena of conflict, and the way in which actors internalized transnational and state cultural politics. Musharraf's national-cultural program of Enlightened Moderation, disseminated by a variety of corporate and NGO interests, "orchestrate[d] meanings and practices of identity, mark[ed] bodies, and condition[ed] political subjectivities."[46] Elites and members of the middle class in metropolitan centers of Punjab, Sindh, and the NWFP could contrast their own forward-thinking, moderate subjectivities with ethnic stereotypes of "Talibanization" on the frontier, stereotypes that legitimated state violence.[47] And poetry – its affective performance in music, its rich yet fluid fields of signification – lent itself especially well to this. In songs that focus only on trauma and not structures, symbols like turbans (equated with obscurantism and extremism) can displace blame for violence onto stereotyped individuals' dispositions, rather than structural factors.

Finally, this affective regime also produces commodities of virtue, allowing audiences to counter-define themselves by performing and internalizing opposition to these fictive character-types. In Swat, a specific performative selfhood was evident, both in remarks at older mushā'ire and in our conversations with elite poets: the phrase da sho'ūr aw aḥsās khāwindān, "men of perception and sensitivity," arose again and again. In some of those conversations, this self-image contrasted with images of both militarist and religious extremists. In the process, the act of adopting this self-image also served to negatively formulate something like a notion of "the unenlightened masses" at large, whose subjectivities have not been formed within liberal binaries.

Muzāḥimat as criticality and subversion within hegemonic spaces

Even amidst all the above, we did not find a totalizing hegemony in these networks. While liberal projects have affected them, they are also shaped by the activist impulse that the conflict created. Muzāḥimat came to be an adoptable, even virtuous, attribute of perception and sensitivity, and subverted elitist elements in it. At times, performative muzāḥimat can be depoliticized. Other times, it performs liberal-ethnonationalist politics that questions disconnections between the ideals of liberalism and the realities of empire, as seen from the state's hinterland. In such cases it opposes military authoritarianism (as seen in Amjad's poem, above). But equally often, it calls for collective revolution against any and all psychosocial, political, and economic structures of oppression. This is particularly true of work by poets like Tahir and Arzu. When we asked Arzu how she responds to the label of inqilābī ("revolutionary") that fans have given her, she agreed that it spoke to a certain reality.[48] All this pulls on the subject-position of poets within the literary formation as a whole.

76

The majority of Pashto poets, including some of the most influential ones, maintain relatively modest day jobs as, for example, tailors or schoolteachers. Highly-politicized muzāḥimat actually received a boost from the overall growth of institutional activity related to peacebuilding. In 2008, a small peace mushāʿira held by the Socha Likwal association included the usually comedic Sajid Afghan reciting a poem that outlined structural factors in militancy, ranging from inequality to repression, and directly countered liberal ideas that violence results from individuals' backwardness, or that education and books are the most important solution. By 2014, muzāḥimatī cross-currents were able to take over even the major officially sponsored events. At a 2014 peace mushāʿira held by PaRRSA in Swat's stately Wadudia Hall, veteran poet Abasin Yousufzai publicly debuted his poem Iḥtijāj ("Protest"). He berated listeners for not protesting attacks on funerals, weddings, jirgas, mosques, and hujras, for not voicing truth despite seeing it, for not combatting antagonism, and for not fulfilling Pashtun ethics. At first, Yousufzai seemed like he wanted to single out extremist thinking and society's failure to condemn it, in keeping with liberal ideas of violence. Using a call-and-response technique, he then recited a litany of traumas, asking each time, "And did you protest?" As choruses of "No!" drowned out his heavily amplified voice, he asked each time, "Why not?" A half-mocking response of Hase! ("We just didn't!") caught on. Yousufzai deftly redirected the collective thought process, positing a depoliticization by internalized imperial structures as the reason "why not." The audience seemed much more sympathetically invested thenceforth.[49]

In drawing out the wider social context that has helped generate poetic ideas in Swat, muzāḥimat interacts with regional registers of neoliberalism and is textured by it, but is not the same thing. It involves collaborative impulses and civic service, but also, counter to depoliticizing impulses, it encourages poets to locate and speak to structural violence. Muzāḥimat reterritorialize formal events and hegemonic narratives, partly because it thrives in crosscurrents. Indeed, its rebelliousness can be antipathetic to participation in overly institutionalized projects. Amjad mentioned that he did not register his organizations with the state (making these ineligible for most donor funds) for the same reasons he did not join any political party: he wanted flexibility, which was, he said, "just part of his āzādāna tabīʿat," or freedom-inclined nature. This was tied to sentiments voiced by every one of our interviewees, that literature should exist "for life," not for its own sake, nor (especially) as a professional industry. Poets like Didar Tahir were highly skeptical of mushāʿire receiving outside funding at all. Most of the organizations we encountered were self-funded by monthly member contributions of 300–500 Pakistan rupees, and only two – Suvastu and Mrastiyal Adabi Likwal (MAL) – were officially registered.

MAL, a literary collective overseen by the poet Iqbal Shakir in the market town of Batkhela, is member-supported but also accepts contributions and other support from local politicians, professionals, and traders. Still, MAL retains a strongly muzāhimatī orientation due to shared networks with other groups, including Pukhtun Adabi Malgari (PAM), of which Didar Tahir was a founder, and MAL propagates this ethos upwards via elite partners, more than its activities are disciplined by them. PAM holds mostly small impromptu meetings, and consciously eschews external fundraising. Tahir noted that PAM has a strong ethos of "literature for life's sake," and a very strong bias against "literature for personal gain" that intersected with the positive value on autonomy noted above. At the same time, MAL has partnered with external civil society groups, especially Strengthening Participatory Organization (SPO), a well-established national NGO. This partnership allowed MAL to fund the printing of the proceedings of one of its mushā'ire in 2009, at the height of the crisis, under the title Sawe Sawe Wāwra ("Burnt Snow"). This anthology's poems examine structural, physical, and emotional aspects of violence. Some even explicitly comment on the politics of epistemology, pre-emptively lampooning any possible fetishization of trauma that would reduce imaginations of Swat to warscape alone.[50] The more MAL worked with SPO, the more autonomy it gained; SPO gave them carte-blanche in arranging events like International Mother Tongue Day, Human Rights Day, even benefits for tuberculosis and HIV treatment. According to Shakir, MAL was ultimately so successful in spreading critical muzāhimat through SPO that SPO's director jokingly remarked that MAL had "hijacked" his organization. MAL's trajectory, then, is a larger institutional manifestation of the same negotiations in which Abasin Yousafzai redirected the state-sponsored PaRRSA event in real-time.

Conclusion

We conclude by relinking the two halves of this article: the imaginative content that draws links between the world and the feeling self, and the networks and institutions that link social selves to the world. Even poetry that, on its surface, expresses nothing but devastation can be a part of this world-building. The following poem, by Malakand poet Rahmat Shah Sayil, was among the most iconic songs circulating throughout our period of concern (2007 to now, and especially since 2009):

78

My land has become chains, entrenchments, garrisons everywhere

Burn on, O my feelings! My land has become a living hell.

No one's deigned to consider contributing anything positive to it;

My land is now an abject begging bowl for its own inhabitants.

I don't have even the authority to shed tears for it;

My land has become just the stake in a pointless game.

In it, I no longer recognize even my own self-image;

My land has sacrificed its head to power and lordship.

This is no small story, Sayil, but here's the nub of it:

My land has become an agonized sigh, caught in my throat.[51]

The sequence of "chains, entrenchments, and garrisons" moves from everyday policing of space and tactical competition between Taliban and Army forces to strategic land occupation. It moves from materiality to affect ("Burn on, O my feelings!"), then speaks to the displacement of both the poet's and the listener's richly-experienced land being reformatted as warscape. To listeners, Sayil evokes how this region, with its discrete histories, has been deprived of selfhood just as individuals have been, as the region has been converted into the frontier of somewhere else, from the British era to now. He then returns to affect, testifying that the situation is so enormous, the repression so extreme, and outsiders so insensitive to Pashtun lives, that things are as unspeakable as they are visceral: home can only exist as a sigh, indefinitely and agonizingly deferred.

But while this poem's content seems to leave little space for preserving life, thought, or even selfhood, the social life of this poem instantiates the reverse: it is a living example of the cross-generational, trans-local poetic conversations that we highlight. This poem was actually first published decades before the current Swat crisis, and portrays how Pashtun regions have been ruled throughout history. But Amjad sang it meaningfully in the 2010 Nishtar Hall inauguration, aimed at Swat solidarity.[52] It was posted on a community Facebook page in April 2015, when an agreement to establish a China–Pakistan Economic Corridor was signed, which many in the province expected would further garrison and marginalize their region.[53] It was tweeted in 2019 by activists protesting curfews in Waziristan, which were in turn aimed at defusing rallies by Pashtun civil rights activists.[54] Its opening lines appeared as a proverb in a 2019 editorial in Pukhtun magazine, protesting the imposition of women's face coverings in Peshawar District schools.[55] For the author of that piece, it encapsulated the trauma of imposing embodied, gendered modes of restriction, and they linked military restrictions of space and mobility to bodily repressions by right-wing political structures. Finally, four of our interviewees quoted this poem to summarize their points about Swat.

Belying the content of what it is saying – War/Truth now is all that there is – this poem became a magnet, attracting the very same cross-temporal and cross-regional community conversation that war seeks to atomize and then reorient elsewhere. And if that is the effect of just one text, then what of many voices and other poems, all in networked conversation? Poetic conversation simultaneously describes effects of the conflict and indexes social spaces that cut across its atomizing destruction, in space and in time.

When we shift the focus away from hegemony, we find autonomy arising from self-organized, informal circles, again and again. Organized activities draw vitality from informal modes of association which are organic with critical community dispositions outside neoliberal subjecthood, and reshape wider worlds as they respond to outside donors. Similar to how Nosheen Ali describes state employees' mushā'ire in another frontierized region, Gilgit-Baltistan,[56] literary activity in Swat thrives within dominant organizations but generates subversive content as a result of external networks. On the frontier, state and international patrons have attempted to harness poetic production for non-local projects, in the process positioning Swat's networks as especially important in Pashto. But in so doing, they have given space to the muzāḥimat generated by these networks to proliferate. Of course, in Swat and on the frontier, as anywhere, emergent fields operate; some people accumulate status and influence through these, and their work interfaces with more powerful fields like international development. But this is not all that is happening in Swat. At least partly due to the civic yet deconstructive ethos of muzāḥimat, institutions are pulled toward horizontality and flexibility, as skepticism toward hierarchized structures becomes a virtue in this emerging affective-discursive-institutional formation.

This also relates to the relative weakness of new elite interventions, compared to the longer-term life of Pashto poetic conversations and their informal institutions. Not supported by the government in education, or in any sector except new campaigns (since 2008 or so) for hearts and minds, most Pashto speakers usually read only in other languages. This is another reason why real-time events preoccupy our account. But the fact of being rooted in mainly face-to-face realms and informal networks seeking to remain informal and autonomous gives muzāhimat an autonomy, allowing it to spin outward and transform public Pashto overall. This is even more the case when such events spread through new pathways that online media platforms offer. The firebrand poet Bakhtzada Daanish said in interview that his 2019 compilation Za ba na Līwanai Keġam! (I Refuse to go Insane!) received critical acclaim because he voiced his refusal of a breakdown of meaning amidst violence, but his compelling live recitations on YouTube are what facilitated this success. Meanwhile, the singer Karan Khan has become one of the most popular performers not only in his native Swat but across the Pashto-speaking region. He has done so by monetizing his online presence, revolutionizing business models for Pashto recording artists everywhere, but most observers, including himself in an interview, attribute his success to the thought-provoking muzāhimatī poetry he selects. Thus, in new realms that circumvent patronage structures in favour of decentralized creation and consumption, Pashto literature has enjoyed mass interest post-2009 as never before, while the rise of critical civic-oriented muzāhimat has been an inseparable part of this phenomenon.

How can we make sense of this simultaneous ontological breakdown and new flourishings that have appeared alongside each other? Heriberto Yépez theorizes frontiers as places where hegemonic political-economic, psycho-social, and epistemic systems meet and fragment. These are processes of fission and mutual destruction, and people and their subjectivities at the borders form the primary battlefield. Yet the fluid recombination of fragments sometimes has productive power to create new forms that ripple back to rework powerful systems.[57] Writing about similar processes, Gloria Anzaldúa highlights such re-combinations while giving them an ethical-normative content; frontier lifeways and subjectivities are more than a power-capitulating form of resilience within a neoliberal age, they demand that fulfilling their potential be therapeutic, transformative of the multiple historic layers of violence that compose hegemonic orders.[58]

Frontier perspectives like muzāhimat critique War/Truth for us all, from a uniquely skilled vantage point – centuries of experience – and show ways out. In this case, the sentiments and strategies underlying muzāhimat gained an explicit, self-conscious critical voice during this period, and just a few years later this conscious ethos pervaded the Pashtun Tahaffuz Movement (PTM), a Pashtun-led national civil rights organization that for the first time united frontier and metropolitan citizens of Pakistan in a widespread critique of both military and Taliban-style aspirations to hegemony.[59] At the same time, Anzaldúa's vision is also permeated with the pain of breakdown as part of this long-term violence, the same thing that our counterinsurgency authors point to: ontological devastation as prelude to resubjectification by powerful projects initiated elsewhere. As in the poetry of Sayil, Arzu, Didar Tahir and others, the vitality of frontier worlds does not minimize this loss, or the fact of long-term war.

Some colleagues that we shared this paper with heard a story about the resilient flourishing of heritage. Others found in it a story about inevitable assimilation and destruction in the face of overwhelming forces beyond any local ability to resist. For our part, we have wanted to highlight the "middle conversation" in its complexity. Studying war, but through this consciously maintained space of "not-war," is the best way not to underline war's erasures, and a way for us not to contribute to those erasures.

CONTACT James Caron james.caron@soas.ac.uk 1 We are both scholars based in London. Salman grew up in Malakand during the conflict this essay addresses and, like many others in this highly poetry-aware society, composed poetry about it in a diary. We both noticed a disjuncture in reading about this war in academic spaces, versus how people in our experience expressed and reflected upon their experiences in Swat and its broader region. We wanted to explore how we could write about this war in a way that would address the latter experience. Poetry seemed a natural route to us. All poems in this article are translated from Pashto to English by James, in consultation with Salman. Interview excerpts have been translated from Pashto to English by Salman in consultation with James. We conducted all interviews together. © 2022 The Author(s). Published by Informa UK Limited, trading as Taylor & Francis Group This is an Open Access article distributed under the terms of the Creative Commons Attribution- NonCommercial- NoDerivatives License (http://creativecommons.org/ licenses/by-nc-nd/4.0/), which permits non-commercial re-use, distribution, and reproduction in any medium, provided the original work is properly cited, and is not altered, transformed, or built upon in any way. Acknowledgements: We thank Robert Shepherd and the editorial team at Critical Asian Studies, as well as our anonymous reviewers, for greatly improving this article. We also thank all the poets and others who continue to share their time and their emotional-intellectual worlds with us for this article, and the larger project of which it is part. Disclosure statement; No potential conflict of interest was reported by the author(s). Additional information. Funding. This research was funded by the British Academy's 2019 program for Heritage, Dignity, and Violence, in turn supported by the Global Challenges Research Fund (GCRF). It forms part of a larger project Mapping the Wounded Landscape of Swat Valley (HDV190288) led by Daanish Mustafa of King's College London. Notes on contributors. James Caron, James Caron is Lecturer in Islamicate South Asia at the

School of History, Religions, and Philosophies, SOAS University of London. James's fields of interest include borderland studies, the history and sociology of knowledge in South, Central, and West Asia, the metaphysics of violence, and materiality and ecocriticism in Islamic world traditions. Salman Khan. Salman Khan is a British Academy postdoctoral research associate in the Department of Geography, School of Social Science and Public Policy, Kings College London. Salman's fields of interest are institutional analysis, local governance, gendered research geographies of entrepreneurship, informal economies, marketplaces and bazaars in South Asia, borderland studies, and materiality and affect. Critical Asian Studies is a peer-reviewed quarterly journal that welcomes unsolicited essays, reviews, translations, interviews, photo essays, and letters about Asia and the Pacific, particularly those that challenge the accepted formulas for understanding the Asia and Pacific regions, the world, and ourselves. Published now by Routledge, part of the Taylor & Francis Group, Critical Asian Studies remains true to the mission that was articulated for the journal in 1967 by the Committee of Concerned Asian Scholars. Print ISSN: 1467-2715 Online ISSN: 1472-6033, 4 issues per year.

Chapter 5

The Taliban, IS-K and the Haqqani Terrorist Network

Terrorist organizations suchlike ISIS, and the Taliban through Facebook, YouTube and Twitter invite young people to join their networks by using various marketing techniques. These terror groups are marketers as well as consumers to a degree; their recruiters 'market' boys and use them as human bombs against civil society and military infrastructure. They supply suicide bombers across Asia and the Middle East in a cheap rate. Religious and political vendettas are being settled by using suicide bombers against rival groups or families. This generation of fear and panic is controlled by extremist elements and non-state actors. Fear and terror marketing systems are updated every year and new techniques of destruction are being introduced. The way the Afghan Taliban design their strategies for training and brainwashing suicide bombers is not quite different from the suicide techniques of the ISIS-K. They market fear and terror according to their demand. If we deeply consider the terrorism marketing techniques of both the Afghan Taliban and the IS-K, we will clearly observe approximation in their way of killing.

The concept of suicide attacks, or dying in order to kill in the name of religion become supreme ideal of Taliban and IS-K groups that have been carrying out suicide attacks against the innocent civilians of Afghanistan and Pakistan. After the US invasion of Afghanistan, Taliban resorted to suicide terrorism to force the United States and its NATO allies to withdraw their forces from the country and restore Emirate Islami of Taliban. Taliban and the IS-K became dominant forces in suicide terrorism to internationalise and justify it. Modern suicide terrorism emerged in Afghanistan after 9/11, but it was introduced in different shapes. Over the past two decades, the tactic of suicide terrorism in Afghanistan and Pakistan were modified and justified by religious clerics. According to expert, Assaf Moghadam (Suicide Terrorism, Occupation, and the Globalization of Martyrdom: A

Critique of Dying to Win, published in 2006), "the growing interest in suicide terrorism in recent years has generated a steep rise in the number of books that address a topic that is inherently fascinating—a mode of operations that requires the death of its perpetrator to ensure its success". In Dying, in order to kill Strategic Logic of Suicide Terrorism is possible to assemble statistical data about terrorist incidents. Experts and analysts, Yoram Schweitzer and Sari Goldstein Ferber, in their research paper (Al-Qaeda and the Internationalization of Suicide Terrorism. Jaffee Center for Strategic Studies, Tel Aviv University. Memorandum No. 78 November 2005) have highlighted some aspects of Istishhad or suicide terrorism:

"The concept of istishhad as a means of warfare is part of an overall philosophy that sees active jihad against the perceived enemies of Islam as a central ideological pillar and organizational ideal. According to al-Qaeda's worldview, one's willingness to sacrifice his or her life for Allah and 'in the path of Allah' (fi sabil allah) is an expression of the Muslim fighter's advantage over the opponent. In al-Qaeda, the sacrifice of life is of supreme value, the symbolic importance of which is equal to if not greater than its tactical importance. The organization adopted suicide as the supreme embodiment of global jihad and raised Islamic martyrdom (al-shehada) to the status of a principle of faith. Al-Qaeda leaders cultivated the spirit of the organization, constructing its ethos around a commitment to self-sacrifice and the implementation of this idea through suicide attacks. Readiness for self-sacrifice was one of the most important characteristics to imbue in veteran members and new recruits. The principal aim of a jihad warrior: sacrifice of life in the name of Allah, is presented in terms of enjoyment: "We are asking you to undertake the pleasure of looking at your face and we long to meet you, not in a time of distress…take us to you." The idealization of istishhad, repeated regularly in official organizational statements, is contained in its motto: "we love death more than our opponents' love life. This motto encapsulates the lack of fear among al-Qaeda fighters of losing temporary life in this world, since it is exchanged for an eternal life of purity in heaven".[1]

Taliban and the IS-K emerged as terrorist organizations with their dynamic structures. The ISIS reshaped jihadist landscape with its bloody strategy more than that of the Taliban. In Afghanistan, US and NATO forces ousted the Taliban and in a way paved the road for establishment of the IS-K terrorist group. In 2006, when NATO deployed its forces across in the south, insurgents shifted to asymmetric tactics. On 19 October 2021, Taliban's acting Interior Minister hosted a ceremony in Kabul to honour suicide bombers responsible for the killings of innocent Afghans, and deployed suicide brigades to take on Pakistani forces on Durand Line. He praised the families of 1,500 suicide bombers in Afghanistan and fixed monthly salary for them. In October 2021, ISIS suicide bombers attacked the Fatemiyyeh Brigade's mosque in Kandahar, killing at least 33 people and injuring 74 others. Another attack in 2022, in which an IS-K suicide bomber hit a mosque in Kunduz, killing at least 100 people. However, BBC in its news story (Iraq bombing: IS says it was behind deadly suicide attacks in Baghdad, published on 22 January 2021) reported attacks of IS-K in Afghanistan. Suicide tactics of ISIS and IS-K in Iraq and Afghanistan are identical but recent development in using Armoured Suicide Vehicles (ASV) in Iraq made a huge difference. Expert, Ellen Tveteraas (Under the Hood– Learning and Innovation in the Islamic State's Suicide Vehicle Industry, Studies in Conflict & Terrorism, 2022) has documented operations of the ISIS armoured Suicide Vehicles in Iraq that emerged around Baghdad in October 2014:

"The first reports of up-armoured suicide vehicles in Iraq emerged around Baghdad in October 2014, with the Islamic State employing Humvees left behind by the Iraqi army following the fall of Mosul in June that same year. Because they were a limited resource and had utility in other aspects of battle, these cars proved impractical to use for suicide bombings in high numbers. Combining the benefits of the Humvee with the requirement for mass production, the group gradually developed a reproducible and bulletproof design based on civilian vehicles. Personnel would cover all or parts of cars with thick iron plates, slanting it in front to increase the effective thickness of the metal and heightening the odds of small arms and heavy munitions ricocheting off. They also added metal grids to increase the distance between exploding munitions and the car. In rural operations, the group would paint the armour beige to blend in with desert terrain and make the discovery by reconnaissance units more difficult. In urban operation the armour would be painted in more radiant colours to mimic civilian vehicles. The added armour initially caught the Iraqi military off-guard, and to effectively stop some of these new contraptions they had to procure Kornet missiles at around $250 000 apiece. Suicide operatives were the purview of the special skills bureau, with prospective bombers organized in a section called the Martyrdom Operatives Battalion (Katibat al-Istishadiin). Members of the suicide battalion would normally arrive at the area of operation shortly before the execution of an attack and spend the preparation period in isolation with clerics to build the mental fortitude required to execute this type of mission. The battalion had no shortage of volunteers and, following the group's acquisition of territory, its size far outgrew the tactical demand for suicide operations."[2]

After the American Army took to one's heels at midnight, Afghanistan faced numerous political, economic and health care challenges. Causes of the failure of the Central Intelligence Agency (CIA) and NATO's intelligence machine to stabilize Afghanistan, or defeat Taliban were multitudinous. First, Afghan Army officers and commanders sold their weapons and check posts to Taliban to address their financial hardship because they were denied their salaries in war zones. Second, they started transporting terrorists in Army vehicles and helped the Islamic State in carrying out suicide attacks against civilians and government installations. Third, they protected foreign intelligence networks, plundered military funds and resources due to their personal and anti-state attitude. Fourth, the Afghan Army and the National Directorate of Security (NDS) intelligence agency were on the payroll of CIA and NATO member states to implement their agendas. Fifth, Generals of Afghan National Army (ANA), directors of foreign office and national security office maintained secret accounts abroad to easily receive funds from foreign intelligence agencies. Some of them were involved in money laundering, and some were tasked to humiliate Afghans in print and electronic media. Sixth, the issue of landmines was also not addressed properly by the US and NATO member states which prompted the death of thousand civilians. Seventh, the Afghan army was personally involved in planting landmines in Pashtun provinces to intercept the Taliban incursions. On 15 March, 2021, Daily Siasat reported the killing of more than 120 Afghans by landmines every month. Directorate of Mine Action Coordination of Afghanistan (DMAC) said in a statement: "An average of 120 people, including children were being killed or maimed by unexploded ordnance and landmines, every month". Expert and analyst, Michael A. Peters in his research paper (Declinism' and discourses of decline-the end of the war in Afghanistan and the limits of American power, Educational Philosophy and Theory) has documented the real failure of US Army in Afghanistan and the abrupt announcement of the Biden administration to leave Afghanistan surprised everyone and caused a rift with NATO allies who wanted to stay in Afghanistan:

"The ignominious end of the Afghan War after twenty long years, often referred to as the 'forever war', was brought to an abrupt end by Joe Biden in such haste that it surprised everyone and caused a rift with NATO allies who wanted to stay a presence in Afghanistan. Whatever spin can be placed on the end of US involvement, the withdrawal was messy and unplanned, air lifting US troops and well over 120,000 Afghan US supporters from Kabul airport. Many more Afghans who were part of the US war effort remain trapped in the country. Even with American support, the Afghan army was routed in a week and the Afghan government also collapsed. The embattled president Ashraf Ghani fled the country reportedly with a 'helicopter full of cash'. His swift departure left the best possible opening for the Taliban, who are talking of forming an 'open, inclusive Islamic government' and have established an interim government yet without the representation of women. President Biden first went on record as saying that nation-building was never part of the original mission yet the official justification for the Americans being in Afghanistan after the killing of Bin Laden had evaporated. Mission-creep set in with the downscaling US forces from 20,000 a couple of years ago to less than 2,000 in the final years".[3]

With the establishment of Taliban government in Afghanistan in 2021, mentally and physically tortured civilians experienced every mischance and stroke of bad luck. The proxy militia inflicted deep pain and torment on minorities by attacking mosques and religious places, and protecting Pakistani and Central Asian terrorist organizations. Women were tortured, humiliated and incarcerated, girls were deprived from education and their schools were shamelessly closed. After taking control of Ghazni province on 21 August 2021, they used inhuman and illegal strategies and policies that resulted in huge barriers to women's health and girls' education. Afghan women experienced collapsed human rights and risk of basic rights, and were treated like goats and dogs. Human Rights Watch (HRW) and SJSU interviewed women in Ghazni province and documented their spiralling prices for food, transportation, and schoolbooks. The poorer and hungry parents sold their girls and sons for a piece of bread. Taliban kidnapped women, sexually abused and tortured transgender then killed them. Some women felt heightened risk because of gender, ethnicity and religious sect. Human Rights Watch in its recent report (Afghanistan: Taliban Deprive Women of Livelihoods, Identity: Severe Restrictions, Harassment, Fear in Ghazni Province-18 January, 2022), noted intimidation of villagers by Taliban fighters: "Taliban authorities have also used intimidation to extract money, food, and services. 'When the Taliban visit a village, they force the households to feed them and collect food items from people,' a woman from a village said. 'The Taliban and their fighters call us in the middle of the night to cure and give special treatment to their patients and families,' a health worker said. They enter the hospital with their guns, it's difficult for the doctors and nurses to manage."[4] HRW noted.

Following the US and NATO withdrawal from Afghanistan, more than 3,000 Hazara Muslims were tortured and forcibly evicted from their homes by Taliban terrorist militia. As mentioned earlier, Taliban and the IS-K terrorist organizations have been killing Hazara Muslims in all provinces of Afghanistan since 1990s, destroying their houses and kidnaping their women and girls for sexual exploitation. After the 9/11 terrorist attacks in the United States, the Hazara Muslims experienced further harassment and intimidation. Successive Afghan governments failed to protect their agricultural land, houses and children. In her recent research paper, analyst and expert, Kate Clark (Afghanistan's conflict in 2021 (2): Republic collapse and Taliban victory in the long-view of history. Afghanistan Analysts Network, published in 30 December, 2021) documented civilian's pain, killings, and destruction after the US withdrawal from Afghanistan:

"The high number of civilians killed and injured in the conflict in 2021 was striking because the war in Afghanistan was then being fought mainly between Afghans. After the US-Taliban February 2020 agreement, which bound the two parties not to attack each other, but allowed the Taliban to attack the Afghan National Security Forces (ANSF), the US largely removed itself from the battlefield. This spared the Taliban their most dangerous enemy, while denying the Afghan National Security Forces US support except in extremes. It translated into the US taking a much reduced and sporadic part in the war after February 2020. According to the US's own published statistics, the number of 'weapons' dropped by the US Air Force in 2020 was 1,631 (almost half of the yearly total came in the two months before the Doha agreement was signed), compared to 7,362 in 2018 and 7,423 in 2019, and 801 in 2021 (first eight months only). In the chart below, it can be seen that the number of air munitions fell after February 2020 and rose somewhat in autumn 2020 as the US used airstrikes, for example, to drive back Taliban offensives in the south (see a call by Amnesty International for safe passage for civilians out of Lashkargah in October and Washington Post reporting on Kandahar in November). The number of munitions that the US Air Force dropped again after Biden's decision to withdraw, rising only in August 2021 as the US Air Force made last-ditch efforts to shore up the ANSF...... The campaign of targeted killings, which were often unclaimed but largely believed to be carried out by the Taleban, that had begun in late 2020, did not let up, but represented the third most likely way for civilians to be injured or killed: UNAMA said the campaign targeted an "ever-widening breadth of types of civilians… human rights defenders, media workers, religious elders, civilian government workers, and humanitarian workers." The campaign also targeted members of the

ANSF. According to one security source in Kabul, twice as many ANSF were targeted and killed or injured as civilians."[5]

The Taliban militia killed more than 5000 members of former Afghan security forces. The HRW accused leadership of "condoning" the "deliberate" killings. Taliban were held responsible for a bloody campaign of murder and torture against journalists and rights activists. Taliban with the assistance of Pakistani ISI located addresses of Afghan soldiers and government officials who helped the US and NATO in the illegal war against Afghanistan. HRW in its report (Afghanistan: Taliban Kill, 'Disappear' Ex-Officials: Raids Target Former Police, Intelligence Officers, published on November 30, 2021) noted, "Taliban forces in Afghanistann have summarily executed or forcibly disappeared more than 100 former police and intelligence officers in just four provinces since taking over the country on August 15, 2021. The 25-page report, "'No Forgiveness for People Like You,' Executions and Enforced Disappearances in Afghanistan under the Taliban," documents the killing or disappearance of 47 former members of the Afghan National Security Forces (ANSF) – military personnel, police, intelligence service members, and militia – who had surrendered to or were apprehended by Taliban forces between August 15 and October 31."[6]

The IS-K group was also in contact with Lashkar-e-Jhangvi (LeJ) and Lashkar-e-Taiba (LeT) in Jalalabad to target the Taliban forces, but failed to gain control of Jalalabad province. On December 11, 2014, former Interior Minister of Pakistan, Rehman Malik told a local news channel that IS-K had established recruitment centres in Gujranwala and Bahawalpur districts of Punjab province. The wall-chalking campaign and leaflets prompted fears about the terrorist group making inroads in the country. According to the leaked government circular in Balochistan and Khyber Pakhtunkhwa provinces, ISIS recruited more than 10,000 to 15,000 fighters in 2015 for the next sectarian war in Pakistan. In Kabul, on 08 December 2014, Reuters reported a 25-year-old student from Kabul University vowed to join the mujahideen of IS-K. "When hundreds of foreigners, both men and women, leave their comfortable lives and embrace Daesh, then why not us?" he asked. The influx of terrorist groups like the Islamic State of Khorasan in Jalalabad province challenged the writ of the Taliban local administration. Former Afghan President Ghani also warned that 30 terrorist groups were operating across the country posed serious threat to the national security of Afghanistan. The UN experts also believed that more than 45,000 terrorists were fighting against the Afghan National army and between 20 to 25 percent were foreigners. Pakistan military establishment secured peace agreements with certain Taliban factions by legitimising the Talibanization of the region. Experts and analysts, Qasim Jan, Yi Xie, Muhammad Habib Qazi, Zahid Javid Choudhary and Baha ul Haq in their research paper (Examining the role of Pakistan's national curriculum textbook discourses on normalising the Taliban's violence in the USA's Post 9/11 war on terror in South Waziristan, Pakistan. British Journal of Religious Education, 2022) have documented talibanization process of Waziristan:

"After 9/11, South Waziristan attracted global attention as an epicentre of terrorism. In the wake of the US invasion of Afghanistan, the Taliban and al-Qaida escaped from Afghanistan through the North-western border to the tribal areas including South Waziristan, Pakistan. Pakistan, as the US ally, launched several military operations against these religious militants, mainly the Taliban, in this hideout. However, Pakistan's military establishment has been accused of playing a 'secret double game', named 'tournament of shadows', clandestinely supporting militants including the Taliban as their 'strategic asset'. At a later stage, the Pakistani establishment secured peace agreements with certain Taliban factions, legitimising the Talibanization of the region. The legitimisation of the Talibanization, in this context, refers to the state of Pakistan's approval of the Taliban's styled Sharia law in South Waziristan. Its practices included public flogging, hand amputation, beheading and stoning to death, proportionate to minor/ major offences of the accused/guilty. Besides eroding the writ of the state (Pakistan), these peace agreements resulted in the creation of new binary i.e. 'Good Taliban' who pointed their guns on Afghanistan and fulfilled the objectives of Pakistan's security establishment, while those who didn't fall in line were called 'Bad Taliban'. The peace deal helped the Taliban and their affiliates in finding safe heavens in South Waziristan. Their commanders visited schools and colleges and delivered speeches about the glorification of Jihad and sacrifices for the cause of Allah/Muslim God. Hence, the Talibanization of the border region of tribal areas seems to be linked to Pakistan's strategic interests in Afghanistan and the South Asian region".[7]

Terrorism, violence and civil war in Afghanistan prompted catastrophe, displacement and financial destruction. With the establishment of the IS-K terrorist group in 2015, and its war against Taliban and the Afghan government further added to the pain of civilian population. The IS-K killed women, children and kidnapped young girls, looted houses and beheaded senior citizens in all provinces of Afghanistan. Both Pakistan and former Afghan government facilitated and financially supported Daesh and transported their terrorist fighters to their destination. The IS-K carried out dozens of terrorist attacks in Pakistan and Afghanistan with the help of ANA. The group has trained its fighters to carry out biological and nuclear terrorist attacks. Expert and analysts, Eric Schmitt (in "ISIS Branch Poses Biggest Immediate Terrorist Threat to Evacuation in Kabul", published on 03 November, 2021, The New York Times) has highlighted rivalries between Taliban and the IS-K terrorist group in Afghanistan:

"The rivalry between the Taliban and its partners and ISIS-K will continue after the last American troops leave, analysts say. And the fragile cooperation between American and Taliban commanders is already fraying, and the two could easily revert to their adversarial stances. The American military is treating the Taliban's red line about Aug. 31 seriously. The recent evacuations have been possible because of Taliban cooperation—in allowing most people to reach the airport unscathed, and in working against the threat of ISIS attacks, commanders say. After Aug. 31, military officials say, there is a real concern that at best, the cooperation with the Taliban will end. At worst, that could lead to attacks on U.S. forces, foreign citizens and Afghan allies, either by Taliban elements or by their turning a blind eye to Islamic State threats. Mr. Biden has pledged to prevent Afghanistan from again becoming a sanctuary for Al Qaeda and other terrorist groups that want to attack the American homeland. Military commanders say that will be a difficult task, with no troops and few spies on the ground, and armed Reaper drones thousands of miles away at bases in the Persian Gulf. In the February 2020 agreement with the Trump administration, the Taliban vowed not to allow Al Qaeda to use Afghan territory to attack the United States. But analysts fear that is not happening and that Al Qaeda remains the longer-term terrorism threat."[8]

In 2015, the IS-K was established to fight and tackle Pakistan based extremist groups who were trying to hijack the US war according to their agenda. Pakistanis from Southern Punjab rushed to join the terrorist infrastructure to sustain their poor families. In 2020, according to former Interior Minister of Pakistan, Rahman Malik, more than 80,000 poor madrasa students from Southern Punjab had joined the IS-K and participated in the civil war in Syria, Iraq and Afghanistan. These revelations generated panic in both Pakistan and Afghanistan that these fighters will further add to the pain of the Pakistan military establishment in the near future. The IS-K's intent is clear, and the Wilayat Khorasan is the ISIS most viable and lethal regional affiliate based on an expansionist military strategy. This is designed to enable the group's encirclement of Jalalabad city and is foundational to its expanded operational reach. Despite their Wahhabi backgrounds, the IS-K and Taliban groups follow a common agenda to destabilise Central Asia. The relationship between the Taliban and ISIS in Afghanistan is friendly. Taliban and ISIS are parts of a broader Deobandi and Wahhabi movements in Afghanistan who want to create misunderstanding between Islam and the west. Clayton Sharb, Danika Newlee and the CSIS iDeas Lab in their joint work (Islamic State Khorasan (IS-K), Center for Strategic and International Studies, 2018) have highlighted the IS-K global agenda and its intentions in Kashmir and Pakistan:

"IS-K carries out its global strategy in different operating environments by curating it to local conditions. Consider, for example, the divided region of Kashmir. It sits at the top of the Indian subcontinent and serves as a flashpoint for conflict between historically feuding nuclear powers, Pakistan and India. With nationalistic leaders dominating politics in both Islamabad and New Delhi, perpetual unrest in the disputed territories, and precedent of state-sponsored terrorism, Kashmir is fertile ground for future IS-K subversion. In Afghanistan and Pakistan, IS-K's strategy seeks to delegitimize the governments and degrade public trust in democratic processes, sowing instability in nation-states, which the group views as illegitimate. Recently, in the lead up to 2018 parliamentary elections in Afghanistan, IS-K warned citizens in Nangarhar province, "We caution the Muslims in the province from approaching election centres, and we recommend that they stay away from them so as to safeguard their blood, as these are legitimate targets for us." IS-K claimed multiple attacks on "elections centres" and security forces during the Afghan parliamentary elections, following through on their warning to "sabotage the polytheistic process and disrupt it."[9]

The IS-K is the strangest non-state actor in Afghanistan that poses a serious security threat to Taliban and Pakistan. The IS-K has deep roots in South Asia, with its branches in Pakistan, India, and some Southeast Asian states. Well-organized and well-established organization with over 250,000 trained fighters that can anytime challenge the authority of the failed state in Afghanistan. There are countless books and journals in markets and libraries that highlight infrastructure of the IS-K with different perspectives and view its operational mechanism and suicide technique with different glasses. My glasses are not as different from them as I have written books on the suicide operation of the ISIS and IS-K, and contributed article to the newspapers and journals. The IS-K threat to the existence of Taliban is intensified by the day as the group consecutively targeted government installations and public places. Expert and analyst, Mohamed Mokhtar Qandi in his paper (Challenges to Taliban Rule and Potential Impacts for the Region: Internal and external factors are weakening the Taliban, making the group's long term stability increasingly unlikely, Fikra Forum, The Washington Institute for Near East Policy, 09 February 2022) has noted the intensifying threat of ISIS and IS-K in Afghanistan, and asserted that the ISIS seeks to be an alternative to the Taliban movement:

"ISIS views the Taliban movement as a major strategic foe in South Asia. From the outset, members of Khorasan Province began questioning the Taliban's legitimacy in jihadi circles, which helped ISIS win new followers who splintered from the movement. Furthermore, ISIS may be attractive to those seeking revenge on the movement. In some cases, ISIS has attracted former Afghan intelligence members as well as younger middle-class youth who may become increasingly disaffected with the Taliban. There is also the dispute between the Taliban and the Salafist current inside Afghanistan that is not affiliated with Khorasan Province. The Taliban's harassment of these Salafists may push them to join the ranks of ISIS, or at least provide a haven for its members. Since the Taliban came to power by force, their lack of legitimacy can quickly lead to a decline in their popular support vis-à-vis ISIS, especially if they fail to meet the needs of the people and improve the economic situation. Despite the power that the Islamic State demonstrated in Khorasan, it is unlikely that the movement will be able to plan or launch attacks on distant targets. However, if ISIS-Khorasan succeeds in controlling more territories in Afghanistan and recruiting elements who resent Taliban, it will be tantamount to reviving the organization in the Middle East. On the one hand, the organization will intensify its propaganda and its claims that it is the sole carrier of the banner of jihad and hence, must be supported in establishing the Islamic caliphate as a global project. This will provide the organization with many opportunities to set up training camps for its elements and export them to the Middle East where they previously experienced a harsh defeat".[10]

Transnational extremist groups suchlike IS-K, Lashkar-e-Taiba, al Qaeda, and Taliban are relying on domestic extremist organizations that control thoughts and minds of citizens. The yesteryear analysis explored survival of groups in alliances. We can find these trends in Afghanistan where Taliban have entered into alliance with different Pakistani and Arab terrorist groups. Although ISIS also collaborated with different Afghan, Pakistani and Central Asian organizations, but it follows American agenda and wants to export jihad and suicide terrorism to Central Asia. In areas under its control, the IS-K terrorist group manage its own strategies of governance. The terrorist group killed hundreds in Afghanistan to justify its presence. In Afghanistan, if other groups leave the area under their control, the IS-K will either kill its members or force them to pledge allegiance and work with IS-K. Experts and analysts, Amira Jadoon, Abdul Sayed and Andrew Mines in their research paper ("The Islamic State Threat in Taliban Afghanistan: Tracing the Resurgence of Islamic State Khorasan", The Combating Terrorism Center at West Point, January 2022, Volum 15, Issue-1) have noted military confrontations between Taliban and the Islamic State of Khorasan:

"Since its inception, ISK has viewed the Afghan Taliban as its main strategic rival in the region.100 In a quest to outbid and outcompete its rival, ISK has not only attacked Afghan Taliban targets regularly since 2015, but also recruited heavily from the organization's ranks and leadership, which ISK has categorized into three general groups: first, the 'sincere Taliban jihadis' who defected to join ISK; second, those who kept a neutral stance toward ISK; and third, the ones who are the puppets of regional governments and motivated by personal interests. ISK has made delegitimizing the Afghan Taliban's purity as a jihadi movement one of its main messaging priorities. This is reflected in ISK's media campaigns for the last several years, which consistently highlight idolatrous Afghan Taliban-supported or tacitly approved religious and cultural practices, as well as relationships with foreign states that ISK views as heretical. Undermining the Afghan Taliban's legitimacy as a jihadi movement is a key pillar to ISK's organizational identity that is unlikely to change. Since the former took power, ISK's strategy has evolved not only to challenge the Afghan Taliban's legitimacy as the predominant jihadi force in the region (given their negotiations with the United States, and links to Pakistan, China, and Iran), but also their competency as a governing actor. ISK's two-pronged attack on the Afghan Taliban's legitimacy is likely to persist as long as the Taliban remain in power."[11]

On 19 April 2022, Radio Free Europe/Radio Liberty reported Uzbek Presidential Spokesman Sherzod Asadov denial of the IS-K claim that it had fired missiles towards Uzbekistan, and called on Uzbek citizens to disregard what he called provocations. According to the Defense Ministry and Uzbekistan's border guard troops, there were no active military developments along the Uzbek-Afghan border, the situation was stable, Asadov said in a statement placed on Telegram. Moreover, Salam Times reported the IS-K claim that a rocket attack against Uzbekistan from neighbouring Afghanistan was fired and it was the first such bombardment of the Central Asian nation by the group. "The group fired 10 Katyusha rockets at Uzbek forces stationed in the border city of Termez in southern Uzbekistan, IS-K said, adding that the attack followed an audio message from an IS-K spokesperson. On April 17, IS-K called on all fighters around the world to carry out "big and painful" attacks targeting officials and soldiers". Salam Times noted.[12] These rocket attacks generated fear in Central Asia amid prevailing political and economic uncertainty in Afghanistan and raised concerns that the group was expanding its recruitment campaign in the country and posed a serious threat to the region. The "ISIS is seizing the current power vacuum in Afghanistan as an opportunity to rapidly increase the number of its militants across the country, said Mohammad Naim Ghayur, a military analyst in Herat. The increasing number of attacks carried out by ISIS in recent months indicated that this terrorist group had not only solidified its footprint but also had built its capacity to challenge Afghanistan›s security,» Salam Times noted. Expert and analyst, Roshni Kapur in his paper (The Persistent ISKP Threat to Afghanistan: On China's Doorstep. Middle East Institute, January 6, 2022), has noted recent attacks of the IS-K in Afghanistan:

Two separate bombs were detonated in Dasht-e-Barchi in Kabul on December 10, killing two and injuring three others. Although no group has claimed responsibility for the attack, the Islamic State of Khorasan Province (ISKP) is likely behind the latest bout of violence. IS-K's fingerprints have been on other attacks. One of the worst, which killed over 180 people and injured hundreds, took place outside the Kabul airport in August 2021 during the final days of evacuations....The Taliban and ISKP will try to project themselves as the authentic representative of Islam and use that as a recruitment and expansion strategy. Nevertheless, experts have said that rivalry between the two is likely to be confined to a protracted guerrilla-style conflict with direct battles and clashes instead of descending into a civil war. While the Taliban has given amnesty to former security members, the same concessions have not been extended to ISKP. The Taliban is likely to carry out raids against ISKP hideouts, similar to the operation in Nangarhar and detainment of 80 ISKP fighters, as the latter seeks to pose a formidable challenge to the Taliban's rule. ISKP is also likely to regroup, change its modus operandi, become more resilient, and recruit more hardliner fighters to enhance its position in Afghanistan and the surrounding region. Although the US launched a drone strike against ISKP in late August 2021, it has not implemented a long-term counter-terrorism strategy against ISKP. The intelligence-gathering and surveillance systems used by the US and its allies have been dismantled. The chief of US Central Command, Gen. Frank McKenzie, also confessed that Washington is providing only limited security assistance to the Taliban to counter the threat from ISKP. Regional countries may step into the security void to prevent the threat of ISKP spilling into their territories".[13]

Concerns of India are genuine that the Taliban and the IS-K terrorist groups can anytime transport their fighters with sophisticated weapon into Kashmir and Punjab. In March 2022, Indian Army seized US made weapons in Kashmir. Now, there were speculations that if the Taliban guaranteed security, South and Central Asian states would recognize the Taliban government. Beijing is also at the spike due the Taliban attitude towards neighbouring states. China is in hot water that if the East Turkestan Islamic Movement (ETIM) collaborated with the IS-K terrorist group they might possibility orchestrate terrorist attacks in Xinjiang province. Editor of Terrorism Monitor, Jacob Zenn in his article (Islamic State in Khorasan Province's One-Off Attack in Uzbekistan, Volium XX, Issue 9, 06 May 2022) has highlighted issue of the IS-K missile attack and response of Uzbekistan:

"On April 18, 2022, the Islamic State (IS) released a short video of Islamic State in Khorasan Province (ISKP) fighters firing rockets from the outskirts of Mazar e Sharif, Afghanistan into Termiz, Uzbekistan.Uzbekistan denied that any ISKP attack took place on its soil. This was in lieu of the fact that IS provinces tend to be accurate about their claims, albeit inflating the severity and casualties of their attacks. According to the Uzbek presidency's spokesperson, the reports of the ISKP attack were not "reality" and there were no military operations on Uzbekistan's territory nor any instability along its borderlands.....A more plausible explanation came from the Taliban's deputy spokesperson, however, who asserted that ISKP did launch rockets toward Uzbekistan from Afghan territory, but the rockets failed to reach the Uzbekistan border. As is typical of Taliban foreign policy, the deputy spokesperson affirmed that Afghan soil would not be allowed to be used by any militant group to attack any external country. Video footage also emerged of the Taliban uncovering the ramshackle hideout that ISKP had used to fire the rockets, including the empty rocket launchers".[14]

Taliban are in deep water due the attitude of international community and domestic sectarian and terrorist organizations that have put their government at spike. Their recognition social problems are associated with their domestic policies, torture, humiliation, arrest and closure of girl's schools. Islamic State-Khorasan Province has retrieved military and financial strength and now challenge their authority and carrying out suicide attacks to target religious places. Expert and analyst, Amy Kazmin in her article (Isis-K insurgency jeopardises Taliban's grip on Afghanistan: New rulers accused of betraying Islam by jihadis intent on creating ideologically pure caliphate, October, 26, 2021) has highlighted military and political rivalries between Taliban and the Islami State of Khorasan in Afghanistan:

"After the Taliban Two months after the Taliban seized power, violence, death and fear still stalk Afghanistan. US troops might have departed but the new Islamist rulers in Kabul are now threatened by an insurgency launched by Islamic State-Khorasan Province, an Isis-inspired jihadi movement that has deep ideological differences with the Taliban. Since the Taliban takeover in August, Isis-K has mounted a series of suicide bomb attacks, including at the Kabul airport and at two Shia mosques, as well as assaults on Taliban convoys, which have killed hundreds. Analysts have warned of further violence as Isis-K tries to prevent the Taliban from consolidating their grip on Afghanistan. Isis-K's more hard-line stance has proved attractive to disgruntled Taliban fighters. Dismayed at the new regime's reluctance to impose tougher restrictions on women and its diplomatic overtures to countries such as the US, China and Russia, former Taliban members have switched allegiance to Isis-K. "The American war is over, but the Afghan wars are not," said Avinash Paliwal, deputy director of the SOAS South Asia Institute, and author of "My Enemy's Enemy", a book about Afghanistan. The Taliban's long time goal has been to establish an Islamic government in Afghanistan. But Isis-K, which has been active in Afghanistan since 2015, wants to establish an Islamic caliphate across Afghanistan, Pakistan and parts of India and Iran. Isis-K militants consider the Taliban, who have held talks with regional powers and the US in a quest for diplomatic recognition, as "filthy nationalists" who have betrayed the greater Islamic cause, according to an analyst. "Isis-K sees the Taliban as just another kind of political outfit- cutting a deal with the Americans- that is ideologically not pure," Paliwal said. "Their aim is to destabilise an already struggling regime."[15]

Taliban's controversial policies and their resentment towards minorities in Afghanistan divided communities on sectarian bases. As there is no state and legitimate government in the country, they arrest, torture and sexually abuse women with impunity. They have arrested dozens of intellectuals, doctors, former military officers, journalists and social media activists. Some were tortured to death and some were hanged publicly. Analyst and expert, Salman Rafi Sheikh in his article (Eight months on, Taliban's rule is far from stable: Resistance groups are mounting an increasingly potent challenge to the Taliban and may have Pakistan's clandestine support, Asia Times, May 2, 2022) has noted internal policies of Taliban of divided and rule. He also painted a picture of their violence and incompetency to stabilise Afghanistan and maintain friendly relations with neighbouring states:

"On April 29, a blast in Kabul in a mosque belonging to a Sunni minority group – the Zikris – killed at least 50 people. On Thursday, a bomb blast in a van carrying Shiite Muslims in the northern city of Mazar-e-Sharif killed at least nine people. The attack on the Shiite van came after Taliban leaders claimed to have captured an ISIS-K mastermind of the previous attack in Mazar-e-Sharif on a Shiite mosque that killed at least 31 people. These attacks challenge the Taliban leadership's claims to have eliminated opposed terror groups like ISIS-K, offered full protection to minorities and claimed groups like ISIS-K do not pose a serious threat. While their claims have by now clearly been proven wrong, there is little denying that the continuing success of ISIS-K is directly tied to the Taliban regime for several reasons. First, some hardliner groups within the Taliban – including the Haqqanis, who control the Ministry of Interior responsible for tackling such threats and whose ties with the ISIS-K go back to their joint attacks on the US-NATO-Afghan forces – are reluctant to take effective tough action against the terror group. It was the same internal division with ISIS-K that led the Taliban, despite their apparent ideological rivalry with the group, to release several hundred ISIS-K fighters after their August takeover, allowing the organization to increase its numbers to 4,000, according to a February 2022 estimate by the UN, from 2,000 previously. This has allowed the ISIS-K to operate freely inside Afghanistan, giving it the leeway to establish cells in almost all of Afghanistan's provinces".[16]

Chapter 6

Taliban, Tablighi Jamaat and Terrorism in Kazakhstan

The United States manages 3,750 nuclear warheads, while press release from the State Department confirmed 2,000 warheads to be dismantled. President Biden announced that under the AUKUS agreement, Australia would retrieve nuclear powered submarine while President Putin exhibited his disagreement on the deteriorating regime of arms control but reduced the number of warheads deployed on Russia's ballistic missiles to meet the New START limit. Nuclear weapons experts and analysts, Hans M. Kristensen and Matt Korda (2021) have noted that 'Russia's nuclear modernization program was motivated in part by Moscow's strong desire to maintain overall parity with the United States'. On 28 July, the United States and Russia restarted bilateral Strategic Stability Dialogue. The Biden administration upheaved the prospect of restricting military manoeuvres and missile deployments in Eastern Europe insomuch as Russia corresponds at the fore of dialogue on its military deployment in Ukraine, but hostile attitude of the Biden administration further caused skepticism when the country's leadership unnecessarily demonstrated superiority and military strength. In January 2022, People's Republic of China, France, Russian, the United Kingdom and the United States in a joint statement declared the avoidance of nuclear war.

The statement of nuclear powers confirmed their commitment to work with all state to create a security environment more conducive. "We intend to continue seeking bilateral and multilateral diplomatic approaches to avoid military confrontations, strengthen stability and predictability, increase mutual understanding and confidence, and prevent an arms race that would benefit none and endanger all. We are resolved to pursue constructive dialogue with mutual respect and acknowledgment of each other's security interests and concerns". The statement noted. The US assertion that Moscow might create environment of a false flag operation in Eastern Ukraine as a pretext for invading all or part of the country was repudiated by Russian military. "Russia is laying the groundwork to have the option of fabricating a pretext for invasion, including through sabotage activities and information operations, by accusing Ukraine of preparing an imminent attack against Russian forces, according to an email of state department sent to the country's bureaucrats and technocrats. In November 2021, President Biden and Chinese President held their first face-to-face conversation on managing great power competition and averting a new Cold War but both sides failed to produce a diplomatic breakthrough.

On January 15, 2022, in his interview with Newsweek, Russia's Ambassador to the United States Anatoly Antonov warned that 'NATO's eastward expansion is one of the major threats to Russia's national security, as the flight time to cities in the country's European part is becoming shorter, Russia's Ambassador to the United States Anatoly Antonov said in an interview with Newsweek. The continuing advance of the North Atlantic bloc to the east is one of the main threats to Russia's national security. As the bloc approaches our border proper, the flight time of NATO air and missile weapons to Moscow, St. Petersburg and other cities in the European part of the country is reduced," Antonov said. "How would the US Government react if Washington, New York or Los Angeles were 'under the bombsight'?"."NATO is constantly building up its offensive potential, demonstrating military force along the perimeter of the Russian territory. "NATO's efforts aimed at the military development of the former Soviet republics are unacceptable to us. This is fraught with the deployment of missile systems and other destabilizing weapons that directly threaten our country. As a result, the risks of escalation and direct military clashes in the region and beyond will increase manifold. Everything has its limits. We are, in fact, on the edge of precipice," the ambassador told Newsweek.

China, Russia and the United States are locked in an intensifying competition to export their respective fifth-generation fighter jets. The Biden administration has been in deep trouble since the test of Russia's anti-satellite missiles, and its contemptable defeat in Afghanistan, and issued warning of Russian hybrid war in Europe, but the US forces continue to destabilise Middle East and Central Asia. Contrariwise, the EU member states are well aware of their security and friendship with Russia by extending hand of cooperation. In this bigger strategic game, Russians and Americans have the same reason for modernising their nuclear forces. In yesteryears, President Vladimir Putin developed modern weapons and restored the real Russian place in the international community. Since

Russia seized Crimea in 2014, the country has begun to build basing sites for their advanced systems, including the Iskanders missile, but nuclear experts warned that if Russia deploys nuclear weapons there, it would spark complex problems. Analyst Scott Ritter (RT News, 28 April, 2020) highlighted the START agreement and complication of US and Russia's inventions of modern technologies and weapons, which could exacerbate the process of nuclear war preparations:

"Both the US and Russia are engaged in the early stages of developing new strategic nuclear weapons to replace older systems. These weapons, which will cost trillions of dollars to develop and deploy, are with few exceptions still many years away from entering into service. A five-year extension of New START would provide both nations time to reach an agreement which responsibly addresses the need for strategic nuclear force modernization while continuing the past practice of seeking additional cuts in their respective nuclear arsenals........China's intransigence runs counter to the official US position, most recently articulated in a State Department report sent to Congress regarding Russian compliance with the New START Treaty. While the report finds that Russia is complying with its treaty obligations, the treaty does not cover enough Russian strategic systems, including several that have been previously announced by President Putin, and leaves China to operate with no restrictions in terms of the size and scope of its strategic nuclear arsenal".[1]

Perhaps, China is also preparing to build new missile technology, expand anti-satellite capabilities and increase nuclear material production. The question is how China can use nuclear weapons as the country maintains policy of peaceful coexistence? In 2019, its Defence White Paper noted the country stickled to the policy of no first use of nuclear weapons at any time, and under any circumstances, but recent hostile nuclear environment has forced the country to deploy a nuclear triad of strategic land, sea, and air-launched nuclear systems to defend its territorial integrity and national security. Despite the progress made by international conventions, biological and chemical weapons are still a precarious threat in Europe and Central Asia.

According to Russia's new military doctrine, the possibility of limited uses of nuclear weapons at the tactical and operational levels and of chemical and biological weapons is possible. As the United States has established biological weapons laboratories in Central Asia and used these weapons against civilian population of Afghanistan, Russian military leadership has taken these developments seriously. Russia is training its chemical and biological army on a modern streak. New CBRN defence vehicles and equipment can be used in the fight against coronavirus. Its forces have also undertaken more CBRN training to the future war effectively. The danger from these weapons is so consternating, and the dirty bomb material and its fatalities diverted attention of terrorist groups to biological weapons. Smuggling of nuclear weapons is a serious challenge in Europe and Central Asia, while smuggling of these weapons in Africa has threatened security of the region.

For more than two decades, the threat of nuclear and biological weapons in Central Asia has been at the forefront of international security agenda. Nuclear experts have often warned that terrorists and extremist organizations operating in Central Asia can anytime use dirty bomb and nuclear explosive. These groups must be prevented from gaining access to weapons of mass-destruction and from perpetrating atrocious acts of bioterrorism. Russia and some Central Asian States have applied professional measures to protect their nuclear weapons sites but nuclear proliferation still poses a grave threat to the national security of all states. Military experts and policymakers have also expressed deep concerns that if the Islamic Movement of Uzbekistan, Chechen extremist groups, Katibat Imam Bukhari and the IS-Khorasan, operating in the region gain access to nuclear explosives, it might cause huge destruction and fatalities. There are several extremist and terrorist groups operating in Tajikistan where they are recruiting members of local religious groups, and civilians from all walks of life to prepare them for the fight against Russia. Analyst Leonid Gusev (01 February 2020) his recent paper noted activities of extremist groups in Tajikistan:

"As in the other countries of the region, the main recruiting platform used by ISIS (a terrorist organization banned in Russia) in Tajikistan is the Internet. There are some 3 million Internet users in Tajikistan, 80 per cent of them accessing extremist content through social media either deliberately or accidentally. During their meeting in May 2018, President of Tajikistan Emomali Rahmon and President of Belarus Alexander Lukashenko expressed their commitment to strengthening cooperation in the fight against terrorism, extremism, drug trafficking and the illegal arms trade. In October 2019, Tajikistan hosted a joint military exercise of the Collective Security Treaty Organization (CSTO) member states, "Indestructible Brotherhood 2019." One of the components of that exercise, according to Commander of the Central Military District of the Russian Federation, Colonel-General Alexander Lapin, consisted of antiterrorist operations.

103

Tajikistan is a tension hotspot in Central Asia in terms of religious extremism and terrorism. A particular source of danger is neighbouring Afghanistan, where about 60 per cent of the lands along the frontier are engulfed in clashes between government forces and the Taliban and other radical Islamist groups. At the same time, there is almost no security along the Afghan-Tajik border, including the issue of drug trafficking. The local Tajik forces supporting border guards are scant, especially since the Kulob Regiment was relocated from the 201st Russian military base to Dushanbe. Yet the government has so far managed to control the situation."[2]

Recent events in Kazakhstan and Tajikistan have raised the prospect of extremist and jihadist groups using biological, radiological and chemical weapons against military installations and critical national infrastructure in both states. Russia is vulnerable to such attacks by these terrorist groups who received military training from the US army in Afghanistan and Pakistan. The greatest threat to the national security of Russia stems from the business of nuclear smuggling of state sponsored terror groups operating in Central Asia. Increasingly sophisticated chemical and biological weapons are accessible to these organizations and ISIS and their allies, which is a matter of great concern. These groups can use more sophisticated conventional weapons as well as chemical and biological agents in near future as the US Special Force is already in control of Pakistan's nuclear and biological weapons. They can disperse chemical, biological and radiological material as well as industrial agents via water or land to target schools, colleges, civilian and military personnel. They were trained by US and NATO forces, and tested these weapons in Afghanistan. These groups also received training of dangerous weapons in different military units of Pakistan army.

As international media focuses on the looming threat of chemical and biological terrorism in Central Asia, the ISIS is seeking access to nuclear weapons. The crisis is going to get worse as the exponential network of ISIS and its popularity in Afghanistan caused deep security challenges. This group could use chemical and biological weapons once it strengthens its bases in Central Asia and Russia. The possibility of a nuclear technology transfer by an irresponsible state like Pakistan and Iran to the ISIS command is still reverberating in international press. In an interview with a local television channel, the late Dr. Abdul Qadir Khan categorically said that Pakistan's nuclear smuggling activities did take place from 1992 to 1998 while both Nawaz Sharif and Benazir Bhutto were in power.

Recent debates in print and electronic media about the possible use of Chlorine Bombs or biological weapons in Central Asia have caused deep concerns in government and military circles that radicalized jihadists returning from Syria and Iraq may possibly use these weapons with the cooperation of local supporters and some states. Yet, experts have warned that the acquisition of nuclear weapons by the Islamic State (ISIS) poses a greater threat to the national security of regional states. The gravest danger arises from access of extremist and terror groups to the state-owned nuclear, biological and chemical weapons. The growing use of Chlorine Bombs is a matter of great concern. The first such incident occurred when the ISIS commanders gained access to the Iraqi nuclear weapons site in Mosul University.

However, recent cases of nuclear proliferation and attacks on nuclear installations across the globe have further exacerbated the concern about the threat of nuclear attacks in Caucasus regions, Russia and Tajikistan. The threat of chemical and biological jihad has raised serious questions about the security of Central Asian states nuclear and biological weapons. Experts have warned that the Central Asia, Pakistan and Afghanistan based jihadists, and the Taliban pose a great security threat. Improvised explosive devices and chemical and biological weapons are easily available in Asian and European markets and can be transported to the region through human traffickers. The influx of trained terrorists and extremist groups from several Asian, African and European states has raised concerns that those who sought asylum through fake documents in Russia could pose a threat to the country. In a press conference in Australia, President Obama declared that if his government discovered that ISIS had come to possess a nuclear weapon, he would get it out of their hands. The fear of such attacks still exists in Central Asia because thousands of European nationals joined ISIS's military campaign in Syria and Iraq.

In 2013, chemical attacks in the outskirts of Damascus posed a direct threat to all Arab states, and forced the UN Security Council to adopt a resolution on chemical weapons in Syria. The international operation of transporting the components of these weapons out of Syria was completed in the first half of 2014. In 2015, the ISIS tried to gain access to these weapons and used chlorine bombs in Iraq and Syria. On 06 January, 2015, cases of ISIS using chemical weapons in Iraq and Syria emerged. These chemical attacks illustrated that ISIS and the Syrian opposition chosen to use chemical weapons preferentially in Iraq and Syria. In Russia and Central Asia, ISIS is seeking these weapons to use them against the armed forces of the region.

In one of its issues magazines (Dabiq), claimed that Islamic State sought to buy nuclear weapons from Pakistan but experts viewed this claim as baseless.

Before the rise of ISIS, the Islamic Movement of Uzbekistan (IMU) was the main Central Asian extremist organisation in the field. Its base of operations is in Afghanistan and Pakistan. Central Asian fighters linked to ISIS headquarters in Syria also participated in acts of terrorism in other countries. The ISIS has previously restrained itself from getting involved in attacks in Central Asia as the group's leadership emphasised that attacking this region was not the highest priority. In July 2018, five Tajik men killed four foreign cyclists in a car-ramming attack, accompanied by an on-foot gun and knife assault in the Khatlon province of Tajikistan. The presence of Daesh in Iraq and Afghanistan, and participation of Central Asian jihadists in it prompted consternation in the region. In Syria, the radical Islamic militants from Central Asia established terrorist organisations of their own. These terrorists have Salafi-Wahhabi inclinations and are among the backers of al-Qaeda, al-Nusra Front, and Daesh group. In his Diplomat analysis (20 September 2016), Uran Botobekov, documented videos and extrajudicial killing in Iraq and Syria:

"Recently, Central Asians saw on YouTube a terrible video of a teenager, Babur Israilov from Jalal-Abad in southern Kyrgyzstan, on his way to becoming a suicide bomber. In the video, Babur cries before being sent to his death in an armoured car laden with explosives in Fua, Syria. One of the fighters gathered around encourages him, saying in Uzbek that Satan intervenes at crucial moments to confuse a Muslim's mind, so he should think only of Allah. Further in the video sentimental Arabic music plays, the armored personnel carrier moves, and, at the fatal moment, the bomb explodes[3]. According to Radio Free Europe/Radio Liberty, Babur Israilov was a member of an extremist group of Uzbeks–Imam Bukhari Jamaat–which fights alongside Jabhat al-Nusra in Syria. Just like the father of the British boy JoJo, resident of Suzak district in the Jalal-Abad region of Kyrgyzstan Tahir Rahitov saw his son Babur via video. According to Tahir, his wife died in 1995 and the boy was raised by his grandmother. In November 2013 Babur left for Russia in search of work. In March 2014 he arrived in Syria via Turkey, joined Imam Bukhari Jamaat, and fought alongside Jabhat al-Nusra against the government of Bashar al-Assad".[3]

On 06 November 2019, Masked Daesh militants attacked a check post on the Tajik-Uzbek border overnight, triggering a gun battle that killed 15 militants, a guard and a policeman.[4] There was no immediate announcement from the militant group, which claimed responsibility for a series of assaults in Tajikistan. Five of the gunmen were captured after the attack on the Tajik side of the border, 50 km (30 miles) southwest of the capital Dushanbe, Tajikistan's National Security Committee noted. The investigation into the 03 April 2017 terrorist attack on the St. Petersburg metro station focused on a man of Central Asian origin with possible ties to Syrian rebel groups. The attack raises concerns about the threat posed both by Daesh and extremists within Russia's sizable Central Asian community. Investigators identified Akhbarzhon Dzhalilov as the prime suspect in the attack on the St. Petersburg metro that left 14 people dead and 49 injured. Dzhalilov is an ethnic Uzbek from the Southern Kyrgyzstani city of Osh who obtained Russian citizenship in 2011. Eight more people, mostly from Kyrgyzstan, were detained in St Petersburg and Moscow on suspicion of assisting Dzhalilov.[5] While Tajikistan remains vulnerable to jihadist extremism due to its proximity to jihadist hotbeds, pre-existing networks and difficult socio-economic conditions, it appears that the central radicalization issue is the diaspora abroad, led by Tajiks living in Russia.

Since the beginning of 2017, a string of jihadist terrorist attacks involved Central Asian citizens, mainly of Uzbek and Kirgiz origin. Russia's Federal Security Service (FSB) detained Abrar Azimov from Central Asia. He was accused as one of the organizers of the attack, and the one who had trained Jalilov. However, Azimov refused to admit his guilt in court during the hearing. By the end of April, the FSB arrested 12 people of Central Asian descent in the Kaliningrad region suspected of involvement with the Jihad-Jamaat Mujahedin extremist group. The alleged leader of the cell was placed by Uzbekistan on a wanted list for extremist crimes.

The rise of ISIS in Afghanistan posed serious security concerns, according to a September 2016 statement of Zamir Kabulov, the Russian Foreign Ministry's Director of the Second Asian Department in Afghanistan. Mr. Kabulov claimed that about 2,500 ISIS combatants were in Afghanistan and the organization was preparing to expand from Afghanistan into other Central Asian countries and Russia, giving Moscow reasons to worry. Nuclear terrorism in Central Asia and Russia has risen important questions about the US and NATO policy towards Russia that without using biological and nuclear weapons against the country, its dream of supreme power will vanish. Authors Christopher McIntosh and Ian Storey (20 November 2019) in their well-written analysis have elucidated the real motive of US and NATO hegemonic design:

"While terrorist organizations vary widely in their internal organization and structure, almost all are highly sensitive to benefits and costs, both external and internal. By examining these, it will become clear that terrorists might have more to lose than gain by proceeding directly to an attack. Doing so might alienate their supporters, cause dissent among the ranks, and give away a bargaining chip without getting anything in return. While there is any number of far more likely scenarios for nuclear terrorism broadly understood, we focus only on groups with a working nuclear device, not a radiological dispersal device or the ability to attack a nuclear reactor. The threat posed by an operational device is fundamentally different, not least because possession would radically change the nature of the organisation as a strategic, warfighting group. A large body of work in terrorism studies teaches us that terrorist groups do behave strategically. Communications within Al Qaeda, Princeton Near Eastern Studies expert Michael Doran has written, have shown that the group behaves "almost exclusively according to the principle of realpolitik," and is "virtually compelled[" to do so by the "central doctrines of Islamic extremism" itself. While it may not appear so based on terrorists' tactics, most groups have all the hallmarks of strategic decision-making, command and control, and sensitivity to costs. This is all the truer for the hypothetical that concerns us: Only a large, well-organized, and heavily funded group would be able to attain operational nuclear capability. Regardless of what one thinks about the debates regarding terrorist organizations and their ability to acquire these weapons—either by theft or gift—acquisition and maintenance is going to be resource-intensive and difficult".[5]

If terrorist groups such as ISIS or Lashkar-e-Taiba and Tablighi Jamaat determine to go nuclear, what will be the security preparations in Central Asia to intercept these groups? These and other Pakistan based groups can attempt to manufacture fissile material needed to fuel a nuclear weapon—either highly enriched uranium or plutonium, and then use it. Moreover, there are possibilities that Pakistan, Afghanistan and Central Asia based extremist and jihadist groups can purchase fissile material in black market or steal it from a military or civilian facility and then use that material to construct an improvised nuclear device. Yet today, with Russia rising again as a military power, the grim logic of nuclear statecraft is returning. In his nuclear risk analysis, Simon Saradzhyan (Russia Matters, Simon Saradzhyan, (August 06, 2019) argued that there is a possibility of nuclear war between Russia and the United States:

"Is the risk of a nuclear war between the U.S. and Russia now higher than at the height of the Cold War? Yes, it is, according to an article former U.S. Energy Secretary Ernie Moniz and former U.S. Sen. Sam Nunn have penned for Foreign Affairs. "Not since the 1962 Cuban Missile Crisis has the risk of a U.S.-Russian confrontation involving the use of nuclear weapons been as high as it is today," the co-chairs of the Nuclear Threat Initiative warn in their commentary published in August. 6, 2019. To back their claim, the two American statesmen describe an imaginary scenario in which Russian air defense systems shoot down a NATO aircraft that has accidentally veered into Russian airspace during a wargame in Russia's Kaliningrad exclave in 2020".[6] All but, 15 years ago, Graham Allison (September/October 2004) noted the possibility of nuclear terrorism in Russia by Chechen terrorists. Chechen have had a long-standing interest in acquiring nuclear weapons and material to use in their campaign against Russia. He is of the opinion that Chechen had access to nuclear materials, and their experts were able to make nuclear explosive devices:

"To date, the only confirmed case of attempted nuclear terrorism occurred in Russia on November 23, 1995, when Chechen separatists put a crude bomb containing 70 pounds of a mixture of cesium-137 and dynamite in Moscow's Ismailovsky Park. The rebels decided not to detonate this "dirty bomb," but instead informed a national television station to its location. This demonstration of the Chechen insurgents' capability to commit ruthless terror underscored their long-standing interest in all things nuclear. As early as 1992, Chechnya's first rebel president, Dzhokhar Dudayev, began planning for nuclear terrorism, including a specific initiative to hijack a Russian nuclear submarine from the Pacific Fleet in the Far East. The plan called for seven Slavic-looking Chechens to seize a submarine from the naval base near Vladivostok, attach explosive devices to the nuclear reactor section and to one of the nuclear-tipped missiles on board, and then demand withdrawal of Russian troops from Chechnya. After the plot was discovered, Russian authorities disparaged it, and yet it is ominous to note that the former chief of staff of the Chechen rebel army, Islam Khasukhanov, had once served as second-in-command of a Pacific Fleet nuclear submarine".[7]

The Islamic State (ISIS) and Central Asian terrorist groups seek biological and nuclear weapons to use it against security forces in Russia and Central Asia. The modus operandi of ISIS or ISIS inspired individuals are diverse and show no moral restraints–as recent attacks in Brussels and Berlin demonstrated. The use of biological and chemical weapons by terrorists has prompted huge fatalities in Iraq and Syria. However, preventing dangerous materials from falling into the hands of ISIS, Pakistani terrorist groups, and Central Asia extremists is a complex challenge. Since 2013, there has been extensive use of chemical weapons in armed conflicts in Syria by US backed terrorist groups. The deadliest attacks were carried out with chemical agents by the ISIS terrorist group in Syria that needed significant knowledge and the specialized resources. In October 2017, Columb Strack in his paper revealed that the ISIS is the first terrorist group that developed chemical weapons:

"The Islamic State is the first non-state actor to have developed a banned chemical warfare agent and combined it with a projectile delivery system. However, it appears to have been forced to abandon its chemical weapons production after the loss of Mosul in June 2017. The absence of chemical attacks outside of Mosul after the city became cut-off from the rest of the 'caliphate' earlier this year indicates that the group has not established alternative production facilities. But U.S. intelligence believes that a new chemical weapons cell has been set up in the Euphrates River Valley. In late July 2015, the Islamic State fired several mortar bombs at Kurdish People's Protection Units (YPG) positions near the city of Hasakah in northeaster Syria. A statement released by the YPG after the attack described how the explosions had released "a yellow gas with a strong smell of onions," and that "the ground immediately around the impact sites was stained with an olive-green liquid that turned to a golden yellow after exposure to sunshine".[8]

The possible use of nuclear and biological weapons by the ISIS, Central Asia extremist groups, Chechens, Taliban and Pakistani sectarian terrorists in Central Asia and Russia would be a greater security challenge for the region and Russia that fights the ISIS in Syria. Pakistan has established its own extremist networks in Chechnya and Central Asia once more to lead the US fight against Russia in the region. The country's army has been training and financing ISIS, Chinese extremist groups and Mujahedeen from Central Asia in various districts since 2001. Connor Dilleen (Asia Times-30 May 2019) in his recent article noted activities of Central Asia terrorists' groups in Afghanistan:

"During a recent visit to Tajikistan, Russian Federal Security Service Director Alexander Bortnikov claimed that around 5,000 militants based in Afghanistan from a group known as Islamic State Khorasan, or IS-K, had been redeployed to the north of the country, near its border with the former Soviet states of Central Asia. Bortnikov's statement has been treated with some skepticism, with Moscow accused of exaggerating the threat posed by IS-K to advance its own objectives in the region. But his comments make it timely to revisit the question of whether IS may emerge as a genuine threat not just to Afghanistan but also to the broader Central Asian region. To date, the states of Central Asia—Kyrgyzstan, Uzbekistan, Tajikistan, Turkmenistan and Kazakhstan—have been relatively free of terrorist incidents involving Islamist groups. Between 2008 and mid-2018, 19 attacks categorized as terrorism occurred across the region, resulting in around 140 fatalities. Most of these attacks targeted law enforcement agencies, and regional governments have claimed that they disrupted another 61 attacks during 2016 alone. IS was involved in several of these events. In July 2018, a group claiming allegiance to IS killed four foreign tourists outside of the Tajik capital of Dushanbe, and in November, Tajik authorities claimed that they had detained 12 suspects with alleged ties to IS who were planning an attack against a Russian military base and school".[9]

However, the return of these groups from Pakistan, Afghanistan and Syria will cause national security challenges. In Sialkot District of Punjab province in Pakistan, the army trains and supports an ISIS women brigade for future war. Dr. Younis Khshi in his research paper has noted activities of these women in Pakistan where many women have impressed and convinced through brainwashing with the concept of Jihad-Bil-Nikah, got divorce from their Pakistani husbands and went to marry a Mujahid of ISIS for a certain period, came back gave birth to the child of Mujahid, and remarried their former husband. Some decide to continue that marriage for the rest of their lives. All of this is being done to obtain worldly wealth and later eternal life in Heaven because ISIS is paying something around RS/50,000 to 60,000 per month to every warrior.

However, Mr. Uran Botobekov (The Diplomat, January 10, 2017) has also reported the presence of Central Asian women in Syria and Iraq: "Based on 2014 and 2015 data, there were around 1,000 women from Central Asia in Iraq and Syria's combat zones. According to Indira Dzholdubaeva, prosecutor-general of the Kyrgyz Republic, there are over 120 Kyrgyz women in Syria and Iraq. Chairman of the National Security Committee (KNB) of Kazakhstan, Nurtay Abykaev, has said there were 150 Kazakh women in ISIS ranks in Syria. The authorities of Uzbekistan, meanwhile, have said that up to 500 Uzbek women are in Syria, Iraq, and Afghanistan with various groups. The Ministry of the Interior of Tajikistan claims that over 200 Tajik women have gone to the war zones in Syria together with their husbands. However, the website of the Ministry of the Interior has published the names and photos of only five Tajik women who are wanted due to their membership in ISIS".[11] Moreover, analyst and expert of current affairs, Nick Mucerino (November 5, 2018) has noted the threat to Russia from Islamic State returnees from Syria, Iraq, Pakistan and Afghanistan:

"The threat posed by Russian speaking fighters who travelled to fight under the Islamic State in Syria presents a complicated problem for both Russia and its allies to address. Just like its Western counterparts, Russia is worried that these returnees will mount deadly attacks on the country's soil. The danger presented by Russian speaking foreign fighters loyal to the Islamic State is not lost on the Kremlin. Since its emergence during Syria's civil war in 2013, Russians and Russian speaking nationals from the former Soviet Union have been a prominent presence among the terror group's fighters. In February 2017, President Vladimir Putin, citing security service figures, stated that approximately 4,000 Russian citizens and 5,000 from Central Asia followed ISIS' appeals for aid. Many took part in helping to establish its 'caliphate', or the proto-state it carved out of the lands ISIS seized from Iraq and Syria. This figure is the largest in Europe and even outnumbers the citizens from Arab states including Saudi Arabia and Tunisia, who travelled to join the Group. The large presence of Russian speakers is further reflected in the fact that it is the second most common language among ISIS fighters and several of its top commanders belong to the former USSR. Independent security experts have estimated that about 400 of those fighters have already returned to Russia after fighting in Syria".[12]

The US-Taliban deal encouraged extremist groups from Central Asia and China that now with the support of Pakistan and Taliban; they will exacerbate operational activities in Central Asia and Russia. They receive training in dangerous weapons and nuclear explosives in Pakistan and Afghanistan. A women military brigade (Dr. Yunis Khushi-June 26, 2017) of the ISIS and Taliban receives training of dangerous weapons under the supervision of Pakistan's army in Sialkot district of Punjab province. In his (The Diplomat, 08 April 2020) article, Uran Botobekov noted the zeal and felicitations of these groups:

"Al-Qaeda-backed Central Asian Salafi-Jihadi groups were highly encouraged by the US-Taliban agreement which was signed in February 2020, aiming to bring peace to Afghanistan. Some Uzbek groups such as Katibat Imam al-Bukhari (KIB), Katibat Tawhid wal Jihad (KTJ), the Islamic Jihad Union (IJU), and Tajik militants of Jamaat Ansarullah (JA), and Uighur fighters of Turkestan Islamic Party (TIP) from China's Xinjiang region, have already expressed their clear opinion about this particular deal through their respective Telegram accounts. Some of the groups congratulated the agreement, while others dedicated emotional eulogies to the Taliban. The KIB, which is formed primarily from Uzbek, Tajik and Kyrgyz militants from Central Asia's Ferghana Valley, was one of the first organisations to congratulate the Taliban, denouncing it as "the great victory of the Islamic Ummah". On February 29, 2020, Abu Yusuf Muhajir, the leader of KIB's Syrian wing, in his congratulatory letter said: "The US and NATO forces, who imagine themselves to be the rulers of the entire world and the divine judges of human destinies, and claim divinity on earth have stunned the world with their humiliation, disgrace, and failure of the crusade." The KIB leader proceeds by saying that "the Americans were forced to sign an agreement with the Islamic Emirate of Afghanistan, which they considered a helpless crowd and below their dignity, but they [the Taliban] survived all difficulties with the support of Allah and gained strength."[13]

Nuclear terrorism remains a constant threat to global peace. Access of terrorist organizations to nuclear material is a bigger threat to civilian population. Terrorist groups can gain access to highly enriched uranium or plutonium, because they have the potential to create and detonate an improvised nuclear device. Since the ISIS has already retrieved nuclear materials from Mosul city of Iraq, we can assert that terrorist groups like ISIS and Katibat Imam Bukhari, and Chechen extremist groups can make access to biological and nuclear weapons with the help of local experts. Nuclear facilities also often store large amounts of radioactive material, spent fuel, and other nuclear waste products that terrorists could use in a dirty bomb. Without access to such fissile materials, extremist and radicalized groups can turn their attention toward building a simple radiological device. The most difficult part of making a nuclear bomb is acquiring the nuclear material, but some Muslim and non-Muslim state might facilitate the ISIS, Lashkar-e-Toiba, Chechen extremist groups and Afghanistan and Pakistan based groups to attack nuclear installations in Russia and Central Asia.

Information on how to manipulate nuclear material to produce an explosive device—an improvised nuclear device, which would produce a nuclear explosion and a mushroom cloud, or a radiation-dispersal device, which would spread dangerous radioactive material over a substantial area—is now available widely. Daesh (ISIS) seized control of the Iraqi city of Mosul in 2014. Pakistan has also been heavily dependent on outside supply for many key direct- and dual-use goods for its nuclear programs. It maintains smuggling networks and entities willing to break supplier country laws to obtain these goods. Many of these illegal imports have been detected and stopped. These illegal procurements have led to investigations and prosecutions in the supplier states, leading to revelations of important details about Pakistan's complex to make nuclear explosive materials and nuclear weapons. According to some reports that weapons-grade and weapons-usable nuclear materials have been stolen by terrorist groups from some states. Once a crude weapon is in a country, terrorists would transport it in a vehicle to city and then detonate it in a crowded area.

The ISIS magazine (Dabiq-May 2015) published article of British journalist John Cantlie, in which he warned that the ISIS terrorist group had gained capabilities to launch major terrorist attack: "Let me throw a hypothetical operation onto the table. The Islamic State has billions of dollars in the bank, so they call on their wilayah in Pakistan to purchase a nuclear device through weapons dealers with links to corrupt officials in the region. The weapon is then transported overland until it makes it to Libya, where the mujahidin move it south to Nigeria. Drug shipments from Columbia bound for Europe pass through West Africa, so moving other types of contraband from East to West is just as possible. The nuke and accompanying mujahidin arrive on the shorelines of South America and are transported through the porous borders of Central America before arriving in Mexico and up to the border with the United States. From there it's just a quick hop through a smuggling tunnel and hey presto, they're mingling with another 12 million "illegal" aliens in America with a nuclear bomb in the trunk of their car".[14]

On 25 March 2016, Daily Telegraph reported militants plan to attack the Brussels nuclear plant: "In the wake of claims the Brussels attackers had planned to set off a radioactive 'dirty bomb', Yukiya Amano, the Director General of the International Atomic Energy Agency said: "Terrorism is spreading and the possibility of using nuclear material cannot be excluded. The material can be found in small quantities in universities, hospitals and other facilities. "Dirty bombs will be enough to (drive) any big city in the world into panic. And the psychological, economic and political implications would be enormous," said Mr Amano. One security expert suggested that the terrorists could have been plotting to kidnap the nuclear researcher they had been filming with a view to coercing the scientist into helping them make a 'dirty bomb'. The Newspaper reported. State sponsorship of nuclear terrorism in Central Asia is matter of great concern as some states support terrorist groups such as the ISIS, Taliban, Katibat

114

Imam Bukhari, Chechen groups, and Lashkar-e-Toiba, and provide dangerous weapons. These states can sponsor terrorist groups to launch nuclear attack inside Russia or Central Asia.[15]

Citizens of five central states have joined the ISIS networks to take the war into the region and inflict fatalities on the civilian population. Russia is a strong country in case of law enforcement and intelligence infrastructure, but newly established commando units of ISIS have gained a professional approach to traditional guerrilla war. As far as foreign fighters and ISIS are concerned, prior to the start of Syria's civil war in 2011, Central Asia had periodically seen trickles of citizens leaving to fight in Syria and Iraq. In domestic stability, states of Central Asia are better than Pakistan, Afghanistan and some states of the Gulf region, but the fear of chemical and biological war has vanished. The threat of returned fighters moving underground and engaging in terrorist attacks is greater if there is no process to reintegrate and absorb them into a reasonably open society.

It is known that the Katibat-i-Imam Bukhari group (KIB) has established two branches. The group's main fighting force of more than 500 militants is led by leader Abu Yusuf Muhojir. The chechen fighters are also looking for material of dirty bomb and nuclear weapons to use it against Central Asian and Russian army, but didn't retrieve so for. They are in contact with some states in South Asia and Middle East to receive fund from these regions, and purchase readymade dirty bomb. Afghan and foreign officials say as many as 7,000 Chechens and other foreign fighters could be operating in the country, loosely allied with the Taliban and other militant groups. According to recent reports, 6,000 militants from Central Asia and the Caucasus have already been enlisted in ISIS ranks. The largest radical group in Uzbekistan, Imam Bukhari Jamaat, has joined ISIS in Syria. Experts say there are over one thousand Uzbek and Tajik militants still fighting under the banner of ISIS.

There are speculations that some Russian technocrats and politicians are stressing the need for the establishing a jihadi group like the ISIS to further the interests of Russia in Central Asia and Middle East and fight against the NATO and American forces in Afghanistan. Russia is now third among top countries from which ISIS receives its recruits. The majority of them come from the North Caucasus, but also increasingly from Central Asia. The most prominent North Caucasians among the ISIS ranks have been the Chechens. Shortly before Russia's Syria intervention, the Russian government claimed that between 2,000 and 5,000 militants had joined ISIS; weeks after the entry of Russia into the conflict, however, that figure jumped to 7,000 out of a total of approximately 30,000 foreign fighters active within the ranks of the Islamic State.

If we look at the expertise of these groups, and their multifaceted military training, on their return to the region, they might possibly target biological and chemical laboratories and nuclear installations in Central Asia and Russia. There are states that will provide weapons and training to make the region a hell. Newsweek's Daily Beast blog provided another version of an overspill, already apparently happening in 2010. They quoted a "Taliban sub-commander in the northern Afghan province of Kunduz": ... jihadist allies from Central Asia have started heading home ... encouraged by relentless American drone attacks against the fighters' back bases in Pakistan's tribal areas ... they're expanding their range across the unguarded northern Afghan border into Tajikistan to create new Taliban sanctuaries there, assist Islamist rebels in the region, and potentially imperil the Americans' northern supply lines ... [beginning] in late winter 2009.... In Kunduz they joined up with fighters from the Islamic Movement of Uzbekistan (IMU).[16]

In his recent research paper, Leonid Gusev, an expert of Institute of International Studies, Moscow State Institute of International Relations of the Ministry of Foreign Affairs of the Russian Federation (MGIMO) has noted some consternating cooperative measures and planning's of the extremist groups of Central Asia: "Central Asian countries experience diverse intersecting influences: they feel changes in the situation in the Caucasus, in the Xinjiang autonomous territory of China, in Afghanistan and the Middle East. Militants from various terrorist groups in the region cooperate, many of them fighting in Syria and Iraq. But the biggest threat to Central Asia's security is the situation in Afghanistan, where the Taliban provide organisational and logistics support to the Islamic Movement of Uzbekistan (IMU). Despite sustaining a significant blow, with its main groups squeezed out of the region, it still maintains a presence in the form of underground groups that could become active at any time, joining forces with the radical Tajik opposition and Uyghur separatists. Cells of the Islamic State (ISIS) (a terrorist organisation banned in Russia) also operate in the region......... Tajikistan is a tension hotspot in Central Asia in terms of religious extremism and terrorism. A particular source of danger is neighbouring Afghanistan, where about 60 per cent of the lands along the frontier are engulfed in clashes between government forces and the Taliban and other radical Islamist groups. At the same time, there is almost no security along the Afghan-Tajik border, including the issue of drug trafficking".[17]

Nuclear trafficking in South Asia and Europe was a key concern while the nuclear blacke marketing networks were uncovered in Libya to Syria, Malaysia and Afghanistan. Recent media reports identified Moldovan criminal groups that attempted to smuggle radioactive materials to Daesh (also known as the Islamic State of Iraq and Syria, or ISIS) in 2015. Cases of nuclear smuggling in Central Asia were made in recent cases. Muhammad Wajeeh, a Research Associate at Department of Development Studies, COMSATS Institute of Information Technology, Abbottabad Pakistan in his research paper (Nuclear Terrorism: A Potential Threat to World's Peace and Security- JSSA Vol II, No. 2) has reviewed a consternating threat of nuclear terrorism in South and Central Asia:

"ISIS is believed to have about 90 pounds of low-grade uranium (which was seized from Mosul University in Iraq were the invasion of the city in 2014) that can be used in the Dirty Bomb's to create serious panic among the public. In 2015 and 2016, ISIS became the leading high profile jihadist group in Iraq and Syria. Moreover, ISIS carried out attacks in Paris on November 13, 2015, killing 130 civilians and injuring more than 100 people. The ISIS carried out a series of three coordinated suicide. Bombings in Belgium: one at Maalbeek Metro Staon, Brussels and two at Brussels Airport in Zaventem, killing about 32 civilians and injuring 300 people. During the attacks, a G4S guard working on the Belgian nuclear research center was also murdered and it le the world believing that the ISIS has a potential plot to attack the nuclear facility either to steal the radioactive material for dirty bomb or to release the radioactive material and waste into the atmosphere. These attacks also raised the issue of nuclear security, a discovery made by the Belgian authorities that the ISIS has kept an eye on the local nuclear scientists and their families. Moreover, two Belgian nuclear power plant workers at Deol having knowledge of the nuclear sites joined ISIS and could provide assistance to exploit them for terrorist purposes. On March 30, al-Furat, the media wing of ISIS, threatened attacks on Germany and Britain on the eve of Washington Nuclear Security Summit 2016".[18]

Chapter 7

Woman, War, and the Politics of Emancipation in Afghanistan

Afzal Ashraf and Caroline Kennedy-Pipe

Abstract

During the twenty years of war in Afghanistan much attention was focussed on the issue of female human rights. The emancipation of women from the rule and legacies of the Taliban was a core objective of Western states. This article traces the resistance within communities and regions to these liberal endeavours and highlights the challenges of imposing rather than embedding values. We note that the Afghan state has always struggled to provide basic human rights for its population, especially for its women. Until those needs are addressed, full emancipation through education and representation of women in society is unlikely. As a case study the country provides an understanding of feminism from a female Afghan perspective as well as an opportunity to explore the human rights context for women generally. Hence, we explain how this war allowed females in Western military forces to operate with greater gender equality on the frontline. Further research has the potential to reveal useful lessons in how female emancipation may be facilitated through an improved understanding of cultural contexts and an appreciation of how basic human rights such as the right to life and security are a prerequisite for female emancipation.

Keywords: Emancipation; Feminism; War; Warlords; Women

Both scholarly and practical interest in the women–security nexus deepened after the terrorist attacks of 9/11 and the wars that followed the assault on the US homeland. Specifically, the wars in Iraq and Afghanistan and the chronic instability in Pakistan caused in part, but not wholly, by the struggle with the Taliban, Al-Qaeda and TTP highlighted how issues of gender affects security locally, nationally, and globally.[1] The rhetorical and practical emphasis on the'emancipation' of women in Afghanistan by Western leaders as well as developments such as the advent of female suicide bombers across the Middle East, in Afghanistan and in Africa have combined to sustain an academic and public curiosity about the woman and war question[2]. The withdrawal of Allied forces from Afghanistan in August 2021 has raised a number of concerns about the future and fate of women after the return of Taliban to power. In this piece we try to explain why attempts to bestow women with human rights have ultimately failed in the country: we point to the many misunderstandings of the cultural and tribal customs by those tasked with the task of liberation.

But we also highlight the fraught local and regional politics which rested ultimately on the resistance to any usurping of traditional female roles. During the recent Afghan campaign, much was made of the imperative to liberate women from the excesses of Taliban and ensure that public life was reordered to include females; their emancipation was deemed vital to the reconstruction of the state. While many of us fell into the trap of believing that this endeavour was somewhat novel, we are indebted to our colleague Nargis Nehan in her contribution for pointing out that the women's movement has been a site of constant battle between the liberals and conservatives in Afghanistan. It was always going to be both controversial and in her words for some women 'deadly'. As Rina Amiri has written 'We see that women have long been the pawns in a struggle between the elite modernists, usually defined as pro-Western, and the religious and tribal based traditionalists[3]. In this piece we wish to explore the complexities of emancipatory politics both for those women living in or deployed as female soldiers to Afghanistan.

Rhetoric

Representations/discourses of women were central to the wars in Iraq and Afghanistan. Both conflicts were constructed as campaigns which would allow virtuous Western men (and women) to save the victimized Afghan (and Iraqi women) from the authoritarian and patriarchal structures which enslaved them. Such narrations were embraced not only by British and American politicians but also by many scholars studying these conflicts. Both wars were supposed to deliver for Iraqi and Afghan women a form of 'emancipation' which was usually couched through a lens of Western values and norms. The seeming importance of women, both Afghan and non-Afghan, to all aspects of the war is striking. Not only was the woman issue highlighted by politicians, but issues of gender affected the very conduct of what, despite the original intent, became a counter-insurgency campaign.

The debacle of the war in Iraq after 2003 for a while concentrated attention on that theatre as Western forces found themselves in the quagmire of what was both a complex civil war and a series of proxy wars. Yet in Afghanistan, after the initial success in toppling Taliban, the West had two missions. One was the hunt to find and kill Osama bin-Laden and eradicate Al-Qaeda within the neighbourhood and the other was to reconstruct the country, enforce human rights and build an effective Afghan security force. Nehan, again in this collection has argued that after the Western interventions there was a period in which gender and minority apartheid, social injustice, suppression, intimidation ......diminished to some extent. It appeared that women were attracting considerable attention and funding from the outside world. Indeed, just after President George Bush declared a War on Terror, the first lady, Laura Bush in a radio address on 17 November 2001 argued that 'the fight against terrorism is also a fight for the rights and dignity of women'[4]. Time magazine followed with a report on the plight of Afghan women entitled 'Lifting the Veil'[5]. All seemed set fair for women in the country to be rescued from the influence of Taliban. Despite this interest in female human rights, Kim Barry has detailed the way the Bush Administration, after 9/11 conveniently ignored the US part in allowing Taliban to emerge as the dominant force in the county. When Taliban forces captured Kabul in 1996, there was a resounding silence despite reports of gross human rights violations[6]. And to qualify Nehan's statement of progress somewhat respectfully there is also considerable evidence of the violence that was enacted against women as the US invaded the country[7], often by the warlords allied to the US cause.

Reality

Many of the Afghan men who served as allies in the US led offensive against bin Laden and Taliban were controversial figures including Rashid Dostum who has been accused of torture, abduction, and rape as well as the infamous Dasht-i-Leili massacre. Dostum became a hugely controversial figure even before he served as Vice President in Ashraf Ghani's administration from 2014–2020. In 2018, the ICC was reported to be considering launching an inquiry into whether Dostum had committed a string of war crimes. Certainly, during the period of civil war and then in the period of the US invasion, he had been a key figure in securing the north of the country. Outside of Kabul and the protection of the International Security Force in the city, the national situation was one of insecurity as the warlords vied for control. In May 2002, Human Rights Watch reported accounts of gang rapes; he ethnic Pashtuns in the north of the country suffered multiple attacks after the fall of Taliban[7]. In the power struggles between the warlords, women for example in Mazar feared physical assault should they venture outside of the home?

So, the rhetoric of emancipation did not easily fit with the reality of everyday life for women as war was waged around them. It is also the case that the US bombing campaign, widely lauded as successful in its initial stages, had profound consequences for those civilians living close to targets or the victims of the bombs that had gone astray. This difference between the reality on the ground and political rhetoric was in part created by the media, at least according to some informed female commentators[8]. The claim is that the western media ignored or underplayed rape and sexual abuse of women in the anarchy that followed the withdrawal of the Soviet Army from Afghanistan and in the abridgement of rights during the two decades of the US led occupation. Media stories in the West of the Afghan women football team are pointed to as evidence of the post-Taliban emancipation of the female but allegations of abuse of these players by the team's male managers and staffs is not reported to anything like the same extent. One way to approach the issue is to ask the question, that if abuse is being reported in a group of women such as the football players under the gaze of the international spotlight, then what levels of abuse may exist in remote communities ruled by thuggish warlords? Afghan feminists and their western counterparts have differing accounts of female emancipation depending upon whether their accounts privilege a commitment to female safety from abuse or the prospects of female social and economic opportunities.

Cultural Perspectives

There is another issue in terms of perspective. Some Western feminists take the issue of female security largely as a given norm. Rape and abuse, when it occurs, is regarded as a crime against the individual female[9]. Afghan social custom regards rape as a crime against the woman's collective identity – that is her family and her tribe. The Pashtunwali (social code), while providing a prominent role for males was, in its own way, protective of an interpretation of female dignity and it was mainly women who perpetuated its gender values through the upbringing of their male offspring. There was an in-built prohibition against rape or kidnapping as these were considered a capital crime resulting in a blood feud between rival tribes or families. Therefore, by empowering non-traditional elites in the form of warlords the consequences of invasions by both of the superpowers worsened, rather than improved, female empowerment and safety. (The prevalence of rape, beatings and kidnappings had also occurred with the emergence of warlords following the US-backed insurgency of the Mujahedeen against the Soviet invasion.) In the most recent war, it was at the point of invasion that the Afghan social equilibrium of roles and order between men and women was upset. There is irony in Western justification of the war against the Taliban on the grounds of female emancipation when sexual abuse had been a significant factor both in the establishment and rise of that group.

In 1994 an Afghan warlord raped and killed three women. Mullah Omar and his Taliban provided swift justice by executing the warlord for his crimes, assuaging the indignation and outrage of local people.[10] The Taliban, which had come into existence a year earlier by opposing the abuse of boys, became even stronger by delivering justice for female victims of 'sexual abuse'. There was therefore a serious question to be asked about the nature of who controlled what outside of Kabul in this early period of supposed emancipation of women from Taliban. One key question was who or what could control and influence the warlords? We should note here that part of the Soviet strategy in its own ill-fated Afghan war after 1979, was to instrumentalize the role of women in public life – precisely to break up tribal allegiances and local power. This strategy had provided some advances under Soviet occupation when women for example almost equalled the number of men attending university. Earlier in the century the Soviet leadership had committed itself to the modernization of the women issue in Central Asia precisely to emancipate Muslim women.[11]

Invasion and Emancipation

In retrospect, the pre-war analysis of the prospects of success in either Iraq or Afghanistan seems at best naïve and at worst delusional. The hope that Western forces would be welcomed had gained some traction, for example, in the justifications of war made by politicians such as Tony Blair or George Bush. In societal terms in Afghanistan the reaction to the US led invasion was not what had been expected. This should and could have been predicted. Historically when external powers have infringed on national culture and religious beliefs, extremist ideologies emerge in reaction. We saw this in many instances throughout the 19th Century when for example the British introduced legislation for example banning Hindu practices of Sati (that is the burning of a widow on her husband's funeral pyre) and in the practice of child marriage.[12] This in turn led to the appearance of the Arya Samaj, a forerunner of the RSS (the world's largest extremist movement, and responsible for Gandhi's assassination) and its mainstream affiliate the BJP, India's current ruling party. According to Sir Olaf, the 19th Century Wazirstan Masood tribe sought to "at all costs to resist subjection and to preserve their own peculiar way of life. To attain this end they were always prepared to make use of adventitious aids such as appeals with a pan-Islamic flavour." In other words, whenever Pushtun tradition is threatened by the West, it has sought to defend its local cultural identity by appealing to a wider Islamic identity and constituency; this factor was greatly helped by the US sanctioned appeals by Saudi Arabia to declare a jihad against the Soviets and to send Islamist militants to fight in Afghanistan. As we described above a catalyst for the emergence of the Taliban was Mullah Omer's repulsion at the increasing practice of male child abuse by the warlords. The practice of sexual abuse of young boys, known as bacha bazi, was a trigger for Mullah Omar to declare opposition to such practices[13].

The use of the women question was not therefore just confined to the US and its Western allies. So too did Taliban utilize the issue. For elements of that group, control of the female population, the symbolic importance of rituals and repression was and remains in part a drive to create an idealized society. This is an authoritarian response, that is a fear of uncertainty caused by an assault on traditional values and structures. We see this reaction playing out not just in Afghanistan but also in the USA albeit for different social reasons[14]. But our concern here is to highlight those Western practices and policy did not take fully into account the local gendered politics and all the sensitivities that lay deep within Afghan culture. In this respect, it is worth considering why on the whole we have and continue to separate out the question of women or perhaps place the issue in isolation from the successes or failures of other initiatives undertaken in for example the military, political and economic spheres. Here we are keenly aware of the endemic corruption within Afghan institutions and how this had a considerable impact, destroying any real chance of political transformation. So, to take the example of Rashid Dostum who benefitted financially from US support for his part in ousting the Soviet Army, but his corruption and debauchery reached new heights under the recent Afghan government.

The Taliban define themselves largely as standing against the character, values and power of such people.[15] So, can any improvement in female rights be advanced without first developing a system of justice in society? According to the 11th century Muslim philosopher Ghazali, the answer is no. In his predecessor to Machiavelli's "The Prince", Book of Counsel for Kings, he observed "Whenever Sultans rule oppressively, insecurity appears. And however, much prosperity there may be, this will not suit the subjects if accompanied by insecurity." Western leaders may be forgiven for their ignorance of what may appear to be obscure Eastern political thinkers but in 2009, ISAF's own anticorruption team wrote that, "the international community has enabled and encouraged bad governance through agreement and silence, and often active partnership" with corrupt and abusive warlords. It identified this as a "key factor feeding negative security trends" and went on to point out that this had resulted in acute disappointment within Afghan society and had "contributed to permissiveness towards or collusion with" the Taliban[16].

One query that lurks unanswered is if the west was at all serious about supporting female rights, then why did it not begin by uprooting the prominent abusers of those rights? It is certainly not because this was an unknown issue. Malalai Joya (named after a 19th-century Afghan female warrior) warned at the outset of the misogyny of the previous Afghan government and the warlords involved. She posed the question "Why would you allow criminals to be present? Warlords responsible for our country's situation … The most anti-women people in the society who brought our country to this state, and they intend to do the same again".[17] Her questions remain unanswered as do the claims of Kathy Gannon who pointed out the many atrocities and crimes committed by the Northern Alliance and other warlords selected as partners for the Western intervention. She points out that "in one grizzly attack five women of the Hazara ethnic group were scalped. The attackers were not Taliban; this was two years before that radical Islamic militia took Kabul".[18] She made pragmatic recommendations on how to remove these men from positions of influence and power, but these were not enacted. It would be reasonable to assume that when there is a choice between the certainties and short-term benefits of power politics and the uncertainties and long-term nature of ethical policy, Western political culture favours the former. Almost by definition, women and other weak members of society will always sadly be victims of power politics.

It would be somewhat misleading though to consider the plight of women as being somehow particular to the Afghans rather than at least in part a consequence of ill-judged external interventions. Here we want to look at how the military campaign itself used the issue of women in a very specific manner. There are two aspects to this. The first is how counter-insurgency developed an emphasis upon women and their roles in the community and the second theme is that military service in Afghanistan opened up possibilities for Western women which had hitherto been closed to them. The irony here is of course that while Afghan women have been returned to Taliban rule, we must consider the possibility that Western female soldiers benefited from service in the country.

Female Counterinsurgency: The Role of Western Women Soldiers

Laleh Khalili[19] has argued that the gendered nature of the wars in Iraq and Afghanistan were patently obvious when soldiers encountered the local population. In these interactions, women in the community were typically perceived as civilians while men—that is all males over the age of fourteen—were 'coded' as combatants. As a consequence, men were targeted as potential enemies both by combat units and by drones. (Under President Obama the armed drone became his weapon of choice with 563 strikes carried out either in signature strikes, where the individual's identity is unknown, or in precision strikes on a named individual) Women, usually were not the actual target of such strikes but were part and parcel of the collateral damage which inevitably accompanied aerial assaults. In Iraq, US forces had initially largely ignored the female population, in part because of the sensitivities of engaging with women in a traditional society. Insurgents in turn took advantage of these cultural sensitivities by disguising themselves in the all-enveloping female clothing to avoid detection whilst perhaps plotting or perpetrating attacks.

(This was not a new tactic as during the 1966 Algerian conflict for example, insurgents cognizant to the ideas of the French army would dress in Burqas and easily cross through checkpoints which were usually closed to men but open for women[20]. This disguise as we may term it in turn forced Western forces to deploy women soldiers at checkpoints precisely to be able to search females without causing offence. During the presidency of George W. Bush, the mission to emancipate Afghan women led to the recruitment of more women into the Armed Services. Following the election of Obama, the focus shifted somewhat. The drive for equality in the armed forces became of paramount importance. This was coupled with new peacebuilding approaches which eventually led to a revaluation of the role of female service members in war zones[21] and active deployment of females on the front line in the post-9/11 operations. Ironically, given the substance of this essay, the Afghan theatre provided Western military women with opportunities which had been long denied to them in terms of front-line operations.[22] Deployment in Afghanistan opened up opportunities in field artillery, combat arms positions and special operations. From 2009 there was a need for American women to accompany American troops on patrol, especially after the military 'surge' and the parallel civilian surge to extend reach into Afghan civilian populations. All of this spearheaded a significant shift in American policy eventually leading to the lifting of the embargo on women in combat.

The Feminization of coin

The US developed two programmes to enable military forces to make contact with Afghan women: the Female Engagement Teams (FETs) and the Cultural Support Teams (CST). It is worth discussing the reasons for this innovation. Some of those who provided briefings to senior commanders deploying to Afghanistan on cultural intelligence and psychological operations have noted that central to Pustunwali is the concept of Nang (honour). Three important factors contribute to Pushtun Honour: Zar (Gold or wealth), Zan (women and girls) and Zamin (land or property).[23] Despite these efforts though, any cultural appraisal and sensitivity collided with a typical western military operation which involved breaking down doors, storming into property and even intruding into female quarters. All this proved counterproductive. Such a single operation could offend all three cultural taboos. It was partly to mitigate such affects that female soldiers were introduced. It at least meant that the handling and interrogation of women could be carried out without the offence that would be keenly felt if men engaged with females. (It is worth remembering that even in recent times, 'we' for example in the UK no longer think it appropriate for male policeman or soldiers to handle females in our own cultural context).

When the training of Western women soldiers is scrutinized it becomes apparent that the military mission or some form of intelligence gathering took priority over any cultural sensitivities. In other words, killing insurgents was more important than protecting and winning over the hearts and minds of the female population. As such and whatever the good intentions, female soldiers perpetuated rather than refined the ill-fated counter insurgency practice put in place by their male comrades. The issue was that in their kill/capture missions the US used a variety of tactics, including precision strikes and night raids on the homes of Afghans suspected of colluding with terrorist groups. These night raids (as described above) caused widespread upset amongst the Afghan community[24] and also caused considerable friction between President Karzai and his allies. Civilians were killed but the domestic space was also violated and what became apparent is that the cultural 'sanctity' of the home was not well understood by many Westerners. Female soldiers were meant to reassure the local women during night raids that they as women would protect the wife, the mother, and the children of the household even as the raid was conducted. This occurred even as the men of the household, the husbands, brothers, fathers and sons were hunted down. Accounts by those female soldiers who served in this capacity have related instances of removing their helmets to show their faces and demonstrate to the household that they too were women and protectors.

The mission was to build relationships with the women even as soldiers collected 'intelligence' and information on the home. There is scant evidence that this type of relationship building with local women actually worked and there have been numerous stories of the inconsistencies in what and how local women were meant to respond as homes and communities were invaded and men folk removed. The detention of men raising questions about how the family could be supported without the presence and activity of male breadwinners. Despite these inconsistencies or perhaps because of them a need for women soldiers was also demanded by the Provincial Reconstruction Teams (PRTs) which were established from 2005 by the US and its allies. This meant military and civilians experts working in conjunction with local Afghan leaders to provide development funding for local projects to try and win 'hearts and minds.' These engagements though also provided intelligence-gathering opportunities.[25] Despite controversy over this intelligence role, and as noted above, the embedding of all female cultural teams alongside special operations forces was regarded as successful in enabling access to the 50 per cent of the population usually side-lined in the business of war. One male veteran I interviewed told me that in his two tours of the country and when engaging with local communities he never encountered a woman. They were always in his words secluded in the back of the compound and unlikely to engage with any men outside of the family. But this is not the whole story. While Western women were quite literally on the frontline, the emergence of an Afghan National Army co-opted women into the armed services.

Female Martyrs

In this complex theatre, women, unusually for a traditional society, were also resorting to violence as in the phenomenon of suicide bombers. In Afghanistan there was, at least initially, a prohibition against the use of female 'martyrs. However, for a multiplicity of reasons, we have witnessed an increase in female suicide bombers since 2009. This followed an open letter issued by Umayama al-Zawahiri (the wife of Al-Qaeda leader Ayman al-Zawahiri) urging her sisters to assist the terrorist groups through suicide missions. The use of females created the conditions for surprise attacks but had the added 'bonuses of creating an additional pool of resources. The experiences of women in the conflict have been represented in the oral tradition of Landays, traditional short verses which reflect the impact of drones strikes, military occupation, and suicide. These verses might speak of the glory of war but also provide telling accounts of what it means to be female. Violent images abound, as in this rhyme: Embrace me in a Suicide Vest but don't say I won't give you a kiss[26] Martin Van Creveld, the military historian, has argued that women are only ever used in battle/conflict when men are not available, or are reluctant to take part.[27]

Indeed, even in supporting roles such as fighter ferry pilots, women in the RAF were used during the Second World War but then excluded from flying aircraft until virtually the end of the last century. They were allowed to fly transport aircraft in the late 1980s and only in the late 1990s where they are permitted to qualify for combat roles. This Western example provides valuable insights into how wartime strategic necessity and peacetime social change work on different timescales. Female emancipation is a social project which in the West has taken over a century and is advancing as part of wider societal changes, by learning from failures of policy and practice. In war women in all societies are invited to fill any gaps left by men in traditionally male roles. Once war ends, progress on female emancipation returns to its usual social speed which can be accelerated or decelerated by the economic and social changes brought about by that war. The return of the Taliban may well accelerate progress against rape and other forms of sexual abuse. It will certainly decelerate progress in wider education and in the workplace for women. These questions point to issues that need some attention. The Afghan conflict and what occurs now is a rich seam of further research and debate on the place of women in society. But there are challenges to any study: any comparison of women's rights under the Western backed government and the Taliban is problematic partly because reporting and analysis are skewed by an apparent bias in favour of the norms espoused by the West.

And here we must acknowledge that there were significant improvements in terms of women's health through intervention. Female life expectancy rose from 56 years in 2001 to 66 years in 2017. Mortality in childbirth also improved from 1,100 per 100,000 deaths in 2000 to 396 per 100,000 in 2015.[28] Those were just some of the gains made for women. There were others made in terms politics and representation. But any future western analysis would need to address the subtle issue of perceptions shaped by power politics, the consequence of which is that Taliban abuse of women's rights appears to have been mostly overt and criticized whereas abuse of women's rights under the previous regime was largely covert and ignored. There is also an issue of which rights are more important: the right to work or the right to life.

Urban versus Rural

We must also unpack the category of Afghan women. There is a significant distinction between urban and rural life. Many of the political gains for women were made in the cities; although it is true that the Taliban had issued some of its most severe edicts in Kabul concerning female apparel, behaviour, and work.[29] Rural women in Afghanistan have, when asked, declared that the right to life was/is the crucial issue. Most Western analysts operate at the pinnacle of Maslow's hierarchy of needs where education and work are understandable priorities. The conditions in Afghanistan are near the bottom of this hierarchy where the right to life and security (against rape etc) is of most importance. It is unsurprising, therefore, that the Taliban rose to power initially on a crusade to stop sexual abuse and managed to reduce the threat to life and rape for more women and girls (and boys) than was the case under the previous regime. These points can partly explain the failure of the Western backed mission in Afghanistan. Another issue is that Western analysts employ different timescales and conditions to judge female emancipation between the experience of the West and places such as Iraq Afghanistan. What took decades in the West is in our view unreasonably expected to take place in just a few years in Afghanistan. For example, the US insisted that parties standing for the January 2005 Iraqi Transitional Government elections should field at least 25 percent female candidates.[30]

In 2005, the UK Parliament had around 20 percent female representation – over 100 years after Nancy Astor was elected in 1919 as the first female MP. The Iraqis were being asked to achieve a level of female political representation in just over two years which the West had failed to achieve in 100 years. Similar attitudes were employed on the female issue in Afghanistan. Western attempts to impose the norms that took so long to develop in a different cultural context, while experiencing the societal equivalent of post-traumatic stress disorder was ill judged. This accounts for some of the policy and strategy failures we see today. Afghanistan, therefore offers a rich case study to understand feminism from the perspective of not just Afghan women but also from the relative standpoint it offers to revaluate female emancipation in the West. It also provides excellent examples of how feminism has been weaponized for power politics and how issues of societal and economic development gave way to the idea that counter insurgency had priority. Finally, Afghanistan has allowed females in Western forces to operate with greater equality on the frontline, principally to extract intelligence from women in Afghan villages. Their overall performance is difficult to judge due to a lack of independent research, but any successes that may have been achieved took place at the tactical level obviously failing to translate into a strategic victory.

Prospects for Women in Afghanistan

Since the takeover by the Taliban, Afghanistan's military has effectively been disbanded along with the return of its female members to the private sphere. If the Taliban remain in power the prospect of female soldiers being part of any future Afghan military is extremely unlikely. The issue of female participation in wider public life, especially in education and the workplace, is an issue on which the Taliban appear to be divided. Several statements indicating the desire to allow women to be educated and work have been made, but they come alongside indications that all of this will be delayed for a variety of reasons. These include an argument that Taliban members are not trained or equipped to deal with women in a public or civic setting. There are also claims that women are being harassed or positively hunted down as punishment for speaking out on other activities in public. Most of these claims are denied by the Taliban.

It is thus difficult to verify or find truth here. There is always a strong possibility that many of the individuals accused of harassing females may well be either criminals posing as Taliban or more likely tribal or other social relations who consider that the women involved have brought dishonour to their traditional codes of behaviour through these public activities. Equally relevant is the fragmentary nature of Taliban policy arising out of the diversity of backgrounds and experiences in its leadership. Some in this group are traditional hard-liners who have spent little time outside of their tight social circles. A small number who have spent time abroad, particularly in Qatar where the Taliban had a headquarters, have indicated a somewhat more liberal approach. Qatar's example would have been particularly inspiring for the Taliban because it is a society which has to a large degree managed successfully to blend highly conservative ideas on female dress codes with remarkable degrees of empowerment of women through education and leadership in the workplace. According to statistics, Qatari women lead the world in studying STEM subjects with 57 percent of Qatari women choosing these subjects compared to 35 percent in the USA[31,32].

Less well-known is the fact that these women can go on to lead organisations in cybersecurity or Fintech to a degree which is rarely seen in western society. It is likely that exposure to this model of successfully combining strict religious interpretations with liberal ideas about female equality of opportunity will have influenced some of the Taliban leadership. Less certain is whether that leadership can come to a united vision of the future. Whatever progress may be made in this area, it is likely to take time because social cultural change inevitably takes time to evolve. One significant factor in discussing the future is the issue, already highlighted, of the political will to restore female rights. The priority, for the Taliban is to provide the necessities for its population in terms of food and fuel necessary for survival. Currently, it is failing to do so partly because of its own inaptitude but largely because of the failure of the international community to coordinate a suitable post-conflict settlement allowing the release of funding and the agreements on trade and aid necessary to help the country establish a sustainable economy. If the West wishes to support female emancipation to allow women to receive an education and have equal opportunities in the workplace it must do all it can to support the basic needs of Afghan society in terms of food shelter and fuel. Only then is there any hope for progress on the higher ideals of female emancipation.

There is much to be gained by studying this topic in detail. In the meantime, it is safe to conclude that geopolitical involvement in Afghanistan has put back rather than advanced the cause of female emancipation. These wars caused instability by deliberately disrupting the delicate power structures of traditional society through the empowerment of alternative leaderships: they were motivated by parochial gains achieved through perpetuating insecurity. Evidence suggests that female emancipation is always culturally contextualised, and advances are best advocated through a complex and probably long drawn out evolutionary socially led process. The Afghan case study highlights the importance of considering the thorny issue that some of the human rights which underpin female emancipation are a precondition for others, that is, the right to life and security over the right to education and equality of opportunity and inclusion. Security, stability and a form of justice in society were considered a prerequisite for social development according to both the values of the region and the findings of some ISAF studies and it seems sadly that in the turmoil of war these were lost.

131

The authors have no competing interests to declare. Afzal Ashraf was a senior officer in the British Armed forces with operational experience in Afghanistan and other conflicts. He served in the UK Foreign and Commonwealth Office and other government departments. A former Research Fellowship at St Andrews University's Centre for the Study of Terrorism and Political Violence and a Consultant Fellow at the Royal United Services Institute think tank, he is currently teaching International Relations, Politics and Security at Loughborough University. His research interest is in beliefs and strategies that motivate conflict and peace. Caroline Kennedy-Pipe is Professor of War Studies at Loughborough University is currently a specialist advisor to the House of Commons Select Committee on Defence. Her research interests include contemporary war, the ethics of war and the legacy of Cold War. She is currently working on a book project entitled 'Counter-Insurgency and getting the Woman Question Wrong'. Afzal Ashraf orcid.org/0000-0003-2039-1603 Teaching international relations and security topics, Loughborough University, UK Caroline Kennedy-Pipe Professor of War Studies, Loughborough University, UK. *Ashraf A, Kennedy-Pipe C. Woman, War, and the Politics of Emancipation in Afghanistan. LSE Public Policy Review. 2022; 2(3): 7, pp. 1–11. DOI: https://doi.org/10.31389/lseppr.58 Submitted: 23 February 2022 Accepted: 11 March 2022 Published: 02 May 2022* *LSE Public Policy Review is a peer-reviewed open access journal published by LSE Press. LSE Public Policy Review is an open-access, peer-reviewed journal which is published quarterly and draws principally (but not exclusively) on authors from across the LSE's 19 departments. Issues are thematic and concentrate on a key topic at the heart of current debates in public policy. Public policy challenges bring to the fore cross-cutting questions which require a global perspective and a focus on their interconnectedness. Articles in each issue take different disciplinary perspectives, encouraging interdisciplinary collaboration and analysis at the forefront of current thinking. As a result, each issue presents a comprehensive approach to the specific theme and an analysis that is academically rigorous but also readily accessible to all readers. All issues are initially proposed as public symposia, with symposia leaders outlining the main themes, suggested papers and authors. The LSEPPR Commissioning Editors regularly review a range of proposals for future issues, and decide amongst them based on the relevance of the topic, the fit of the proposed approach with the aims and scope of the journal and the level of scholarship of the proposed contributions. Given the thematic nature of the LSE Public Policy Review's issues, we cannot accept open submission of individual manuscripts. The LSEPPR publishes original research papers, conceptual articles, review papers written for a general readership, in non-technical language aimed at a wide audience including government, business and policy-makers, as well as academics and students. LSEPPR seeks to actively contribute to the study and development of public and social policy, public administration and public management. The journal publishes four issues quarterly online throughout the year. 'Guest' issues are*

Chapter 8

Humour in Jihadi Rhetoric: Comparative Analysis of ISIS, Al-Qaeda, TTP, and the Taliban

Weeda Mehran, Megan Byrne, Ella Gibbs-Pearce, Archie Macfarlane, Jacob Minihane and Amy Ranger

Abstract

Research shows that humour plays a significant role in the formation of a collective identity and 'creates a sense of internal cohesion' based on shared experiences [Fominaya, C. F. (2007). The role of humour in the process of collective identity formation in autonomous social movement groups in contemporary Madrid. International Review of Social History, 52(S15), 243–258. https://doi.org/10.1017/S0020859007003227]. In this paper, we focus on humour in jihadi English magazines. This study is based on 82 English magazines published by the Taliban, ISIS, Al-Qaeda and Tahrik-e Taliban Pakistan (TTP). This research takes a mixed method of analysing data both qualitatively and quantitatively. The findings point to a statistically significant difference amongst these groups in the type of humour they utilise. In general, Al-Qaeda, the Taliban, and TTP show similar patterns in the types of humour they employ, a pattern that often stands in stark contrast with ISIS. ISIS is more likely than Al-Qaeda, the Taliban or TTP to use dehumanising and mocking humour while less likely than these groups to use situational humour, which is a less negative form of humour.

Keywords: Humour jihadi rhetoric ISIS Al Qaeda Taliban TTP

Introduction

In studying the cultural dimensions of jihadism, Hegghammer writes that militancy is not just about operations, objectives, and strategic thinking.

Militancy is about rituals, costumes and dress codes (Hegghammer, 2017). It is also about music, film and storytelling. 'It is about sports, jokes, and food' (Creswell & Haykel, 2017, p. 1). As observed by the author, this 'soft dimension of military life' has not received its due attention by scholars (Creswell & Haykel, 2017). Looking inside any radical group, we can observe a range of daily social practices that have no obvious strategic purpose (Creswell & Haykel, 2017). Jihadis use poetry; they speak about dreams, weep openly and value personal humility, artistic sensitivity, and displays of emotion (Creswell & Haykel, 2017). More recently, research has picked up on this topic and has explored various softer aspects of jihadi militancy. Pieslak and Lahoud (2020) for example, explore jihadi music. Creswell and Haykel (2017) analyse the role of poetry in jihadi culture whilst Weinrich (2020) examines Islamic chanting and jihadi hymns. Furthermore, Mehran and Lemieux (2021) have studied the role of narrated stories in jihadi propaganda, highlighting how these serve to provide information, motivate followers, and offer advice for conducting jihad and hijra.

Hegghammer (2017) observes that militants do not waste time by engaging in poetry recitation, singing hymns, and other activities that have no apparent strategic purpose. It is not difficult to imagine that jihadi militants do not spend 'all' their time on their bomb-making skills. The downtimes and the soft dimensions of militants' life are depicted in the media products of the groups, in fact, play a 'strategic purpose'. When a jihadi militant who is about to go on an 'istishhadi mission'–suicide mission – is shown laughing and playing football with village children in a Taliban video (Mehran et al., 2021), or militants are described to be laughing, smiling, and joking in Al-Qaeda magazines, the question remains, what are the strategic purpose of depicting laughter, humour, jokes, and smiling militants in jihadi rhetoric? After all, jihad is a serious business, and the pages of magazines and minutes of videos are finite. Why spend time showing smiling militants or writing about their jokes?

When it comes to the realm of politics, humour has been studied and explored in various contexts and across different cultures. For example, humour has been studied as an American national tradition (Fry, 1976); it has been analysed in the political context of socialist states (Davies, 2015); investigated as a form of resistance in the Arab world (Kishtainy, 2009), and resistance in the workplace in Brazil (Rodrigues & Collinson, 1995) to name a few. As a means of popular communication, humour has the potential to enhance common-sense views on political issues (Tsakona

& Popa, 2011). Political criticism is often encoded in humorous terms, softening the serious subject matter with playfulness and wit (Tsakona & Popa, 2011). Nonetheless, as observed by Tsakona and Popa, 'politics can be represented in a humorous manner and humour can have a serious intent' (2011, p. 1). In fact, humour takes many different forms, is extremely context dependent, and performs varied functions. In this paper, we study different types of humour and their function in jihadi rhetoric.

One of the most significant functions of humour within politics and social movements is its power to strengthen social identities. Understanding the contexts of jokes alongside their targets and purposes often clarify who is 'us' and who is 'them', thereby fostering a sense of cohesion for the group 'in on the joke' (Fominaya, 2007). Furthermore, adherence to the understood social dynamics of a group is a source of mutual solidarity and community reinforcement, particularly when the humour is more aggressive (Terrion & Ashforth, 2002). In light of theoretical discussions on the role of humour in politics, we analyse humour as a soft dimension of jihadi militancy and its strategic purpose in jihadi rhetoric. This is an attempt at answering Hegghammer's call for more research on jihadi culture (Hegghammer, 2017). As such, our primary research questions are:

What constitutes acceptable humour for violent jihadi groups?

What is the role of humour in jihadi rhetoric?

Do violent jihadi groups differ in how they use humour?

The findings are based on an analysis of 82 English language magazines by Al-Qaeda, ISIS, Taliban, and Tahrik-e Taliban Pakistan. The results illustrate that groups differ in terms of the frequencies and kinds of humour they use. Broadly speaking, Al-Qaeda, the Taliban, and TTP show similar patterns in types of humour they use, a pattern that often stands in contrast with how ISIS employs political humour. For example, ISIS is more likely than Al-Qaeda, the Taliban, or TTP to use dehumanising and mocking humour while less likely than these groups to use situational humour.

Conceptual Framework: Political humour, context, and functionality

Much of the research on political humour describes the concept as an umbrella term depicting irony, satire, ridicule, parody, mockery, and scorn (Tsakona & Popa, 2011). Political humour is highly context dependent to the extent that without contextual knowledge of political issues, political humour cannot be processed and interpreted (Tsakona & Popa, 2011). The same utterance can have different meanings and connotations for different audiences.[1] Dynel, for example, observes that speakers' utterances can have both humorous and derogatory meanings which can only be recognised by the receptive audience that can appreciate the effect it would have on other parties (Dynel, 2011).

The context of political humour varies, such that humour by politicians happens in settings where the political discourse is serious (Tsakona & Popa, 2011). For example, humour by politicians often aims at undermining their opponents, while journalists and commentators use humour to criticise politics and politicians (Morreall, 2005). In comparison, political humour by the media and ordinary people occurs in the form of humorous genres such as jokes, cartoons, satirical shows on various platforms such as TV shows, radio shows, and online (Kuipers, 2008). Political humour highlights the inconsistencies and inadequacies of political decisions and actions and the 'incompetence, recklessness, and corruption of politicians and political leaders' (Tsakona & Popa, 2011, p. 6). It contrasts 'political reality' with observable reality. A shared language and understanding are needed to distinguish between sincerity, jocularity, and irony. To joke is to speak without meaning and joking can obviate responsibility for the consequences of the utterance (Stevens, 2021).

Humour, in addition to having a subversive power as a strategy for communication, also plays a key role in the conceptualisation of direct actions whose intended audience is the general public (Fominaya, 2007). The subversive role of humour has also been practiced by political extremists. For example, Billig's analysis of websites supportive of the Ku Klux Klan found that their extensive racism was de-emphasised by disclaimers that online discourse and humour were sequestered from real racism (Billig, 2005). More recently, far-right groups have turned to memes as vehicles of humour, enabling repackaging their ideologies into more accessible and acceptable formats (Askanius, 2021).

Theorising humour has been rooted in ontological reductivism, in that theoretical discussions have primarily identified humour in terms of its effect of laughter. Humour is often associated with, if not identified and confused with laughter. This is primarily because of the close relationship between humour and enjoyment (Tsakona & Popa, 2011). However, humour and laughter are two separate phenomena (Greatbatch & Clark, 2003). Laughter is certainly not a ubiquitous concept. A joyous laugh, for instance, is different from that of a dark realisation that would 'leave one without any breath at all' (Sontag, 2002, p. 34). As such, humour does not need to lead to laughter. For example, Arendt warns against viewing idiotic or humorous behaviour as mutually exclusive with danger. Using Hitler as a case study, she notes that [w]hat is really necessary is–if I want to keep my integrity under these circumstances – then I can do it only if by remembering my old way of looking at such a thing and say: No matter what he [Hitler] does, if he killed ten million people, he is still a clown. (Arendt, 2018, p. 504) Thus, Arendt asserts that to view Hitler as a clown and laugh at him is to 'already know what he really is and still laugh' (in Stevens, 2021, p. 13).

In an attempt to clarify the nuances of this phenomenon, Stevens proposes a typology of humour along dry or wet lines. In its archetypal form, dry humour is 'signified by an absence of passion or intentionally comic delivery' (Stevens, 2021, p. 4). Dry humour intends to unveil and divulge, despite the fact that these intentions might be missed by the audience (Stevens, 2021). Dry humour is witty or clever. In comparison, wet humour is hinged on shared belief or knowledge and 'operates within a logic of confirmation' (Stevens, 2021, p. 4). Continuing with this distinction between dry and wet humour, Stevens argues that while dry humour is an invitation to a new view; wet humour 'invites us to come to an extant view again' (Stevens, 2021, p. 4). Wet humour is about what should not need saying yet is said again anyway (Stevens, 2021). This confirmatory logic of wet humour is the core of the entertainment aspect of humour in social media (Stevens, 2021). Stevens contends that the most basic form of dry humour is puns (Stevens, 2021). As Cavell observes, puns are often uncomfortable as they alter the rules that language traditionally follows (Cavell, 2005). This in turn divides people based on whether they find such instances comical or not, reinforcing the boundary between insiders and outsiders. In contrast, Stevens provides the example of impressions as a form of wet humour which instead functions by creating a bond of unity through shared understanding of a topic (Stevens, 2021). Impressions or impersonations are easy for an audience to understand as they are simply a reiteration of something or someone with whom they are already familiar, yet they also allow for new layers of critique to be added by highlighting specific matters (Sørensen, 2013). Such examples highlight the differing ways in which humour can manifest itself, and the consequential impacts these can have beyond just being 'funny'.

It should be noted, however, that Stevens is quick to explain that his approach to dry and wet humour is not dichotomous and should be seen as a continuum. Stevens' notion of dry and wet humour is also akin to Tsakona and Popa's (2011) description of humour along two lines based on functionality: (a) humour conveys criticism against the political status quo (dry humour), and (b) humour reinforces and recycles dominant values and views about politics (wet humour). Tsakona and Popa (2011) give examples of political satire and cartoons as forms of political criticism. In the twentieth century, socio-political humour was synonymous with satire, a form of dry humour (Stevens, 2021). This traditional style of humour is 'dusty and desiccated' while political humour nowadays is received as 'entertainment' (Stevens, 2021, p. 3). Other scholars investigating online humour highlight the maliciousness of employing humour to troll. Young, while underlining the ambiguous nature of some online discourses, describes it as a 'contemporary digital culture of an irony of infinite reversibility, of texts that offer no critical vantage point for determining to what extent they mean what they say' (Young, 2019, para. 51).

Humour can also have a subversive function and lead to political change by offering different perspectives on political issues that lead audiences to question political decisions, representing a form of resistance (Tsakona & Popa, 2011). Subversive humour in the workplace, for example, is conveyed through 'discourse strategies which create social distance, and emphasize social boundaries between the speaker and the target of the humour' (Holmes & Marra, 2002, p. 65). Humour plays a significant role in the process of identity construction and identity reinforcement. For example, in the context of social movements, Fominaya's ethnographic study points to the importance of humour in the process of collective identity formation within anti-capitalist groups in Madrid. The author asserts that humour generates a sense of internal cohesion and helps project an alternative identity (Fominaya, 2007). The mechanism through which humour contributes to identity construction is by both delineating and ratifying a collective (Stevens, 2021).

A shared humour creates an environment that fosters internal cohesion and contributes to social bonding between interlocutors who agree on both the content and targets of humour, which is referred to as the inclusive function of humour (Dynel, 2011; Fominaya, 2007). It also plays an exclusive function by enhancing the gap between those who do and do not adopt the same stance towards the humour's themes and targets (Tsakona & Popa, 2011). Research in the field of film and television studies, illustrate that in movies ridicule and contempt are used to portray weakness of victims – paradigmatically women and children–as lack of physical power

(Jasper et al., 2020). Stereotypes can be reinforced through contemptuous and ridiculous depiction of groups. For example, Jasper et al. (2020) claims that at the height of American racism, films like The Birth of a Nation portrayed black people as both silly and threatening at the same time.

At times humour is expected to take the place of physical retaliation (Stevens, 2021). As such, derogatory humour and ridicule are a 'critical part' of a delegitimization strategy in which people 'are categorized into negatively valued social groups that are not afforded protection or rights otherwise considered normative, for the purposes of justifying maltreatment' (Hodson & Macinnis, 2016, p. 69). Such disparaging inter-group humour works in tandem with processes such as dehumanisation and system justification with its specific function to label social groups as acceptable targets for devaluation (Hodson & Macinnis, 2016). In this way, more mundane forms of disparaging humour can 'play a key role in delegitimizing out-groups, trivializing their rights, concerns, and right to protection' (Hodson & Macinnis, 2016, p. 70). Furthermore, humour as a deviation from the norm has a social function that Tsakona and Popa argue constitutes a 'social corrective', that aims at 'highlighting, eliminating, and even preventing any disruption from what is socially accepted and approved of' (Tsakona & Popa, 2011, p. 4). Therefore, humour is viewed as a means of criticism as well as social control, as it implicitly projects norms and values of a specific community, and heightens boundaries between in- and out-group members (Archakis & Tsakona, 2005). For example, Fominaya compounds that deliberate use of humour in social movements represents 'a fundamental declaration of political orientation' and signals distancing from the status quo (Fominaya, 2007, p. 246).

Humour can also be geared towards controlling the target and fostering conflict (Holmes & Marra, 2002; Rodrigues & Collinson, 1995). This type of humour, often dubbed as 'aggressive humour', stands in stark contrast with solidarity-building and affiliative functions of humour (Hay, 2000; Luginbühl, 2007). Aggressive humour distinguishes between an in-group of those who enjoy such utterances, and out-group(s) comprising the individuals/groups who are lambasted, criticised, or humiliated. This type of 'disaffiliate humour'–where the speaker uses aggressive utterances to be humorous to one group and abusive towards another group, is associated with sarcasm (Dynel, 2009; Partington, 2006), disparagement (Ferguson & Ford, 2008), ridicule (Billig, 2005) or mocking (Everts, 2003). As such, the audience is imperative in determining the type of humour. In the absence of a listener beside the one attacked, Dynel (2011, p. 112) expounds that, an aggressive utterance may be altogether devoid of any humorous capacity. Therefore, disaffiliate humour, is simultaneously affiliative, because 'it demonstrates camaraderie, and strengthens bonds of solidarity between those who laugh' (Dynel, 2011, p. 112). As such, central to such humour experiences are feelings of superiority, mockery, and amusement at the expense of the othered (Dynel, 2011, p. 113).

While this discussion highlights the functionality of humour and the debate surrounding various types of humour, less explored is the functionality of political humour in the context of extremism. Most recently, the use of humour by extremist actors has been revolutionised by online subcultures of the far-right. Scholarly attention has been especially drawn to the use of memes (Bogerts & Fielitz, 2019; Dafaure, 2020; Fielitz & Ahmed, 2021) that develop and spread virally by copying or combining with other units of meaning such as texts and images (Fielitz & Ahmed, 2021, p. 7). The visual culture of certain alt-right online communities share 'a cynical style of humour intended to numb and desensitise its consumers to the use of violence' (Fielitz & Ahmed, 2021, p. 4) with several violent far-right attacks in recent years closely connected to this 'chan culture' (Crawford et al., 2020). Memes are a form of countercultural irony used by far-right movements to shift what is acceptable discourse, gradually exposing users to increasingly virulent content by concealing it as ironic parody (Crawford et al., 2020). This parody also creates a sense of community by presupposing certain knowledge and hence excluding those who don't get the in-jokes (Lamerichs et al., 2018).

A recent study by Ayad reveals that a younger generation of Salafis, 'Gen-Z Salafis', are appropriating the tropes, language and visual culture originally espoused by the alt-right and far-right (Ayad, 2021). These online subcultures include members of 'Islamogram',[2] the akh-right,[3] as well as younger supporters of Islamic State, al-Qaeda and the Taliban who have adopted culture war tropes that attack the inherent degeneracy of western culture. By repurposing popular memes and video aesthetics to define themselves and their enemies, Gen-Z Salafis' use humour to engage and entice a younger generation towards a Salafi ideology and identity. The importance of identity construction as a feature of strategic communications by violent jihadist organisations is well established. For example, ISIS communications aim to provide readers with a 'competitive system of meaning' to shape supporters' perceptions, polarise and convince them to mobilise (Ingram, 2018). Reicher et al. argue that the effectiveness of discursive strategies in mobilising violence is determined by the extent to

141

which skilled entrepreneurs of identity can construe speaker and audience in a common social category, defining an in-group so as to exclude an out-group (Reicher et al., 2005). Humour is just one way in which violent actors use strategic communications to project norms and values of a specific community in order to heighten boundaries between in-group and out-group members (Archakis & Tsakona, 2005). This research speaks to this line of literature by focusing on the role humour plays in the jihadi rhetoric.

Research Methodology

This study utilises 82 English magazines published by the Taliban, ISIS, Al-Qaeda and Tahrik-e Taliban Pakistan (TTP). The data is analysed both qualitatively and quantitatively. All data analysed within this paper was accessed and retrieved from Jihadology.net, which provides access to primary source material from a range of global jihadi groups for research purposes. Although Al-Qaeda, ISIS, the Taliban and TTP have produced magazines in languages other than English (e.g. Urdu magazines by the Taliban and TTP, Pashtu by the Taliban, and Arabic by Al-Qaeda, ISIS, and the Taliban), for the purpose of this project we focus on English language material as it is the only language shared by all four groups analysed. Furthermore, the messaging strategies of a group will often differ depending on the language. For example, Lahoud observes that ISIS's al-Naba magazine – published in Arabic – uses stereotypical gender descriptions for women which are found to be demeaning and offensive even to female ISIS supporters. In comparison, the author contends that the English and French magazines produced by ISIS (Dabiq and Dar al-Islam respectively) widely avoid using demeaning language within their prose when addressing or discussing women (Lahoud, 2018).

Furthermore, the choice of English language for these magazines is also indicative of an audience that has English language competency; this can apply to Muslims living in the West or the Western audience in general. As observed by Ingram, messaging strategies implemented by ISIS play on factors connected to identity, solution and crisis constructs (Ingram, 2018). Likewise, the Taliban (Johnson, 2018), Al Qaeda (Gohel, 2017), and TTP (Siddique, 2010), discuss grievances, provide solutions, and build identities within their rhetoric to attract potential recruits. Therefore, a comparative analysis of these magazines can shed light on the nuances and differences between these groups in how they depict humour and for what purposes.

Conceptual definitions and operationalisation

It should be noted that different categories of humour, for example dehumanising humour, ironic and sarcastic humour, mocking humour, and situational humour are not necessarily mutually exclusive.

Data Analysis

The study implemented a two-step coding process, which allowed for consistency with the process of a grounded theory approach (Glaser & Strauss, 2003). The data was manually coded by five coders using computer-assisted qualitative data analysis software, NVivo Initially, the team coded for text referring to humour and laughter identified through a broad definition of humour. Next, through a process of inductive coding, the team coded various types of humour and its contexts (subcategories) which were identified in the first round of coding. In the second step, all the entries that had been coded broadly for humour were analysed and coded into the identified subcategories.

To assess the inter-rater reliability, all coders separately coded a randomly selected trio of issues (Al Risalah Issues 1, 2, 4). Based on our independent codes, we calculated Cohen's Kappa coefficients. The results showed high levels of agreement on most coding categories (Kappa value of 0.88). Coders resolved the differences in this initial stage of coding by discussing the parameters of the codes and reaching an agreement as a group. In the second stage, each member of the team coded a separate set of magazines individually, which were in turn checked by at least one other member of the team. In this stage, the Kappa Coefficients were calculated for the pair of coders and the results in general indicated high levels of agreement (Kappa values ranging between 0.498 and 1.00). Any resultant disagreements were discussed and finalised by the coders. A final diagnostic test was performed by a single coder who conducted a 'constant comparison' process (George & Apter, 2004) by checking all entries for each category and subcategories of codes to ensure consistency (Carcary, 2009; Gwet, 2008). This process of detailed coding generated more than 1068 references allowing for rich quantitative discussion of the data, a practice that enhances the credibility of qualitative data (Patton, 1999).

Findings

The overall findings of this research point to various forms of political humour being used by Al-Qaeda, ISIS, TTP, and the Taliban. In this section, we first provide an overall view of the frequencies of humour in jihadi rhetoric while discussing how each group perceives of acceptable or unacceptable humour. This discussion is based on descriptive statistics and provides counts and percentages of references to humour, regardless of type, and whether the jihadi group in question discusses what it believes is permissible or forbidden humour. This discussion is followed by analysing inter-group differences in various types of humour and what purposes they serve. Our findings illustrate that groups differ in terms of the frequencies and kinds of humour they use. Statistics provide purely descriptive statistics based on counts and percentages of references to humour per group. The first column illustrates the percentage of humour references per group. As the table demonstrates Al Qaeda and ISIS have the highest number of humour references. We also investigated whether each group discusses what constitutes acceptable and unacceptable of humour. These are counts of number of times a group discusses directly what is acceptable or unacceptable humour. We treat these categories as proxies for a definition of humour by the jihadi group.

Boundaries of Humour

Boundaries of humour refer to language employed to distinguish what is and is not allowed to be discussed in a funny or comedic nature. Due to humour's inescapable subjectivity, there are no unanimous rules for what can be considered comedic. Instead, what is deemed humorous is predominantly determined by the social context it is being used in (Purcell et al., 2010). For example, Western boundaries of humour tend to be focused on ethics, political correctness, and the line of what is 'too far' in comedy (Peifer, 2012). This differs greatly from the boundaries posed in jihadi rhetoric where topics that many would consider 'off limits' such as people being killed are frequently mocked or ridiculed. Instead, boundaries for these jihadi groups are most frequently centred on religion, specifically regarding what constitutes appropriate humour for a 'good Muslim' and how the West is particularly disrespectful (Macdonald & Lorenzo-Dus, 2021).

By splitting humour into these two categories, norms can be developed on what and who should be mocked (Tsakona & Popa, 2011) strengthening the 'us versus them' narrative many groups aim to impose onto their readers. Quantitatively, table demonstrates statistically whether each individual group implements boundaries of humour and if so the percentages of usage in relation to the acceptable or unacceptable subcategories. Although the chi-squared test does not yield any statistically significant results, it can be observed that 48 percent of the references made to setting boundaries are by ISIS, with the Taliban being the next group (34 percent of references) that delineates what is unacceptable humour. For example:

If a claimant of Islam worships anything or anyone besides Allah, mocks Allah, or completely abandons submission to Him, then he cannot be considered a Muslim.[4]

Throughout publications from ISIS, similar sentiments are made on multiple occasions, setting the boundary that mocking Allah or religious figures such as the Prophet Mohammed is to be considered an extreme offence.[5] In addition, unacceptable religious discourse is also further divided between rules for 'good Muslims' such and critiquing enemies for unacceptable humour in the form of disparaging remarks or content relating to Islamic figures. We as Muslims do take Islām seriously and we take it literally. We also take the honor of Muḥammad seriously and we love him dearly. Cartoons defaming Muḥammad are no joke and Muslims have made that very clear, yet the defamation continues as we have recently seen with the South Park affair.[6] Furthermore, analysing Al-Qaeda's magazines also provided insight into the group's general attitude towards humour. For example, in an issue of Inspire, the author advises:

[…] to fear Allah in your akhlaq or behavior. Refrain from excessive joking and laughing. The more one laughs, the less dignity he will possess.[7]While it is evidently unacceptable for Muslims to mock Islamic figures, humorous content deriving from enemies, particularly Western nations and their citizens, is presented as among the gravest of offences. For example: I do not see what happened at Charlie Hebdo as a tragedy. Rather the tragedy is that people think it is OK to demean the sacred and belittle that which is more beloved to us Muslims than their own souls.[8] This statement suggests that partaking in overt expressions of humour is unacceptable behaviour for a principled Muslim who respects Allah. However, this sentiment is juxtaposed alongside a density of references to these very actions. Particularly this is visible for situational humour where in regular reference point to members making jokes and laughing among themselves or laughing at others. This contradiction supports Hellmich's contention that Al-Qaeda's messages are pervaded with hypocrisy, which undermines the organisation (Hellmich, 2008). The two groups with the highest frequencies for discussing unacceptable humour boundaries (ISIS and the Taliban) are also the only groups to show concern for acceptable humour boundaries, albeit at a much lower rate than the former. Therefore, it follows that these two groups may have stronger beliefs on how and when humour should be used to communicate messages. Nonetheless, all four groups use humour throughout their English magazines. This is evidence that Al-Qaeda, ISIS, the Taliban, and TTP consciously utilise humour to promote their own group's strategic aims, centred along the lines of group cohesion and group identity formation.

Types of Humour

In this step, we calculate the differences between the groups in the type of humour they use.

Since all the variables are nominal and the sample size of the material for each group is different, we used a Chi-squared test to analyse if the differences between the observed and expected values happened by chance. According to Yates et al., for tables larger than 2×2, a condition for Chi-squared test is that at least 80 percent of expected values should be equal to greater than 5 (Yates et al., 1999). As such, our analysis meets the accepted criteria as described above. The p-value is .00001, which indicates that the probability that the differences between the observed and expected values occurring by chance is below 1 percent. The general rule is that the larger the difference between the observed and expected value, the higher the contribution that value has made to the overall Chi-squared test.

Dehumanising humour

As illustrated, all groups employ dehumanising humour in varying degrees. By applying dehumanisation techniques to a person or group, targets of the dehumanising humour will no longer be seen to have hopes, feelings, and concerns in the way a sentient human has. Instead, they will be considered subhuman entities (Bandura et al., 1996). Research shows that dehumanising humour deployed by extremist groups indicates mindlessness or insentience within the targeted opposition (Wahlström et al., 2020). As such, when utilising dehumanisation within the framework of humour, terrorist organisations are able to contrast the more graphic imagery dehumanisation elicits with the softer aspect of humour as 'the communication vehicle that legitimises the derogation' (Hodson & Macinnis, 2016, p. 70), thereby strengthening the development of in/out-group dynamics through the use of othering.

The findings demonstrate that ISIS is more likely than Al-Qaeda, the Taliban, or TTP to use dehumanising humour (observed frequency is 29 while expected frequency is 19.05 with the results significant at the p-value of <.0001 and the adjusted residual differences is more than

2). This finding is not surprising given the well-documented scathing and uncompromising discourse ISIS uses within its rhetoric. Shaw and Bandara, for example, note the comparative prominence of inflammatory claims of *takfir* or heresy against certain groups as well as a different tone for ISIS magazines compared to Al-Qaeda's, which are 'wry, humorous, even temperate at times' (Shaw & Bandara, 2018, p. 1329). The noticeable use of dehumanisation within ISIS rhetoric has been previously examined by Ramsay, who argues animalistic dehumanisation is deployed to express moral judgement primarily against treacherous members of the Muslim community, especially Shi'ites and hypocrites (*munafiqun*) (Ramsay, 2016). Meanwhile, mechanical dehumanisation, i.e. comparing the enemy to machines and robots was only found in ISIS magazines indicating a broader and more developed use of this type of humour, especially compared with the Taliban and TTP (with observed frequencies of only 3 and 1 respectively).

In terms of types of dehumanisation, humour using animalistic dehumanisation is the most prevalent form implemented by all four groups, involving the denial of uniquely human characteristics such as refinement, civility and morality (Haslam, 2006). By attributing bestial qualities to the target through animalistic labelling such as vermin, pig, donkey or ape, the perceived primitiveness of the subject is demonstrated mockingly and humorously. Rhetoric which attributes animalistic qualities relates to the development of class structure as well as in and out-group dynamics (Loughnan et al., 2014). The target of animalistic dehumanisation is presented as 'coarse, uncultured, lacking in self-control, and unintelligent' (Haslam, 2006, p. 258). The use of this humour therefore delineates clear social boundaries (Loughnan et al., 2014) in which the deliverer of the remark indicates to the reader that the target is of lesser social and cognitive standing.

Indeed, dehumanising humour lends itself to the mocking and scathing rhetoric implemented by all four groups analysed. Animalistic dehumanisation deploys overtness as a humour mechanism, which when paired with a mocking delivery, signals to the reader in a clear manner where they should place their allegiance within the dialogue. However, it should also be noted that different animalistic comparisons will serve different humorous purposes. For instance, the repeated use of the term 'dog'[9] to describe President Bush refers to an animal considered culturally unclean; the term 'donkey'[10] to describe Americans indicates laziness, stupidity, and sexual promiscuity; whilst the more sinister comparison of

American troops to vermin (see Note 10) functions to cause emotional disgust justifying their slaughter. Therefore, as with all forms of humour context is vital to understand its specific function. The following extract from ISIS's *Dabiq* magazine serves to mock the target reinforcing the boundary between in- and out-group, but in this instance does it through highlighting their subhuman stupidity:

I found out that she was the wife of the donkey that was coming to me almost every day to rebuke me and to 'teach' me my religion, or so he claimed![11] A different form of dehumanisation, mechanical dehumanisation, was also observed to use humour within our study: The governments are like a robot that is stuck on a loop, continually performing the wrong sequence despite repeated instructions by its master to the contrary. Master to robot: You have to find a different way of addressing the danger the mujāhidīn pose to the west. 'Cannot ... compute ... ' Military action does not work, what about negotiations? 'Must ... obey ... programming ... ' Everything you've done since 9/11 has put us in more danger, not less. 'Zzzzz ... syntax ... error ... ' Of course, Robo-Obama doesn't listen to voices of reason and thus programs himself with the same corrupted old data, making the same mistakes over and over again .... [12]

This excerpt from the ISIS's magazine *Dabiq* demonstrates how humanness can be further conceptualised in relation to inanimate objects like robots. This form of dehumanisation denies 'human nature' characteristics such as emotionality, vitality, and warmth and is intended to make the target seem superficial, inert and cold (Haslam, 2006; Loughnan et al., 2014). In this context, ISIS portrays Obama as obsessed with military action and beholden to 'the wrong sequence' making him appear lacking in any agency or remorse for his actions. Dehumanisation is one of the most extreme forms of negative out-group identity construction, essentialising group boundaries by accentuating the difference between in and out-group members (Baele, 2019). Dehumanisation when used in a humorous context reinforces the exclusive function of humorous forms such as ridicule and mocking by justifying the derogation of certain groups.

Ironic and sarcastic humour

Our definition of ironic and sarcastic humour is language that conveys a distinction between what is literally said and the intended meaning of the statement (Gal, 2019). Sarcastic humour aims to unveil and divulge using clever or subtle language (Stevens, 2021). Subtlety distinguishes sarcastic humour from other more overt forms such as mocking humour and it often invites a new perspective which challenges the status quo. Sarcastic humour is also closely associated with 'disaffiliate humour', whereby the speaker uses utterances that are humorous to one group and humiliating or critical towards another, reinforcing a sense of 'us' versus 'them' (Dynel, 2011; Fominaya, 2007). In the context of jihadist propaganda, sarcastic humour serves as one of the tools to strengthen camaraderie between those who laugh, promoting feelings of superiority at the expense of the othered group.

TTP is more likely than ISIS, the Taliban and Al-Qaeda to resort to ironic and sarcastic humour. As shown in Table 4, observed frequencies of ironic and sarcastic humour are higher than their expected values. The observed frequency for TTP is 16, while the expected frequency is 9.21 with a p-value <.000. Comparing the quantitative findings, Al-Qaeda's and the Taliban's rhetoric contain markedly less ironic and sarcastic humour. Therefore, sarcastic humour's subversive function – fostering resistance through novel perspectives (Rodrigues & Collinson, 1995; Tsakona & Popa, 2011). In comparison, Al Qaeda is less likely than any group to use sarcastic humour. When Al Qaeda uses sarcastic humour it is aimed at ridiculing enemies, as shown by Al-Qaeda lambasting Donald Trump in the following example: Trump and many of his aides vehemently opposed the military option. They prefer to rely on economic sanctions, besides of course 'Presidential' tweets, which might force Tehran to bend to American demands or, after another forty years, somehow bring about the collapse of the regime![13] Herein, Trump is the humour's target, with the suggestion that his tweets might bring the collapse of the Iranian regime representing sly mockery of the former president's intellect and policies.

In general, the use of sarcastic humour is employed as criticisms of enemy politicians and their policies. By highlighting visibly hypocritical or thoughtless Western policies, an audience is left to infer the meaning of the critique within the joke and act themselves to challenge the status quo. The attempt to delegitimize and expose western systems and established authorities (such as the Nobel Peace Prize) is a recognised feature within violent political language, functioning to reinforce the in-group as the 'sole holder of truth' (Baele, 2019, p. 712).

Mocking humour

In comparison to ironic and sarcastic humour, mockery is direct and aggressive in style; it converts characteristics of its targets into accusations of incompetence (Everts, 2003). Attributes are presented in isolation or with egregious exaggeration until they become vices; an accent may become a speech impediment, or caution turned into indecision, while speed becomes recklessness. However, this requires the target audience to be receptive to the original qualities of the individual being mocked. Thus, for jihadi magazines trying to penetrate the Anglosphere, frequent targets of mockery are expected to be well-known individuals, especially internationally recognisable politicians and organisations. For example, ISIS labelled Joe Biden as 'the Senile Crusader' in a parody of domestic political bickering between former President Trump and President Joe Biden.[14] Mockery easily extends to ascriptive characteristics as well, such as the corruption of former Israeli Prime Minister's surname 'Netanyahu' into 'Rottenyahu' by Al-Qaeda.[15] Quantitatively, ISIS is much more likely to resort to mocking humour than Al-Qaeda, the Taliban, or TTP (with an observed frequency of 47 versus an expected frequency of 33.70). This relationship is illustrated in Table 4, which is based on the differences between observed and expected values. As demonstrated, ISIS is the only jihadi group in this study that demonstrates higher observed frequencies for mocking humour than what would have been expected.

Stylistically, ISIS's mocking humour is particularly aggressive, sacrificing subtlety in favour of imagery that turns countries into individuals and people into animals, as demonstrated below:

According to Scheuer, the only time airstrikes alone succeeded in determining the end of a war was the airstrikes of Hiroshima and Nagasaki! Indeed, America has been caught once again in a quagmire.[16] In another example, we read: Indeed, the people today are like a hundred camels amongst which you almost can't find any that are fit for riding.[17] To a lesser extent, other jihadi groups also use mocking humour to denigrate the enemy and create a well-demarcated in-group/out-group identity. Mocking humour is a diverse rhetorical toolkit for the authors of jihadist magazines and, although it can be used rather bluntly through simple animalisation – as conceptualised in the discussion of dehumanising humour – there is also evidence of more complex, strategic deployments. Al-Qaeda and the Taliban in particular use mockery and parody to galvanise the curious by placing emphasis on an 'us versus them' mentality, permitting careful blame attribution.

Situational humour

Situational humour is defined as the use of humour, typically nostalgic, contextualised in narratives or 'first-hand accounts of event[s] experienced by jihadi militants' (Mehran & Lemieux, 2021, p. 3). It is often characterised by humour that is incorporated into narrating a situation, for example through storytelling, and describing past jihadi operations in a nostalgic way to evoke a sense of idyllic brotherhood. Situational humour is specifically used in these narratives for the strategic purpose of telling stories to motivate audiences and demonstrate privileged knowledge (Mehran & Lemieux, 2021). Statistically, while situational humour is rather common amongst Al-Qaeda, it appears less often in the rhetoric of ISIS, distinguishing it from the other groups. For Al Qaeda, the observed value for this category is 82 versus an expected value of 65.31, while the p-value is .000 and the results fall within two standard deviations from the mean. References to smiling and laughing are common elements within situational humour. This relates to research by Hegghammer regarding the cultural dimensions of jihadism about the use of 'storytelling [and] jokes' in jihadi literature (Hegghammer, 2017, p. 1). Examples such as, '[i]t's a funny story, and actually (the brothers in) Al-Qaeda found it hilarious!'[18] demonstrate the use of situational humour to create an idyllic and nostalgic frame of events experienced by the jihadis. Or in the following example, situational humour is used to valorise a martyred Al-Qaeda leader:

Khattab was a very simple guy. He would make jokes, laugh a lot and form good ties and relationships with the people.[19] Furthermore, situational humour is utilised to juxtapose perspectives between in- and out-groups within jihadist literature. In the example below, situational humour is used by the narrator to contrast his and his compatriots' experiences with those of his captors in a wistful yet mocking tone whilst recounting their time in Guantanamo Bay: 'We can't do anything, our hands are tied' was his reply. Months later, in Guantanamo, whilst looking back on these days, we would laugh and sing: They took us to Guantanamo, and (they said) their hands were tied.[20] By framing, the clearly contrasted in- and out-groups of the story within a nostalgic sentiment, the perceived injustice of the narrator's captivity is signalled to the reader in a more strategic manner than if the same message had been stated more plainly and without using humour. Even though Al-Qaeda uses situational humour more than other jihadi groups studied in this paper, it is not unique to the group. The following is an example from ISIS's Dabiq magazine: Upon entering the blessed land of Sham, his heart was full of joy and he became the youngest brother among the Bengali muhajirin [...] He was always cheerful and smiling.[21]

ISIS magazines typically reference smiling and laughing within the context of jihad. Examples such as 'I just smiled. This is the Decree and Will of

Allah'[22] and 'Until they meet their Lord, for He has laughed and is pleased with them'[23] demonstrate how the use of situational humour within ISIS publications are often contextualised within the religious associations of jihadi acts. These literary narratives further help to mobilise individuals by emphasising the delight felt by those who participate in acts in the name of jihad. Consequently, situational humour is used strategically to enrich narratives of past events and develop a religious rationale for conducting jihad, as well as motivating individuals to carry out their own operations. This humour depicts a softer side of jihad by emphasising the comradery and brotherhood of carrying out 'istishhadi' missions and the peaceful, even joyful, nature of martyrdom.

Conclusion

Through a comparative analysis of jihadi magazines, this research discusses boundaries of humour and inter-group differences in the types of humour each group focuses on. The findings of this research point to various forms of political humour being used by Al-Qaeda, ISIS, the Taliban, and TTP. In this paper, we categorised the humour appearing in jihadi rhetoric in the form of dehumanising humour, ironic and sarcastic humour, mocking humour, and situational humour. We also have demonstrated that groups differ in terms of the frequencies and kinds of humour they prefer. Broadly speaking, Al-Qaeda, the Taliban, and TTP show similar patterns in the types of humour they use, a pattern that often stands in contrast with how ISIS employs political humour. For example, ISIS is more likely than Al-Qaeda, the Taliban, or TTP to use dehumanising and mocking humour while less likely than these groups to use situational humour.

In general, political humour is used to build an in-group out-group identity; however, different types of humour have particular focus on how identities are constructed. Our findings illustrate that ISIS is more likely to use dehumanising and mocking humour than any other group. The increased regularity of dehumanising humour in ISIS's magazines reflects their overall aggressive and uncompromising stance on out-group members and combative opponents. Both dehumanising and mocking humour are more negative and sinister types of humour compared to sarcastic and situational humour. Situational humour on the other hand, demonstrates the formation of an in-group identity among jihadis based on shared experiences and depicts a sense of collective identity amongst them. Situational humour is often used to contextualise a narrative of events experienced by jihadi militants as it is incorporated into storytelling narratives with the objective to motivate individuals to mobilise. Situational humour is also used to demonstrate solidarity within jihadi organisations and foster the narrative of an idyllic brotherhood of jihadis. Ironic and sarcastic humour plays an inclusive role in identity formation, because it is often necessary to relate to a jihadi ideology and political outlook for an audience to understand and enjoy the nuances of these jokes. A shared humour in turn creates an environment that fosters internal cohesion and creates social bonding while playing a role in construction and reinforcement of in-group identity.

The broader implications of these findings indicate that humour plays an important role in jihadi text as it can reinforce identity, establish group cohesion, and have an exclusive or inclusive functionality. Text containing humour, e.g. situational humour, normalises jihadi life and demonstrates a focus beyond the commonly perceived notion of militancy. This can be an effective persuasive tool to attract potential recruits who are given vison of a romanticised jihadi life and a venue to channel their shared frustrations and anger towards the othered enemy responsible for their grievances. As such, humour is an effective communication strategy. Our analysis also showed that jihadi groups utilise this strategy differently, for example building an identity by vilifying and dehumanising the enemy as in the case of ISIS and dehumanising humour, or by looking inwards and focusing on group cohesion, and shared experiences as in the case of situational humour used by Al Qaeda.

While this paper sheds light on a less studied aspect of jihadi rhetoric – jihadi humour – the findings are limited to the analysis of written text and English magazines only. To provide a more comprehensive picture of the functionality of humour in jihadi rhetoric, future research ought to focus on non-English textual material. Furthermore, the paper did not analyse any visual imagery encountered within the magazines, yet this component remains important and understudied. Exploring spoken humour in jihadi videos or humour depicted in images and memes and comparing it with written humour can be enlightening.

No potential conflict of interest was reported by the author(s). This work was supported by Minerva Research Initiative [grant number FA9550-15-1-0373]. Dr Weeda Mehran is co-director of Centre for Advanced International Studies and the programme director for MA degree in Conflict, Security and Development at the University of Exeter. Her research focuses on security and terrorism. Megan Byme recently obtained her MA degree in Conflict, Security and Development Programme from the University of Exeter. Ella Gibbs-Pearce is a recent MA graduate from the University of Exeter in Conflict, Security and Development. Currently Ella works as a Research Assistant in the Sociology Department at the University of

Oxford. Archie Macfarlane is a Junior Research Analyst at Tech Against Terrorism, focusing on understanding and contextualising terrorist and violent extremist behaviour online. Jacob Minihane is a postgraduate student at the University of Exeter. His research examines extremism alongside its radicalisation pathways and mechanisms. Amy Ranger is a Threat Intelligence Analyst, focusing on terrorists' use of the internet to insight violence. Her research interests include counter terrorism, OSINT and geolocation techniques and counter insurgency theory. Terrorism as a tactic has been used by political and ideological actors and groups for thousands of years. Humour in jihadi rhetoric: comparative analysis of ISIS, Al-Qaeda, TTP, and the Taliban Behavioural Sciences of Terrorism and Political Aggression addresses the complex causation and effects of terrorist activity by bringing together timely, scientifically and theoretically sound papers addressing terrorism from a behavioural science perspective. The Journal publishes empirical and theoretical papers, letters to the Editor and invited visionary pieces by leading experts in the field, which have a strong base in behavioural science research. The articles will also draw in insights from related disciplines, including anthropology, criminology, economics, history, political science, nonlinear dynamic systems, linguistics and sociology. Terrorism as a tactic has been used by political and ideological actors and groups for thousands of years. Behavioural Sciences of Terrorism and Political Aggression addresses the complex causation and effects of terrorist activity by bringing together timely, scientifically and theoretically sound papers addressing terrorism from a behavioural science perspective. The Journal publishes empirical and theoretical papers, letters to the Editor and invited visionary pieces by leading experts in the field, which have a strong base in behavioural science research. The articles will also draw in insights from related disciplines, including anthropology, criminology, economics, history, political science, nonlinear dynamic systems, linguistics and sociology. Print ISSN: 1943-4472 Online ISSN: 1943-4480. 4 issues per year. Humour in jihadi rhetoric: comparative analysis of ISIS, Al-Qaeda, TTP, and the Taliban Weeda Mehran, Megan Byrne, Ella Gibbs-Pearce, Archie Macfarlane, Jacob Minihane & Amy Ranger To cite this article: Weeda Mehran, Megan Byrne, Ella Gibbs-Pearce, Archie Macfarlane, Jacob Minihane & Amy Ranger (2022): Humour in jihadi rhetoric: comparative analysis of ISIS, AlQaeda, TTP, and the Taliban, Behavioral Sciences of Terrorism and Political Aggression, DOI: 10.1080/19434472.2022.2075028 To link to this article: https://doi. org/10.1080/19434472.2022.2075028 © 2022 The Author(s). Published by Informa UK Limited, trading as Taylor & Francis Group. © 2022 The Author(s). Published by Informa UK Limited, trading as Taylor & Francis Group This is an Open Access article distributed under the terms of the Creative Commons Attribution-NonCommercial-NoDerivatives License (http://creativecommons.org/licenses/by-nc-nd/4.0/), which permits non-commercial re-use, distribution, and reproduction in any medium, provided the original work is properly cited, and is not altered, transformed, or built upon in any way.

Notes to Chapters

Chapter 1: Implications of the New Taliban Government for the Biden Administration. Richard J. Chasdi

1. Baitullah Massoud crafted Tehrik-e-Taliban Pakistan (TTP) in 2007 to confront Pakistani national security forces in the Federally Administered Tribal Areas (FATA), a geographical locale now incorporated into Khyber Pakhtunkhwa.

References

Ahmadi, M., Yusufi, M., & Fazlidden, N. (2021). Exclusive Taliban puts Tajik militants partially in charge of Afghanistan's Northern border. Retrieved from https://www.rferl.org/a/taliban-tajik-militants-border/31380071.html [Google Scholar]

Al-Jazeera. (2021, June 2). Military chief says Sudan reviewing naval base deal with Russia. Retrieved from https://www.aljazeera.com/news/2021/6/2/military-chief-says-sudan-reviewing-naval-base-deal-with-russia [Google Scholar]

Anderson, L. (1987). The State in the Middle East and North Africa. Comparative Politics, 20(1), 1, 4, 13–15, 15n3. doi:https://doi.org/10.2307/421917 [Crossref], [Web of Science ®], [Google Scholar]

Central Intelligence Agency. (2021a). Appendix-T-Terrorism, terrorist group(s) - Harakat ul-Mujahidin (HUM). Retrieved from https://www.cia.gov/the-world-factbook/references/terrorist-organizations/ [Google Scholar]

Central Intelligence Agency. (2021b). Appendix-T-Terrorism, terrorist group(s) – Islamic Jihad Union (IJU). Retrieved from https://www.cia.gov/the-world-factbook/references/terrorist-organizations/ [Google Scholar]

Central Intelligence Agency. (2021c). Appendix-T-Terrorism; terrorist group(s) – Islamic Movement of Uzbekistan (IMU). Retrieved from https://www.cia.gov/the-world-factbook/references/terrorist-organizations/ [Google Scholar]

Central Intelligence Agency. (2021d). Appendix-T-Terrorism, terrorist group(s) - Islamic State of Iraq and ash-Sham-Khorasan Province (ISIS-K). Retrieved from https://www.cia.gov/the-world-factbook/references/terrorist-organizations/ [Google Scholar]

Central Intelligence Agency. (2021e). Appendix-T-Terrorism, terrorist group(s) – Lashkar-e-Taiba (LeT). Retrieved from https://www.cia.gov/the-world-factbook/references/terrorist-organizations/ [Google Scholar]

Central Intelligence Agency. (2021f). Explore All Countries -Tajikistan: Central Asia: Ethnic groups. Retrieved from https://www.cia.gov/the-world-fact-book/countries/tajikistan/ [Google Scholar]

Central Intelligence Agency. (2021g). Explore All Countries - Turkmenistan: Central Asia: Ethnic groups. Retrieved from https://www.cia.gov/the-world-factbook/countries/turkmenistan/ [Google Scholar]

Central Intelligence Agency. (2021h). Explore All Countries – Uzbekistan: Central Asia: Ethnic groups. Retrieved from https://www.cia.gov/the-world-factbook/countries/uzbekistan/ [Google Scholar]

Chasdi, R. J. (1999). Serenade of suffering: A portrait of Middle East Terrorism, 1968-1993. Lanham, MD: Lexington Books. [Google Scholar]

Chasdi, R. J. (2002). Tapestry of terror: A portrait of Middle East terrorism, 1994-1999. Lanham, MD: Lexington Books. [Google Scholar]

Constable, P. (2021, July 5). Afghan Hazaras bear cumulative traumas. Washington Post, p. A–11. [Google Scholar]

Dixon, R. (2021, August 31). A worried Russia urges cooperation with Taliban leaders. Washington Post, p. A–11. [Google Scholar]

Fair, C. C. (2014). Insights from a database of Lashkar-e-Taiba and Hizb-ul-Mujahidden. Journal of Strategic Studies, 37(2), 261–262260, 262, 270–272. doi:https://doi.org/10.1080/01402390.2013.811647 [Taylor & Francis Online], [Web of Science ®], [Google Scholar]

Felbab-Brown, V. (2021, August 31). Order from Chaos: Will the Taliban regime survive? Retrieved from https://www.brookings.edu/blog/order-from-chaos/2021/08/31/will-the-taliban-regime-survive/ [Google Scholar]

George, S. (2021, September 20). For Taliban Fighters in Kabul, a big adjustment. Washington Post, p. A–14. [Google Scholar]

Gohain, H. (2007). Chronicles of violence and terror: Rise of the United liberation front of asom. Economic and Political Weekly, 42(12), 1015–1017. [Google Scholar]

Gorman, S., & Spiegel, P. (2009, September 17). Drone attacks target Pakistan militants. Wall Street Journal. https://www.wsj.com/articles/SB125315344115718571 [Google Scholar]

Hinnebusch, R. (2016). The politics of identity in Middle East international relations. In L. Fawcett (Ed.), International relations of the Middle East (4th ed., pp. 156–157). New York: Oxford University Press. [Crossref], [Google Scholar]

Khemnar, S. (2018). Causes and effects of terrorism in India: An overview. International Journal of Applied Information Systems, 12(15), 1. [Google Scholar]

Lawson, F. H. (2018). International relations theory in the Middle East. In L. Fawcett (Ed.), International relations of the Middle East (4th ed., pp. 26, 417). New York: Oxford University Press. [Google Scholar]

Lemon, E. J. (2014). Mediating the conflict in the Rasht Valley, Tajikistan: The hegemonic narrative and anti-hegemonic challenges. Central Asian Affairs I, 261-263, 256, 259, 248. https://brill.com/view/journals/caa/1/2/article-p247_5.xml [Google Scholar]

Meghalaya Times (India). (2013, February 15). Trader escapes unhurt in militant firing. Meghalaya Times (India). [Google Scholar]

Pike, J. (2004). Lashkar-e-Taiba-Lashkar-e-Taayiba (Army of the Righteous). Retrieved from https://fas.org/irp/world/para/lashkar.htm [Google Scholar]

Sahni, A. (2019). A Peaceful Northeast is Imperative for India's Act Easy Policy. World Affairs: The Journal of International Issues, 23(3), 123. http://www. https://jstor.org/stable/10.2307/48531055 [Google Scholar]

Saif, S. K. (2020, November 12). Key leader of terror group killed in Afghanistan. Anadolu Agency (https://www.aa.comtr). [Google Scholar]

SATP. (2001). Harakat-ul-Mujahideen (HuM): Assam. Retrieved from https://www.satp.org/satporgtp/countries/india/states/jandk/terrorist_outfits/harkatul_mujahideen.htm [Google Scholar]

Taylor, A. (2021, August 30). Growth of opium trade may undermine Taliban pledge to kick the habit. Washington Post, p. A–12. [Google Scholar]

Wagner, R. H. (2007). War and the State: The theory of international politics (pp. 105–129). Ann Arbor: The University of Michigan Press. [Crossref], [Google Scholar]

Washington Post. (2021, September 11). Disputed Nord Stream pipeline completed. Washington Post, p. A–17 [Google Scholar]

World Population Review. (2021). Afghanistan. Retrieved from https://worldpopulationreview.com/countries/afghanistan-population [Google Scholar]

Chapter 2: China's Engagement with Taliban after American Withdrawal: Implications for Pakistan. Jalal Ud Din Kakar and Asad ur Rehman

Abdul, L. (2021, Sep 14). "Afghanistan's Muttaqi urges continue to Engage with new Goverment".

Aljazera. Retrieved from www.aljazeera.com/news/2021/9/14

Acemoglu, D. (2021, Aug 20). "Why nation building failed in Afghanistan". Project Syndicate. Retrieved from https://www.project-syndicate.org/

Amy. (2021). "Militant group ETM, which has been targetted by China, remains active in Afghanistan". South China Morning Post. Retrieved from https://www.scmp.com/weekasia/politics/article/3143053/militant-group-etim-which-has-been-targeted-china-remains-active

Attanayake, D., & Haiqi, Z. (2021, Aug 25). "Understanding China in Taliban-led Afghanistan". IndoPacific Affairs. Retrieved from https://www.airuniversity.af.edu/JIPA/Display/Article/2746135/understanding-china-in-talibanled-afghanistan/

Barr, h. (2021, Sep 29). "List of Taliban policies violating Women's Right in Afghanistan". Human Right Watch. Retrieved from https://www.hrw.org/news/2021/09/29/list-taliban-policies-violatingwomens-rights-afghanistan

Bura, S. (2012). "Geo-economics and Startegy. Routledge, 1-13. Retrieved from http;//www.tandfonline.com

CGNT. (2021, June 4). "China-Afghan, Pakistan reach 8-piont consensus on Promoting Peace Process".

GGNT. Retrieved from https://newsaf.cgtn.com/news/2021-06-04/China-Afghanistan-Pakistanreach-8-point-consensus-10NWx1Q50Iw/index.html

Chaudhury, D. R. (2021, Sep 07). ETIM's move to align with ISIS Khorasan or the ISIS-K. Economic Times. Retrieved from https://m.economictimes.com/?back=

Cordesman, A. H. (2021, March 29). "China and Iran; A major chinese gain Chinese Gain in White Area

Warfare in the Gulf". Retrieved from CISI. Center for Strategic and International Studies: https://www.csis.org/analysis/china-and-iran-major-chinese-gain-white-area-warfare-gulf

Dutta, P. K. (2021, August 17). "Najeeb ullah and Gahni: Taliban and a tale of tow Afghan presidents, 25 years apart". Retrieved from https://www.middleeast-eye.net/opinion/afghanistan-us-chinaEmily, S. (2021, Aug 21). "The history of U.S. intervention in Afghanistan, from the cold war to 9/11". VOX. Retrieved from https://www.vox.com/world/22634008/

Fassihi, F., & Myers, S. L. (2021, Mar 27). "China, With $400 billion in Iran Deal Could Deepen Influnce in Mideast.". Retrieved from New York Time: https://www.nytimes.com/2021/03/27/world/middleeast/china-iran-deal.html

Gillani, D. (2020). The US in Afghhanisan; consequences of an ultimate withdrawal. South Asian Studies, 34(2).

Glazbrook, D. (2021, September 20). "A stable Afghanistan is a huge win for China. That's why the US won't allow it". Retrieved from https://www.middleeast-eye.net/opinion/afghanistan-us-chinaGreen, M. J. (2018, April 2). "China's Maritime Silk Road; Strategic and economic implications". Retrieved from

Center for Strategic and Interntional Studies: https://www.csis.org/analysis/chinas-maritimesilk-road

Haass, R. N. (2021). America's Withdrawal of Chioce. Retrieved from Council on Foreign Relation: https://www.cfr.org/article/americas-withdrawal-choice

Hass, R. (2021, March 1). "How China is respomding to escalating strategic competition with US".Brooking. Retrieved from https://www.brookings.edu/articles/how-china-is-responding-toescalating-strategic-competition-with-the-us/Hass, R. (2021, Aug 18). "How China wil seek profit from the Taliban takeover in Afghanistan. Brooking. Retrieved from https://www.brookings.edu/blog/order-from-chaos/2021/08/18/

Hillman, J., & Sacks, D. (2021, March 30). " The China-Pakitan Economic Corridor- Hard realiy Greets BRI'ss Signature Intitative". Retrieved from Council on Foreign Relations: https://www.cfr.org/blog/china-pakistan-economic-corridor-hard-reality-greets-bris-signatureinitiative

House, The White. (2021). "Five Piont Agenda On Afghanistan, Washington,D.C". Whit House. Retrieved from The White House: ://www.whitehouse.gov/briefing-room/statementsreleases/2021/08/14/statement-by-president-joe-biden-on-afghanistan

Kaur, V. (2021). The Pakistan Factor in China's Afghanistan Foreign Policy: Emerging regional Faultlines Amid US-Withdrawal". The Middle East Institute, 1-24.

Kissinger, H. (2021, Aug 25). "The future of American power, Why American failed in Afghanistan". Retrieved from The Economist: https://www.economist.com/by-invitation/2021/08/25/henrykissinger-on-why-america-failed-in-afghanistan

Lodhi, M. (2021). Back to The Future. Retrieved from Dawn News: https://www.dawn.com/news/1638306/back-to-the-future.

M.Lederer, E. (2021, Oct 11). "United Nation: Afghanistan faces' make-or-break moment". Yahoo News. Retrieved from https://news.yahoo.com/un-chief-afghanistan-faces-break185544379.html?fr=sycsrp_catchall

Maizland, L. (2021, Sep 15). "The Taliban in Afghanistan". Retrieved from https://www.cfr.org/backgrounder/taliban-afghanistan

MFAPRC. (2021). "Wang Yi meets with Acting Deputy Prime Minister of Afghan Taliban's Interm Goverment Mullah Ghani Bardar". Ministry of Foreign Affairs, the People's Republic of China. Retrieved from www.fmprc.gov.cn/mfs_

Mir, N. (2021). "Geo-political Pakistan". University of the Punjab Press.

Nagesh , A. (2020, August 25). "Afghanistan economy in crisis after Taliban tale-over". BBC NEWS. Retrieved from https://www.bbc.com/news/world-asia-58328246

RFERL. (2021, Sep 21). "Taliban says China will be 'Main Partner" to rebuild Afghanistan.". Gahandara Afghanistan. Retrieved from http//gandahara.rferl. org

Schar, A. J., & Leffler, D. D. (2021, Aug 14). "Time is running out for Afghanistan". Retrieved from Tolo News Afghanistan: https://tolonews.com/opinion-174229

Sun, Y. (2020, April 8). "China's Strategic Assessment of Afghanistan". War on the Rock. Retrieved from warontherocks.com/2020/04/chinas-strategic-assessment-of-afghanistan/

Thames, K. (2021). "My Future is Now: An Afghan Women from a Threatened Minority wrestles with what happens When the U.S. withdraws. Time.

Thelked , E., & Easterly, G. (2021). "Afghan-Pak ties and Future stblity in Afghanistan". United States Institute of Peace, 175.

Wigell, M. (2018). "Geo-Economics as Concept And Practice in International Relations". FIFA Working Paper, 102-12. Retrieved from https://storage. googleapis.com/upi-live/2018/04/wp102_geoeconomics.pdf

Xiaoqian, F. (2021, Aug 23). " Free for All" Full text. Retrieved from China Institute of Contemporary International Relations.: http://www.cicir.ac.cn/ NEW/en-us/opinion.html?id=971bf2f8-bf96-4c47-928b-af7fd8b70ff9.

Chapter 3: China's New Engagement with Afghanistan after the Withdrawal. Feng Zhang

1. Garver JW. China's Quest: The History of the Foreign Relations of the People's Republic of China. Oxford: Oxford University Press. 2015; 416. DOI: https:// doi.org/10.1093/acprof:oso/9780190261054.001.0001

2. Clarke M. "One Belt, One Road" and China's Emerging Afghanistan Dilemma. Australian Journal of International Affairs. 2016; 70(5): 563–579. DOI: https://doi.org/10.1080/10357718.2016.1183585

3. Hirono M. China's Conflict Mediation and the Durability of the Principle of Non-Interference: The Case of Post-2014 Afghanistan. The China Quarterly. 2019; 239: 614–634. DOI: https://doi.org/10.1017/S0305741018001753

4. Zhu Y. China's Afghanistan Policy since 9/11. Asian Survey. 2018; 58(2): 281–301. DOI: https://doi.org/10.1525/as.2018.58.2.281

5. Zhao H. Afghanistan and China's New Neighborhood Diplomacy. International Affairs. 2016; 92(4): 891–908. DOI: https://doi.org/10.1111/1468-2346.12654

6. Weitz R. China and Afghanistan after the NATO Withdrawal. Washington, DC: The Jamestown Foundation; 2015.

7. Stanzel A. Fear and Loathing on the New Silk Road: Chinese Security in Afghanistan and Beyond. Berlin: European Council on Foreign Relations; 2018.

8. Yan X. From Keeping a Low Profile to Striving for Achievement. Chinese Journal of International Politics. 2014; 7(2): 153–184. DOI: https://doi.org/10.1093/cjip/pou027

9. Zhang F. China as a Global Force. Asia & the Pacific Policy Studies. 2016; 3(1): 117–125. DOI: https://doi.org/10.1002/app5.115

10. Wang Y. Offensive for Defensive: The Belt and Road Initiative and China's New Grand Strategy. The Pacific Review. 2016; 29(3): 455–463. DOI: https://doi.org/10.1080/09512748.2016.1154690

11. Fallon T. The New Silk Road: Xi Jinping's Grand Strategy for Eurasia. American Foreign Policy Interests. 2015; 37: 140–147. DOI: https://doi.org/10.1080/10803920.2015.1056682

12. Roy MS. Afghanistan and the Belt and Road Initiative: Hope, Scope, and Challenges. Asia Policy. 2017; 24: 103–109. DOI: https://doi.org/10.1353/asp.2017.0027

13. Zhu Y, Wei L. Afuhan anquan xingshi jiqi dui sichou zhilu jingji dai de yingxiang (Afghanistan's Security Prospects and Implications for the Silk Road Economic Belt). Nanya yanjiu (South Asia Studies). 2017; 3: 100–116.

14. Mei X. Dui houmeiguo shidai afuhan jingji buke mangmu kuanghuan (Do Not Blindly Revel in Afghanistan's Economy in the Post-American Era) [Internet]; 2021 Aug 18 [cited 2022 Feb 10]. Available from: http://www.aisixiang.com/data/128108.html.

15. Zhu Y. Professor of Lanzhou University. Author Interview. January 2022.

16. Small A. The China-Pakistan Axis: Asia's New Geopolitics. Oxford: Oxford University Press; 2015: 160. DOI: https://doi.org/10.1093/acprof:oso/9780190210755.001.0001

17. Small A. From Bystander to Peacemaker: China, the Taliban, and Reconciliation in Afghanistan. Berlin Policy Journal; 2015 April 27.

18. Risen J. U.S. Identifies Vast Mineral Riches in Afghanistan [Internet]; 2010 June 13 [cited 2022 Feb 07]. Available from: https://www.nytimes.com/2010/06/14/world/asia/14minerals.html.

19. China's Ministry of Commerce: zhongguo-afuhan jingmao hezuo jiankuang, 2020.01–12 (Brief Introduction of China-Afghanistan Economic and Trade Cooperation, January to December 2022) [Internet]; [posted 2021 May 03; cited 2022 Feb 07]. Available from: http://yzs.mofcom.gov.cn/article/t/202103/20210303042321.shtml.

20. Ministry of Foreign Affairs: Wang Yi huijian afuhan taliban zhengzhi weiyuanhui fuzeren Baradar (Wang Yi Meets with Baradar of the Afghan Taliban's Political Committee) [Internet]; [posted 2021 July 28; cited 2022 Feb 07]. Available from: https://www.mfa.gov.cn/wjbzhd/202107/t20210728_9137717.shtml.

21. Ministry of Foreign Affairs: Wang Yi huijian afuhan taliban linshi zhengfu daily fuzongli Baradar (Wang Yi Meets with the Acting Deputy Prime Minister of the Interim Government of the Afghan Taliban Baradar) [Internet]; [posted 2021 Oct 26; cited 2022 Feb 07]. Available from: https://www.mfa.gov.cn/wjbzhd/202110/t20211026_10035260.shtml.

22. Ministry of Foreign Affairs: Wang Yi chuxi dierci afuhan linguo waizhanghui (Wang Yi Attends the Second Foreign Ministers' Meeting of Afghanistan's Neighboring Countries) [Internet]; [posted 2021 Oct 28; cited 2022 Feb 07]. Available from: https://www.mfa.gov.cn/wjbzhd/202110/t20211028_10348761.shtml.

23. Ministry of Foreign Affairs: Xi Jinping chuxi shanghai hezuo zuzhi he jiti anquan tiaoyue zuzhi chengyuanguo lingdaoren afuhan wenti fenghui (Xi Jinping attends Shanghai Cooperation Organization and Collective Security Treaty Organization Leaders' Summit on Afghanistan) [Internet]; [posted 2021 Sep 17; cited 2022 Feb 08]. Available from: https://www.mfa.gov.cn/zyxw/202109/t20210917_9604460.shtml.

24. Ministry of Foreign Affairs: Wang Yi guowu weiyuan jian waizhang zai afuhan linguo waizhanghui shang de jianghua (State Councilor and Foreign Minister Wang Yi's Speech at the Conference of the Foreign Ministers of Afghanistan's Neighboring Countries) [Internet]; [posted 2021 Sep 08; cited 2022 Feb 08]. Available from: https://www.mfa.gov.cn/wjbzhd/202109/t20210908_9604940.shtml.

25. Detsch J. 'Not His Money': Biden Splits Afghanistan's Reserves [Internet]; 2022 Feb 11 [cited 2022 Feb 13]. Available from: https://foreignpolicy.com/2022/02/11/biden-afghanistan-currencytaliban/?utm_source=PostUp&utm_medium=email&utm_campaign=Editors percent20Picks percent20 OC&utm_term=39415&tpcc=Editors percent20Picks percent20OC.

26. Ministry of Foreign Affairs: Wang Yi chuxi zhongebayi siguo afuhan wenti feizhengshi huiyi (Wang Yi Attends China-Russia-Pakistan-Iran Informal Meeting on Afghanistan) [Internet]; [posted 2021 Sep 17; cited 2022 Feb 09]. Available from: https://www.mfa.gov.cn/web/wjbz_673089/xghd_673097/202109/t20210917_9883084.shtml.

27. Ministry of Foreign Affairs: Wang Yi zhuchi zhongaba sanfang waizhang duihua (Wang Yi Chairs China-Afghanistan-Pakistan Trilateral Foreign Ministers' Dialogue) [Internet]; [posted 2021 Jun 06; cited 2022 Feb 08]. Available from:https://www.mfa.gov.cn/web/wjbz_673089/xghd_673097/202106/t20210604_9175321.shtml.

28. Ministry of Foreign Affairs: Wang Yi tan afuhan wenti (Wang Yi on Problems in Afghanistan) [Internet]; [posted 2021 Jul 03; cite 2022 Feb 09]. Available from: https://www.mfa.gov.cn/web/wjbz_673089/xghd_673097/202107/t20210703_9175385.shtml.

29. Ministry of Foreign Affairs: Wang Yi: meiguo ruguo buneng chedi gaixiangengzhang, jiu shibi cong zai afuhan de shibai zouxiang gengda de shibai (Wang Yi: the United States Will Suffer Even Greater Defeat than Its Defeat in Afghanistan If It Does Not Completely Change Its Approach) [Internet]; [posted 2021 Sep 04; cited 2022 Feb 09]. Available from: https://www.mfa.gov.cn/web/wjbz_673089/xghd_673097/202109/t20210904_9175495.shtml.

30. The White House: United States Strategic Approach to the People's Republic of China [Internet]; [posted 2020 May 26; cited 2022 Feb 10]. Available from: https://trumpwhitehouse.archives.gov/ wp-content/uploads/2020/05/U.S.-Strategic-Approach-to-The-Peoples-Republic-of-China-Report5.24v1.pdf.

31. The White House: Interim National Security Strategic Guidance [Internet]; [posted 2021 Mar 03; cited 2022 Feb 10]. Available from: https://www.whitehouse.gov/wp-ontent/uploads/2021/03/NSC-1v2.pdf.

32. Zhou B. In Afghanistan, China Is Ready to Step into the Void [Internet]; 2021 Aug 20 [cited 2022 Feb 10]. Available from: https://www.nytimes.com/2021/08/20/opinion/china-afghanistan-taliban.html.

33. Zhang J. Meiguo liuxia afuhan "sida" xianjing (The United States Has Left Four Major Traps in Aghanistan). Shijie zhishi (World Knowledge). 2021; 8: 70–71.

34. Sun Y. China's Strategic Assessment of Afghanistan [Internet]; 2020 Apr 08 [cited 2022 Feb 13]. Available from: https://warontherocks.com/2020/04/chinas-strategic-assessment-of-afghanistan/.

35. Zhang F, Lebow RN. Taming Sino-American Rivalry. Oxford: Oxford University Press. 2020; 1. DOI: https://doi.org/10.1093/oso/9780197521946.003.0001.

Chapter 4: Writing war, and the politics of poetic conversation. James Caron & Salman Khan

1   We are both scholars based in London. Salman grew up in Malakand during the conflict this essay addresses and, like many others in this highly poetry-aware society, composed poetry about it in a diary. We both noticed a disjuncture in reading about this war in academic spaces, versus how people in our experience expressed and reflected upon their experiences in Swat and its broader region. We wanted to explore how we could write about this war in a way that would address the latter experience. Poetry seemed a natural route to us. All poems in this article are translated from Pashto to English by James, in consultation with Salman. Interview excerpts have been translated from Pashto to English by Salman in consultation with James. We conducted all interviews together.

2   Bhambra 2014.

3   Barkawi 2016.

4   Barkawi and Brighton 2011; 127.

5   Tillotson and Mustafa 2020.

6   Rivas 2020; Hyndman 2019; Sharp 2011.

7   Rubaii 2018; 6.

8   See Qadir and Ahmed 2013; Raza 2014. We should note that we did not engage poetry that was transparently part of hegemonic or counterhegemonic projects, like poetry that was directly sponsored by liberal peacebuilding initiatives, although we do mention it here. Similarly, we did not engage the vast body of Taliban songs that also arose in this period. The reasons for this latter choice were compounded by risk and ethical considerations. On this, though, see Caron 2012; two of the sources therein are drawn from this conflict.

9   Districts Swat, Malakand, and Lower Dir.

10   This article draws on 11 of our interviews, conducted electronically due to the Covid-19 pandemic. We have reconstituted quotations from notes in most cases, due to various sensitivities. Swat remains tense. Some statements, if attributed to specific individuals, might jeopardize respondents' places in networks. Others might bring unwanted state or other political attention. If individuals spoke about themselves, however, and said we should indicate this, we have done so.

11   We use the term "literary formation" following Mir 2010: "those individuals who shared practices of producing, circulating, performing, and consuming ... literary texts" (6).

12   Conducting these interviews electronically meant interviewees could calibrate how they would be seen and heard. While we as researchers were transparent about our positions and our professional interests, this medium fostered much more emotionally rich conversations across lines of gender, nationality, and other sites of belonging than either of us had experienced before when conducting interviews in person.

13   Khanna 2020, 4.

14   G. W. Bush. Address to a Joint Session of Congress. Sept. 20, 2001. https://georgewbush-whitehouse.archives.gov/news/releases/2001/09/20010920-8.html. Accessed 12/30/2021

15   Naqvi 2011.

16   Recited in interview, July 31; 2020.

17   Tahir 2010, 4.

18   Interview, August 14; 2020.

19   Devji 2009

20   Tahir 2010, 5.

21 This refers to the Army's siege on the Red Mosque/Jāmiʻa Ḥafṣa compound in Islamabad, amidst accusations that weapons were be8ing stockpiled in the men's and women's madrasas located in the compound (just opposite the military's intelligence headquarters). This was the first time that army violence played out in real-time in national media, and its location not on the frontier but in the capital led to a newfound skepticism about the War on Terror among Pakistan's metropolitan citizens.

22 August 11; 2020.

23 Arzu 2018, 69.

24 Poetic-images: khayal.

25 Arzu 2018; 68.

26 Majeed 2016, 73. See also various contributions in Marsden and Hopkins 2013 on the roots of Taliban social history in Swat and elsewhere in Pakistan.

27 This interviewee, who lived in Swat's center of Mingora during the war, requested anonymity for reasons of sensitivity, but also requested that this excerpt from our interview be printed.

28 Interview, Anonymous, July 25, 2020.

29 Ahmad (2019) calls this phenomenon a "technology of destruction" that atomizes the present and severs it from previous subjective histories and geographies, rendering any existing sense of causality unintelligible.

30 This is similar to what Kusha Sefat notes in his work on language, materiality, and the person/rule of Khomeini in revolutionary Iran. See Sefat 2020.

31 The "faculty of image-creation" (takhayyul) is the level of cognition that relies on a creative recombination of concrete sensory-based mental images, rather than a discursive processing of abstract concepts. See Key 2018; Rahman 2012.

32 Arzu 2018; 60.

33 See Pritchett 1994.

34 Interview, Anonymous, July 25; 2020.

35 Anźor 1993.

36 See Shahid 2013.

37 On gham-xādī in Swat see Grima 1992.

38 Press release, BKTEF, November 30; 2010.

39 Kashwan, Maclean, and García-López 2018.

40 Naviwala 2010.

41 Kluttz and Fligstein 2016.

42 Ulusyar, interview, July 30, 2020.

43 AkzoNobel Foundation was a corporate social responsibility body attached to Imperial Chemicals Industries Ltd. (Pakistan) from 2008 to 2012, the time during which ICI Pakistan was a subsidiary of the multinational AkzoNobel Corporation.

44 None of those who participated in this effort would name the project or its donors.

45 July 31; 2020.

46 Naqvi 2011; 116.

47 Mustafa, Anwar, and Sawas 2019.

48 August 11, 2020.

49 We thank Ulasyar for sharing these videos from his archive.

50 See, among others, Abasin Yousafzai's free-verse contribution that opens the volume and sets its tone.

51 As performed by Amjad Shahzad, November 1, 2012; video courtesy of Usman Ulasyar.

52 Again, thanks to Usman Ulasyar for sharing his archived video of this event.

53 https://www.facebook.com/277217232328165/posts/807872102596006, accessed August 17, 2020.

54 https://twitter.com/TuriNaeem/status/1139966949025300480, accessed August 17; 2020.

55 Pukhtun 2019.

56 Ali 2010.

57 Yépez 2007.

58 Anzaldúa 1987.

59 See Mallick 2020.

References

Ahmad, Mahvish.. 2019. Destruction as Rule: Containment, Censuring and Confusion in Pakistani Balochistan." PhD Dissertation, Sociology, Cambridge University, Cambridge, UK. [Google Scholar]

Ali, Nosheen. 2010. "Poetry, Power, Protest." Comparative Studies of South Asia, Africa, and the Middle East 32 (1): 13–24. [Crossref], [Google Scholar]

Anzaldúa, Gloria. 1987. Borderlands/La Frontera: The New Mestiza. San Francisco, CA: Aunt Lute Books. [Google Scholar]

Anźor, Zarīn. 1993. Da Ŝawr pa Trāzhedey ke Farhang, Adabiyāt, aw Azadey. Peshawar: Da Āzād Afghānistān da Līkwālo Ṭolana. [Google Scholar]

Arzu, Neelum. 2018. Da Sāzūno Bārān. Mingora: Noor. [Google Scholar]

Barkawi, Tarak. 2016. "Decolonizing War." European Journal of International Security 1 (2): 199–214. [Crossref], [Web of Science °], [Google Scholar]

Barkawi, Tarak, and Shane Brighton. 2011. "Powers of War: Fighting, Knowledge, and Critique." International Political Sociology 5 (2): 126–143. [Crossref], [Web of Science °], [Google Scholar]

Bhambra, Gurminder. 2014. Connected Sociologies. London: Bloomsbury. [Crossref], [Google Scholar]

Caron, James. 2012. "Taliban, Real and Imagined." In Under the Drones: Modern Lives in the Afghanistan-Pakistan Borderlands, edited by Shahzad Bashir and Robert Crews, 60–82. Cambridge, MA: Harvard University Press. [Crossref], [Google Scholar]

Daanish, Bakhtzada. 2019. Za ba na Līwanai Keġam!. Peshawar: Mayhan Khparandūya Ṭolana. [Google Scholar]

Devji, Faisal. 2009. "Pakistan, the Privatized State." The Guardian, October 16. Accessed August 17, 2020: https://www.theguardian.com/commentisfree/2009/oct/16/pakistan-government-militants. [Google Scholar]

Grima, Benedicte. 1992. The Performance of Emotion among Paxtun Women. Austin: University of Texas Press. [Google Scholar]

Hyndman, Jennifer. 2019. "Unsettling Feminist Geopolitics: Feminist Political Geographies of Violence and Displacement." Gender, Place, and Culture 26 (1): 3–29. [Taylor & Francis Online], [Web of Science °], [Google Scholar]

Kashwan, P., L. M. Maclean, and G. A. García-López. 2019. "Rethinking Power and Institutions in the Shadows of Neoliberalism." World Development 120: 133–146. [Crossref], [Web of Science °], [Google Scholar]

Key, Alexander. 2018. Language Between God and the Poets. Berkeley: University of California Press. [Google Scholar]

Khanna, Neetu. 2020. The Visceral Logics of Decolonization. Durham, NC: Duke University Press. [Google Scholar]

Kluttz, Daniel, and Neil Fligstein. 2016. "Variety of Field Theories." In Handbook of Contemporary Sociology, edited by Seth Abrutyn, 185–204. Cham: Springer. [Crossref], [Google Scholar]

Majeed, Tabassum. 2016. Insurgency in Swat. Mingora, Pakistan: Shoaib Sons. [Google Scholar]

Mallick, Ayaz. 2020. "From Partisan Universal to Concrete Universal? The Pashtun Tahaffuz Movement in Pakistan." Antipode 52 (6): 1774–1793. [Crossref], [Web of Science °], [Google Scholar]

MAL (Mrastiyal Adabi Likwal). 2009. Sawe Sawe Wāwra (Batkhela and Peshawar: MAL and SPO). [Google Scholar]

Marsden, Magnus, and Ben Hopkins, eds. 2013. Beyond Swat: History, Society, and Economy Along the Afghanistan-Pakistan Frontier. London: Hurst. [Google Scholar]

Mir, Farina. 2010. The Social Space of Language: Vernacular Culture in British Colonial Punjab. Berkeley: University of California Press. [Crossref], [Google Scholar]

Mustafa, D., N. Anwar, and A. Sawas. 2019. "Gender, Global Terror, and Everyday Violence in Urban Pakistan." Political Geography 69: 54–64. [Crossref], [Web of Science ®], [Google Scholar]

Naqvi, Tahir. 2011. "Private Satellite Media and the Geo-Politics of Moderation in Pakistan." In South Asian Media Cultures, edited by Shakuntala Banaji, 109–122. London: Anthem Press. [Google Scholar]

Naviwala, Nadia. 2010. Harnessing Local Capacity: US Assistance and NGOs in Pakistan. Harvard Kennedy School Policy Exercise, USAID Afghanistan-Pakistan Task Force. Accessed September 14, 2017: http://www.hks.harvard.edu/cchrp/sbhrap/forum/article_0003/HarnessingLocalCapacity.pdf. [Google Scholar]

Pritchett, Frances. 1994. Nets of Awareness. Berkeley: University of California Press. [Google Scholar]

Pukhtun (staff writer, anon.). 2019. "Da Alif Jān Khaṭake Nazm aw da Taḥrīk-i Inṣāf Burqʻa." Pukhtun, n.d., accessed August 17, 2020: http://pakhtoonmagazine.com/pukhtoonwriters/pakhtoon/2054/. [Google Scholar]

Qadir, Altaf, and Ishtiaq Ahmed. 2013. "The Reflection of Swat Crisis in Folk Poetry." Pakistan Perspectives 18 (2): 103–120. [Google Scholar]

Rahman, Fazlur. 2012. "Avicenna, [Section] vi: Psychology." Encyclopædia Iranica III (1): 83–84. [Google Scholar]

Raza, Aamer. 2014. "Voices of Resistance: Pashto Poetry as Bulwark Against Extremism." In Dynamics of Change in Conflict Societies: Proceedings, edited by Ayub Jan and Shahida Aman, 61–70. Peshawar: University of Peshawar. [Google Scholar]

Rivas, Althea-Maria. 2020. Security, Development, and Violence in Afghanistan: Everyday Stories of Intervention. Abingdon: Routledge. [Crossref], [Google Scholar]

Rubaii, Kali. 2018. "Counterinsurgency and the Ethical Life of Material Things in Iraq's Anbar Province." PhD Dissertation. Anthropology, University of California, Santa Cruz. [Google Scholar]

Sefat, Kusha. 2020. "Things and Terms." International Political Sociology 14 (2): 175–195. [Crossref], [Web of Science ®], [Google Scholar]

Shahid, Taimoor. 2013. "The Politics of Enchantment." Annual of Urdu Studies 28: 215–248. [Google Scholar]

Sharp, Joanne. 2011. "A Subaltern Critical Geopolitics of the War on Terror: Post-colonial Security in Tanzania." Geoforum; Journal of Physical, Human, and Regional Geosciences 42: 297–305. [Crossref], [Web of Science °], [Google Scholar]

Tahir, Didar. 2010. Or pa Chīnārūno. Baṭkhela: Mazhar Press. [Google Scholar]

Tillotson, Matthew, and Daanish Mustafa. 2021. "An Arendtian Geopolitics: Action, Power, and the Deferral of Work." Progress in Human Geography 45 (3): 548–565. [Crossref], [Web of Science °], [Google Scholar]

Yépez, Heriberto. 2007. "La frontera como falla." Metapolítica 11 (52): 49–53. [Google Scholar]

Chapter 5: The Taliban, IS-K and the Haqqani Network

1. Yoram Schweitzer and Sari Goldstein Ferber, in their research paper (Al-Qaeda and the Internationalization of Suicide Terrorism. Jaffee Center for Strategic Studies, Tel Aviv University. Memorandum No. 78 November 2005

2. Ellen Tveteraas (Under the Hood–Learning and Innovation in the Islamic State's Suicide Vehicle Industry, Studies in Conflict & Terrorism-2022

3. Michael A. Peters in his research paper (Declinism' and discourses of decline-the end of the war in Afghanistan and the limits of American power, Educational Philosophy and Theory, DOI: 10.1080/00131857.2021.1982694.

4. Afghanistan: Taliban Deprive Women of Livelihoods, Identity: Severe Restrictions, Harassment, Fear in Ghazni Province-18 January, 2022)

5. Kate Clark (Afghanistan's conflict in 2021 (2): Republic collapse and Taliban victory in the long-view of history. Afghanistan Analysts Network--30 Dec 2021.

6. Afghanistan: Taliban Kill, 'Disappear' Ex-Officials: Raids Target Former Police, Intelligence Officers- November 30, 2021

7. Qasim Jan, Yi Xie, Muhammad Habib Qazi, Zahid Javid Choudhary and Baha Ul Haq in their research paper (Examining the role of Pakistan's national curriculum textbook discourses on normalising the Taliban's violence in the USA's Post 9/11 war on terror in South Waziristan, Pakistan. British Journal of Religious Education-2022.

8. Eric Schmitt, "ISIS Branch Poses Biggest Immediate Terrorist Threat to Evacuation in Kabul", November 3, 2021, the New York Times

9. Clayton Sharb, Danika Newlee and the CSIS iDeas Lab in their joint work (Islamic State Khorasan (IS-K). Center for Strategic and International Studies-2018.

10. Mohamed Mokhtar Qandi in his paper (Challenges to Taliban Rule and Potential Impacts for the Region: Internal and external factors are weakening

the Taliban, making the group's long term stability increasingly unlikely. Fikra Forum. The Washington Institute for Near East Policy-09 February 2022.

11. Amira Jadoon, Abdul Sayed and Andrew Mines in their research paper (The Islamic State Threat in Taliban Afghanistan: Tracing the Resurgence of Islamic State Khorasan. The Combating Terrorism Center at West Point. January 2022, Volum 15, Issue-1.

12. April 17, ISIS called on all fighters around the world to carry out "big and painful" attacks targeting officials and soldiers". Salam Times

13. Roshni Kapur in his paper (The Persistent ISKP Threat to Afghanistan: On China's Doorstep. Middle East Institute-January 6, 2022

14. Editor of Terrorism Monitor. Jacob Zenn in his article (Islamic State in Khorasan Province's One-Off Attack in Uzbekistan. Volium XX. Issue 9, 06 May 2022.

15. Amy Kazmin in her article (Isis-K insurgency jeopardises Taliban's grip on Afghanistan: New rulers accused of betraying Islam by jihadis intent on creating ideologically pure caliphate-October, 26, 2021.

16. Salman Rafi Sheikh in his article (Eight months on, Taliban's rule is far from stable: Resistance groups are mounting an increasingly potent challenge to the Taliban and may have Pakistan's clandestine support-Asia Times, May 2, 2022.

Chapter 6: Taliban, Tablighi Jamaat and Terrorism in Kazakhstan

1. Scott Ritter, RT News, 28 April, 2020

2. Leonid Gusev. 01 February 2020

3. Diplomat analysis. 20 September 2016

4. Christopher McIntosh and Ian Storey 20 November 2019

5. Ibid

6. Simon Saradzhyan (Russia Matters, Simon Saradzhyan, August 06, 2019

7. Graham Allison (September/October 2004

8. October 2017, Columb Strack

9. Connor Dilleen. Asia Times-30 May 2019

10. Uran Botobekov. The Diplomat, January 10, 2017

11. Nick Mucerino (November 5, 2018

12. Ibid

13. The Diplomat, 08 April 2020

14. ISIS magazine (Dabiq-May 2015

15. 25 March 2016, Daily Telegraph

16. Newsweek's Daily Beast blog provided another version of an overspill, already apparently happening in 2010.

17. Leonid Gusev, an expert of Institute of International Studies, Moscow State Institute of International Relations of the Ministry of Foreign Affairs of the Russian Federation (MGIMO) has noted some consternating cooperative measures and planning's of the extremist groups of Central Asia

18. Muhammad Wajeeh, a Research Associate at Department of Development Studies, COMSATS Institute of Information Technology, Abbottabad Pakistan. Nuclear Terrorism: A Potential Threat to World's Peace and Security- JSSA Vol II, No. 2

Chapter 7: Woman, War, and the Politics of Emancipation in Afghanistan. Afzal Ashraf and Caroline Kennedy-Pipe

1.   We should note here the valuable contributions made by feminist scholars in alerting us to the multiple issues of gender and power. See Jacqui True, 'Gender Mainstreaming in Global Public Policy' International Feminist Journal of Politics 5. No.3.2003. pp 368–96.

2.   There has been a 'Shocking Disregard for Civilians as US drone strike adds to death toll.' See Amnesty International. http//www.amnesty. org>latest>news>2019>09.

Notes

1. Kennedy C, Dingli S. Gender and Security. In: Alan, C (ed.). Contemporary Security Studies. Oxford University Press. 2022; 159. DOI: https://doi.org/10.1093/hepl/9780198804109.003.0011

2. Sjoberg L. Gender, justice, and the wars in Iraq: a feminist reformulation of just war theory. Lanham,Md. Lexington Books; 2006.

3. Amiri Rina. Muslim Women as Symbols — and Pawns. The New York Times [Internet]; 2001 Nov 27 [cited 2022 Mar 7]. Available from: https://www.nytimes.com/2001/11/27/opinion/muslim-womenas-symbols-and-pawns.html.

4. Bush LW. Radio Address Crawford, TX [Internet]; 2001 [cited 2022 Mar 2]. Available from: https://www.bushcenter.org/publications/articles/2013/02/radio-address-by-mrs-laura-w-bush-crawford-txnovember-17-2001.html.

5. Lifting the Veil (Vol.158, No-24-videos) [Internet]. Time Magazine; 2001 [cited 2022 Mar 1]. Available from: http://content.com>time>magazine.

6. Berry K. The Symbolic Use of Afghan Women in the War on Terror. Humboldt Journal of Social Relations [Internet]. 2003; 27(2): 137–60. Available from: http://www.jstor.org/stable/23524156

7. Taking Cover: Women in Post-Taliban Afghanistan [Internet]; 2002 May [cited 2022 Mar 1]. Available from: https://www.hrw.org/legacy/backgrounder/wrd/afghan-women-2k2.htm.

8. Ridley Y. Feminists have scored an own goal over Afghanistan's 'Me Too' moment – Middle East Monitor [Internet]. MEM; 2021 [cited 2022 Feb 26]. Available from: https://www.middleeastmonitor. com/20211201-feminists-have-scored-an-own-goal-over-afghanistans-me-too-moment/.

9. Kennedy-Pipe C, Stanley P. Rape in war: Lessons of the Balkan conflicts in the 1990s. The International Journal of Human Rights [Internet]. 2000 Sep [cited 2022 Mar 2]; 4(3–4): 67–84. Available from: https://www.tandfonline. com/action/journalInformation?journalCode=fjhr20.   DOI:https://doi. org/10.1080/13642980008406893

10. Honour among them. Economist. 2006 Dec 23; 381(8509): 38–41.

11. Massell GJ. The surrogate proletariat: Moslem women and revolutionary strategies in Soviet Central Asia, 1919–1929. Princeton, New Jersey: Princetone University Press. 1974; 492.

12. Bhatt C. Hindu nationalism: origins, ideologies and modern myths. Oxford: Oxford: Berg; 2001.

13. Prey E, Spears K. What About the Boys: A Gendered Analysis of the U.S. Withdrawal and Bacha Bazi in Afghanistan. New Lines Institute [Internet]. New Lines Institute for Strategy and Policy; 2021 [cited 2022 Feb 27]. Available from: https://newlinesinstitute.org/afghanistan/what-about-the-boysa-gendered-analysis-of-the-u-s-withdrawal-and-bacha-bazi-in-afghanistan/.

14. Taub A. Authoritarianism: The political science that explains Trump – YouTube [Internet]. Vox.Com. 2016 [cited 2022 Feb 27]. Available from: https://www. youtube.com/watch?v=5YU9djt_CQM.

15. Taliban's luxury after long war: Indoor pool, sauna, gym in Dostum's palace now under new rulers – YouTube [Internet]. Hindustan Times; 2021 [cited 2022 Feb 27]. Available from: https://www.youtube. com/watch?v=Clej5iLY7nA.

16. Chayes S. 1962. Thieves of state: why corruption threatens global security. W. W. Norton & Company. 2016; 262.

17. Saner E. Malalai Joya|Afghanistan|The Guardian [Internet]. The Guardian. London; 2011 [cited 2022 Feb 27]. Available from: https://www.theguardian. com/world/2011/mar/08/malalai-joya-100-women.

18. Gannon K. Afghanistan Unbound. Foreign Affairs [Internet]. 2004; 83(3): 35–46. Available from:http://www.jstor.org/stable/20033974. DOI: https://doi.org/10.2307/20033974

19. Khalili L. Gendered practices of counterinsurgency. Review of International Studies [Internet]. 2011 Oct [cited 2022 Mar 1]; 37(4): 1471–91. Available from: https://www.cambridge.org/core/journals/review-of-international-studies/

article/abs/gendered-practices-of-counterinsurgency/7226869010B937A9A3 6D15DFCD92041F. DOI: https://doi.org/10.1017/S026021051000121X

20. Evangelista M. Gender, nationalism, and war: Conflict on the movie screen. Gender,Nationalism, and War: Conflict on the Movie Screen [Internet]; 2011 Jan 1 [cited 2022 Mar 1];1–289. Available from: https://www.cambridge.org/ core/books/gender-nationalism-and-war/C8211287405E473DE77F02B8744 4BD6D.

21. Stachowitsch S. Military Privatization and the Remasculinization of the State: Making the Link Between the Outsourcing of Military Security and Gendered State Transformations: [Internet].2013 Mar 22 [cited 2022 Mar 1]; 27(1): 74–94. Available from: https://journals. sagepub.com/doi/10.1177/0047117812470574. DOI: https://doi. org/10.1177/0047117812470574

22. Stachowitsch S. Professional Soldier, Weak Victim, Patriotic Heroine. [Internet]. 2013 Jun 1 [cited 2022 Mar 1]; 15(2): 157–76. Available from: https://www.tandfonline.com/doi/abs/10.1080/14616742.2012.699785. DOI: https://doi.org/10.1080/14616742.2012.699785

23. Wyatt CM, Dunn DH. Seeing Things Differently: Nang, Tura, Zolm, and Other Cultural Factors in Taliban Attitudes to Drones. Ethnopolitics [Internet]. 2019 Mar 15; 18(2): 201–17. DOI: https://doi.org/10.1080/17449057.2018.1527086

24. The Cost of Kill/Capture: Impact of the Night Raid Surge on Afghan Civilians [Internet]. Kabul; 2011 Sep [cited 2022 Mar 1]. Available from: https://www. opensocietyfoundations.org/publications/costkillcapture-impact-night-raid-surge-afghan-civilians.

25. Katt M. Blurred Lines: Cultural Support Teams in Afghanistan. Joint Force Quarterly 75 [Internet];2014 Oct [cited 2022 Mar 1]; Available from: https:// ndupress.ndu.edu/JFQ/Joint-Force-Quarterly-75/Article/577569/blurred-lines-cultural-support-teams-in-afghanistan/.

26. Landays: Poetry of Afghan Women [Internet]; 2013 [cited 2022 Mar 1]. Available from: https://static.poetryfoundation.org/o/media/landays.html.

27. van Creveld M. Men, women, and war. Do Women Belong in the Front Line? Cassell & Co; 2001.287 p.

28. Allen JR, Felbab-Brown V. The fate of women's rights in Afghanistan [Internet]; 2020 Sep [cited 2022 Feb 28]. Available from: https://www.brookings.edu/ essay/the-fate-of-womens-rights-inafghanistan/.

29. Rashid A. Taliban: The story of the Afghan warlords [Internet]. Pan; 2001 [cited 2022 Mar 1]. Availablefrom:https://books.google.com/ books?hl=en&lr=&id=_GR5tXpppS0C&oi=fnd&pg=PR7&dq=a hmed+rash id+taliban&ots=YqyiTDiHSR&sig=s1yKxQ-pnPWp8ZzI0aclRMlotJU.

30. CNN.com – Women gain attention in Iraqi elections – Jan 26, 2005 [Internet]. [cited 2022 Feb 28]. Available from: https://edition.cnn.com/2005/WORLD/meast/01/25/iraqi.women/index.html.

31. UNESCO (Paris). Cracking the code girls' and women's education in science, technology, engineering and mathematics (STEM); 2017 [cited 2022 Mar 7]. Available from: https://unesdoc.unesco.org/ark:/48223/pf0000253479.

32. Raising Gender Equality in STEM Careers – Scientific American [Internet]. [cited 2022 Mar 7]. Available from: https://www.scientificamerican.com/custom-media/a-new-dawn-for-innovation-in-qatar/raising-gender-equality-in-stem-careers/.

Chapter 8: Humour in jihadi rhetoric: comparative analysis of ISIS, Al-Qaeda, TTP, and the Taliban. Weeda Mehran, Megan Byrne, Ella Gibbs-Pearce, Archie Macfarlane, Jacob Minihane and Amy Ranger

1   These semantic changes can also be affected by linguistic differences across audiences. Humour is an advanced employment of language that is sensitive to and dependent upon listeners' knowledge of a joke's language. Puns, for example, are very difficult to translate effectively.

2   Ideologically heterogeneous, 'Islamogram' is a network of young Salafi propagators who use the Instagram platform but draw heavily on the visual and linguistic culture of 4Chan, Reddit and Discord. https://www.isdglobal.org/wp-content/uploads/2021/11/Islamogram.pdf, p. 12.

3   The akh-right is a specific set of young Salafis who use elements borrowed from white supremacists in their posts. https://www.isdglobal.org/wp-content/uploads/2021/11/Islamogram.pdf, p. 20.

4   Dabiq Magazine, Issue 13.

5   See for example, Dabiq Magazine, Issue 9.

6   Inspire Magazine, Issue 1.

7   Inspire Magazine, Issue 9.

8   Inspire Magazine, Issue 14.

9   Inspire Magazine, Issue 10; Rumiyah Magazine, Issue 12.

10   Rumiyah Magazine, Issue 10.

11   Dabiq Magazine, Issue 10.

12   Dabiq Magazine, Issue 5.

13   Ummah Magazine, Issue 2.

14   Voice of Hind Magazine, Issue 13.

15   Inspire Magazine, Issue 9.

16   Dabiq Magazine, Issue 4.

17 Dabiq Magazine, Issue 2.

18 Al Risalah Magazine Issue 2.

19 Al Risalah Magazine, Issue 1.

20 Al Risalah Magazine, Issue 3.

21 Dabiq Magazine, Issue 14.

22 Inspire Magazine, Issue 13.

23 Rumiyah Magazine, Issue 11.

References

Archakis, A., & Tsakona, V. (2005). Analyzing conversational data in GTVH terms: A new approach to the issue of identity construction via humor. Humor, 18(1), 41–68. https://doi.org/10.1515/humr.2005.18(1).41 [Crossref], [Google Scholar]

Arendt, H. (2018). Thinking without a banister: Essays in understanding, 1953–1975 (J. Kohn, Ed.). Knopf Doubleday. [Google Scholar]

Askanius, T. (2021). On frogs, monkeys, and execution memes: Exploring the humor-hate nexus at the intersection of neo-Nazi and alt-right movements in Sweden. Television & New Media, 22(2), 147–165. https://doi.org/10.1177/1527476420982234 [Crossref], [Web of Science ®], [Google Scholar]

Ayad, M. (2021). Islamogram: Salafism and alt-right online subculture. Institute for Strategic Dialogue. https://www.isdglobal.org/wp-content/uploads/2021/11/Islamogram.pdf [Google Scholar]

Baele, S. J. (2019). Conspiratorial narratives in violent political actors' language. Journal of Language and Social Psychology, 38(5–6), 706–734. https://doi.org/10.1177/0261927X19868494 [Crossref], [Google Scholar]

Bandura, A., Barbaranelli, C., Caprara, G. V., & Pastorelli, C. (1996). Mechanisms of moral disengagement in the exercise of moral agency. Journal of Personality and Social Psychology, 71(2), 364–374. https://doi.org/10.1037/0022-3514.71.2.364 [Crossref], [Web of Science ®], [Google Scholar]

Billig, M. (2005). Laughter and ridicule: Towards a social critique of humour. Sage. [Crossref], [Google Scholar]

Bogerts, L., & Fielitz, M. (2019). "Do you want meme war?": Understanding the visual memes of the German far right. In M. Fielitz & N. Thurston (Eds.), Post-digital cultures of far right: Online actions and offline consequences in Europe and the US (pp. 137–154). Transcript Publishing. [Crossref], [Google Scholar]

Carcary, M. (2009). The research audit trial—Enhancing trustworthiness in qualitative inquiry. Electronic Journal of Business Research Methods, 7(1), 11–23. [Google Scholar]

Cavell, S. (2005). Cavell on film (W. Rothman, Ed.). State University of New York Press. [Google Scholar]

Crawford, B., Keen, F., & Suarez de-Tangil, G. (2020). Memetic irony and the promotion of violence within Chan cultures. CREST (Centre for Research and Evidence on Security Threats). https://crestresearch.ac.uk/resources/memetic-irony-and-the-promotion-of-violence-within-chan-cultures/ [Google Scholar]

Creswell, R., & Haykel, B. (2017). Poetry in jihadi culture. In T. Hegghammer & T. Hegghammer (Eds.), Jihadi culture: The art and social practices of militant Islamists (pp. 22–42). Cambridge University Press. [Crossref], [Google Scholar]

Dafaure, M. (2020). The "great meme war:" The alt-right and its multifarious enemies. Angles. New Perspectives on the Anglophone World (10), 1–29. https://doi.org/10.4000/angles.369 [Google Scholar]

Davies, C. (2015). Political ridicule and humour under socialism. The European Journal of Humour Research, 2(3), 1–27. https://doi.org/10.7592/EJHR2014.2.3.davies [Crossref], [Google Scholar]

Dynel, M. (2009). Beyond a joke: Types of conversational humour. Language and Linguistics Compass, 3(5), 1284–1299. https://doi.org/10.1111/j.1749-818X.2009.00152.x [Crossref], [Google Scholar]

Dynel, M. (2011). Entertaining and enraging: The functions of verbal violence in broadcast political debates. In V. Tsakona & D. E. Popa (Eds.), Studies in political humour: In between political critique and public entertainment (pp. 109–136). John Benjamins Publishing. [Crossref], [Google Scholar]

Everitt, B., & Skrondal, A. (2010). The Cambridge dictionary of statistics. Cambridge University Press. https://www.amazon.co.uk/Cambridge-Dictionary-Statistics-B-Everitt/dp/0521766990 [Crossref], [Google Scholar]

Everts, E. (2003). Identifying a particular family humor style: A sociolinguistic discourse analysis. Humor – International Journal of Humor Research, 16(4), 369–412. https://doi.org/10.1515/humr.2003.021 [Crossref], [Google Scholar]

Ferguson, M., & Ford, T. (2008). Disparagement humor: A theoretical and empirical review of psychoanalytic, superiority, and social identity theories. Humor-International Journal of Humor Research – HUMOR, 21(3), 283–312. https://doi.org/10.1515/HUMOR.2008.014 [Crossref], [Web of Science °], [Google Scholar]

Fielitz, M., & Ahmed, R. (2021). It's not funny anymore. Far-right extremists' use of humour. https://ec.europa.eu/home-affairs/system/files/2021-03/ran_ad-hoc_pap_fre_humor_20210215_en.pdf [Google Scholar]

Fominaya, C. F. (2007). The role of humour in the process of collective identity formation in autonomous social movement groups in contemporary Madrid. International Review of Social History, 52(S15), 243–258. https://doi.org/10.1017/S0020859007003227 [Crossref], [Google Scholar]

Fry, W. (1976). The power of political humor. The Journal of Popular Culture, X(1), 227–231. https://doi.org/10.1111/j.0022-3840.1976.1001_227.x [Crossref], [Google Scholar]

Gal, N. (2019). Ironic humor on social media as participatory boundary work. New Media & Society, 21(3), 729–749. https://doi.org/10.1177/1461444818805719 [Crossref], [Web of Science °], [Google Scholar]

George, M., & Apter, A. (2004). Gaining insight into patients' beliefs using qualitative research methodologies. Current Opinion in Allergy and Clinical Immunology, 4(3), 185–189. https://doi.org/10.1097/00130832-200406000-00008 [Crossref], [PubMed], [Web of Science °], [Google Scholar]

Glaser, B. G., & Strauss, A. L. (2003). The discovery of grounded theory: Strategies for qualitative research (PEN 300.72 GLA). Aldine de Gruyter. https://uoelibrary.idm.oclc.org/login?url=http://search.ebscohost.com/login.aspx?direct=true&db=cat07716a&AN=pclc.992172393405136&site=eds-live&scope=site [Google Scholar]

Gohel, S. M. (2017). Deciphering Ayman Al-Zawahiri and Al-Qaeda's strategic and ideological imperatives. Perspective on Terrorism, 11(1), 54–67. [Google Scholar]

Greatbatch, D., & Clark, T. (2003). Displaying group cohesiveness: Humour and laughter in the public lectures of management gurus. Human Relations, 56(12), 1515–1544. https://doi.org/10.1177/00187267035612004 [Crossref], [Web of Science °], [Google Scholar]

Gwet, K. (2008). Intrarater reliability. In Narayanaswamy Balakrishnan (Ed.), Methods and applications of statistics in clinical trials (Vol. 1 & 2, pp. 334–339). https://doi.org/10.1002/9780471462422.eoct631 [Crossref], [Google Scholar]

Haslam, N. (2006). Dehumanization: An integrative review. Personality and Social Psychology Review, 10(3), 252–264. https://doi.org/10.1207/s15327957pspr1003_4 [Crossref], [PubMed], [Web of Science °], [Google Scholar]

Hay, J. (2000). Functions of humor in the conversations of men and women. Journal of Pragmatics, 32(6), 709–742. https://doi.org/10.1016/S0378-2166(99)00069-7 [Crossref], [Web of Science °], [Google Scholar]

Hegghammer, T. (Ed.). (2017). Jihadi culture: The art and social practices of militant Islamists. Cambridge University Press. https://doi.org/10.1017/9781139086141 [Crossref], [Google Scholar]

Hellmich, C. (2008). Creating the ideology of Al Qaeda: From hypocrites to Salafi-jihadists. Studies in Conflict & Terrorism, 31(2), 111–124. https://doi.org/10.1080/10576100701812852 [Taylor & Francis Online], [Web of Science °], [Google Scholar]

Hodson, G., & Macinnis, C. (2016). Derogating humor as a delegitimization strategy in intergroup contexts. Translational Issues in Psychological Science, 2(1), 63–74. https://doi.org/10.1037/tps0000052 [Crossref], [Google Scholar]

Holmes, J., & Marra, M. (2002). Over the edge? Subversive humour between colleagues. Humor-International Journal of Humor Research – HUMOR, 15(1), 65–87. https://doi.org/10.1515/humr.2002.006 [Crossref], [Web of Science °], [Google Scholar]

Ingram, H. (2018). Islamic state's English-language magazines, 2014-2017: Trends & Implications for CT-CVE strategic communications. ICCT Research Papers, 8 (15), 1–48. https://doi.org/10.19165/2018.1.15 [Google Scholar]

Jasper, J. M., Young, M. P., & Zuern, E. (2020). Ridicule and contempt for minions. In J. M. Jasper, M. P. Young, & E. Zuern (Eds.), Public characters (pp. 148–163). Oxford University Press. https://doi.org/10.1093/oso/9780190050047.003.0007 [Crossref], [Google Scholar]

Johnson, T. (2018). Taliban narratives: The use and power of stories in the Afghanistan conflict. Oxford University Press. https://doi.org/10.1093/oso/9780190840600.001.0001 [Crossref], [Google Scholar]

Kishtainy, K. (2009). Humour and resistance in the Arab World and greater Middle East. In M. Stephan (Ed.), Civilian jihad: Nonviolent struggle, democratization, and governance in the Middle East (pp. 53–63). Palgrave Macmillan US. https://doi.org/10.1057/9780230101753 [Crossref], [Google Scholar]

Kuipers, G. (2008). The sociology of humour. Electronic resource. In Victor Raskin (Ed.), The primer of humor research (pp. 361–398). Humor Research 8. Mouton de Gruyter. https://ebookcentral.proquest.com/lib/exeter/detail.action?docID=370770 [Crossref], [Google Scholar]

Kuipers, G. (2009). Humor styles and symbolic boundaries. Journal of Literary Theory, 3(2), 219–239. https://doi.org/10.1515/JLT.2009.013 [Crossref], [Google Scholar]

Lahoud, N. (2018). Empowerment or subjugation: An analysis of ISIL's gender messaging. UN Women | Arab States/North Africa. http://arabstates.unwomen.org/en/digital-library/publications/2018/6/empowerment-or-subjugation [Google Scholar]

Lamerichs, N., Nguyen, D., Puerta Melguizo, M. C., & Radojevic, R. (2018). Elite male bodies: The circulation of alt-right memes and the framing of politicians on social media. Participations Journal of Audiences & Receptions Studies, 15(1), 180–206. [Google Scholar]

Loughnan, S., Haslam, N., Sutton, R. M., & Spencer, B. (2014). Dehumanization and social class. Social Psychology, 45(1), 54–61. https://doi.org/10.1027/1864-9335/a000159 [Crossref], [Web of Science °], [Google Scholar]

Luginbühl, M. (2007). Conversational violence in political TV debates: Forms and functions. Journal of Pragmatics, 39(8), 1371–1387. https://doi.org/10.1016/j.pragma.2007.04.003 [Crossref], [Google Scholar]

Macdonald, S., & Lorenzo-Dus, N. (2021). Visual jihad: Constructing the "good Muslim" in online jihadist magazines. Studies in Conflict & Terrorism, 44(5), 363–386. https://doi.org/10.1080/1057610X.2018.1559508 [Taylor & Francis Online], [Web of Science °], [Google Scholar]

Mehran, W., Al Bayati, U., Mottet, M., & Lemieux, A. F. (2021). Deep analysis of Taliban videos: Differential use of multimodal, visual and sonic forms across strategic themes. Studies in Conflict & Terrorism, 0(0), 1–21. https://doi.org/10.1080/1057610X.2020.1866739 [Taylor & Francis Online], [Google Scholar]

Mehran, W., & Lemieux, A. F. (2021). 'My journey to jihad': Featured stories in jihadi propaganda. Behavioral Sciences of Terrorism and Political Aggression, 13(1), 1–19. https://doi.org/10.1080/19434472.2021.1886154 [Taylor & Francis Online], [Google Scholar]

Morreall, J. (2005). Humour and the conduct of politics. In S. Lockyer & M. Pickering (Eds.), Beyond a joke: The limits of humour (pp. 63–78). Palgrave Macmillan UK. https://doi.org/10.1057/9780230236776_4. [Crossref], [Google Scholar]

Partington, A. (2006). The linguistics of laughter: A corpus-assisted study of laughter-talk (1st ed.). Routledge. https://www.routledge.com/The-Linguistics-of-Laughter-A-Corpus-Assisted-Study-of-Laughter-Talk/Partington/p/book/9780415544078 [Crossref], [Google Scholar]

Patton, M. Q. (1999). Enhancing the quality and credibility of qualitative analysis. Health Services Research – Chicago, 34(5), 1189–1208. [PubMed], [Web of Science °], [Google Scholar]

Peifer, J. T. (2012). Can we be funny? The social responsibility of political humor. Journal of Mass Media Ethics, 27(4), 263–276. https://doi.org/10.1080/08900523.2012.746110 [Taylor & Francis Online], [Web of Science °], [Google Scholar]

Pieslak, J., & Lahoud, N. (2020). The anashid of the Islamic state: Influence, history, text, and sound. Studies in Conflict & Terrorism, 43(4), 274–299.

https://doi.org/10.1080/1057610X.2018.1457420 [Taylor & Francis Online], [Google Scholar]

Purcell, D., Brown, M. S., & Gokmen, M. (2010). Achmed the dead terrorist and humor in popular geopolitics. GeoJournal, 75(4), 373–385. https://doi.org/10.1007/s10708-009-9258-9 [Crossref], [Google Scholar]

Ramsay, G. (2016). Dehumanisation in religious and sectarian violence: The case of Islamic state. Global Discourse, 6(4), 561–578. https://doi.org/10.1080/23269995.2016.1253271 [Taylor & Francis Online], [Google Scholar]

Reicher, S., Hopkins, N., Levine, M., & Rath, R. (2005). Entrepreneurs of hate and entrepreneurs of solidarity: Social identity as a basis for mass communication. International Review of the Red Cross, 87(860), 621–637. https://doi.org/10.1017/S1816383100184462 [Crossref], [Google Scholar]

Rodrigues, S. B., & Collinson, D. L. (1995). 'Having fun'?: Humour as resistance in Brazil. Organization Studies, 16(5), 739–768. https://doi.org/10.1177/017084069501600501 [Crossref], [Web of Science °], [Google Scholar]

Romero, E. J., & Cruthirds, K. W. (2006). The use of humor in the workplace. Academy of Management Perspectives, 20(2), 58–69. https://doi.org/10.5465/amp.2006.20591005 [Crossref], [Web of Science °], [Google Scholar]

Shaw, M., & Bandara, P. (2018). Marketing jihad: The rhetoric of recruitment. Journal of Marketing Management, 34(15–16), 1319–1335. https://doi.org/10.1080/0267257X.2018.1520282 [Taylor & Francis Online], [Web of Science °], [Google Scholar]

Siddique, Q. (2010). Tehrik-e-Taliban Pakistan: An attempt to deconstruct the umbrella organization and the reasons for its growth in Pakistan's northwest. Danish Institute for International Studies. [Google Scholar]

Sontag, S. (2002). Styles of radical will (1st ed.). Picador. [Google Scholar]

Sørensen, M. J. (2013). Humorous political stunts: Speaking "truth" to power? The European Journal of Humour Research, 1(2), 69–83. https://doi.org/10.7592/EJHR2013.1.2.sorensen [Crossref], [Google Scholar]

Stevens, K. (2021). The politics of humor, from dry to wet. Cultural Critique, 112(1), 1–23. https://doi.org/10.5749/culturalcritique.112.2021.0001 [Crossref], [Google Scholar]

Terrion, J. L., & Ashforth, B. E. (2002). From 'I' to 'we': The role of putdown humor and identity in the development of a temporary group. Human Relations, 55(1), 55–88. https://doi.org/10.1177/0018726702055001606 [Crossref], [Web of Science °], [Google Scholar]

Tsakona, V., & Popa, D. E. (2011). Studies in political humour: In between political critique and public entertainment. John Benjamin's. [Crossref], [Google Scholar]

Wahlström, M., Törnberg, A., & Ekbrand, H. (2020). Dynamics of violent and de-humanizing rhetoric in far-right social media. New Media & Society, 23(11), 3290–3311. https://doi.org/10.1177/1461444820952795 [Crossref], [Google Scholar]

Weinrich, I. (2020). 'Nashīd' between Islamic chanting and jihadi hymns: Continuities and transformations. In C. Günther & S. Pfeifer (Eds.), Jihadi audiovisuality and its entanglements, meanings, aesthetics, appropriations (pp. 249–273). Edinburgh University. https://library.oapen.org/bitstream/handle/20.500.12657/47099/external_content.pdf?sequence=1#page=166 [Crossref], [Google Scholar]

Yates, D., Moore, D., & Mccabe, G. (1999). Practice of statistics. W H Freeman and Co. [Google Scholar]

Young, D. R. (2019, May 2). Ironies of web 2.0. Post45. https://post45.org/2019/05/ironies-of-web-2-0/ [Google Scholar]

Index

About the Author

Musa Khan Jalalzai is a journalist and research scholar. He has written extensively on Afghanistan, terrorism, nuclear and biological terrorism, human trafficking, drug trafficking, and intelligence research and analysis. He was an Executive Editor of the Daily Outlook Afghanistan from 2005-2011, and a permanent contributor in Pakistan's daily *The Post*, *Daily Times*, and *The Nation*, *Weekly the Nation*, (London). However, in 2004, US Library of Congress in its report for South Asia mentioned him as the biggest and prolific writer. He received Masters in English literature, Diploma in Geospatial Intelligence, University of Maryland, Washington DC, certificate in Surveillance Law from the University of Stanford, USA, and diploma in Counter terrorism from Pennsylvania State University, California, the United States.

CPSIA information can be obtained
at www.ICGtesting.com
Printed in the USA
LVHW110846030922
727496LV00002B/57